A GUIDE TO ETHICS

A GUIDE TO ETHICS

Steven Luper

Trinity University

Boston   Burr Ridge, IL   Dubuque, IA   Madison, WI   New York
San Francisco   St. Louis   Bangkok   Bogotá   Caracas   Kuala Lumpur
Lisbon   London   Madrid   Mexico City   Milan   Montreal   New Delhi
Santiago   Seoul   Singapore   Sydney   Taipei   Toronto

McGraw-Hill Higher Education ⚛

*A Division of The **McGraw-Hill** Companies*

1 2 3 4 5 6 7 8 9 0 DOC/DOC 0 9 8 7 6 5 4 3 2 1

Library of Congress Cataloging-in-Publication Data

Luper, Steven.
  A guide to ethics / Steven Luper.
     p.   cm.
  Includes bibliographical references and index.
  ISBN 0-7674-1181-1
    1. Ethics. I. Title.
  BJ1012 .L87 2001
  170–dc21   00-065367

Sponsoring Editor, Kenneth King; *production editor,* April Wells-Hayes; *manuscript editor,* Joan Pendleton; *design manager and cover designer,* Susan Breitbard; *text designer,* Anne Flanagan; *manufacturing manager,* Randy Hurst. The text was set in 10/13 Berthold Baskerville by G&S Typesetters, Inc., and printed on 50# Williamsburg Offset by R. R. Donnelley and Sons.

Cover image: © Alinari/Art Resource NY

www.mhhe.com

Preface

A Guide to Ethics is designed to introduce the beginner to ethics, or moral philosophy. The field is too vast for any book to cover everything, but my goal is to outline moral philosophy and discuss its main areas of controversy.

Perhaps the most fundamental question in ethics is, How ought we to live? This question, in turn, gives rise to two others: What are our obligations? and What is the best life like? Like other introductions to ethics, *A Guide* discusses the first of these questions extensively; it surveys the leading accounts of moral obligation and probes their strengths and weaknesses. Unlike most, however, *A Guide* devotes substantial space (two chapters—5 and 6) to the second question and considers not just Western ideas but also a few fascinating Eastern views. We all struggle to make our lives worthwhile, and asking how it can be done is at least as important as asking about our moral obligations. We need answers to both questions if we are to know how we ought to live.

The chapters are designed to stand on their own. They can be read in any order. However, there is a natural development of ideas from one chapter to the next, starting with Chapter 1, which is a general introduction. Readers who are already acquainted with the field will recognize the following organization:

Chapter 1, Introduction: What Is Ethics?

• Metaethics (What is the status of moral claims?):

Chapter 2, Subjectivism: Is Morality an Illusion?

Chapter 3, Cultural Relativism: Does Each Culture Invent Its Own Morality?

Chapter 4, The Divine Command View: Is Morality God's Invention?

- Normative ethics (How ought we to live?)

  The good (What does the best life include?)

  Chapter 5, Hedonism: Is the Pleasant Life the Best Life?

  Chapter 6, Perfectionism: Do We Live Best When We Excel?

  The right (What are our obligations?):

  Teleological views (explaining proper behavior in terms of the good):

  Chapter 7, Ethical Egoism: Is Duty a Matter of Self-Enhancement?

  Chapter 8, Utilitarianism: Does Duty Consist in Maximizing the Collective Good?

  Deontological views (explaining proper behavior in terms of duty):

  Chapter 9, Kantianism: Is Duty Respect for Humanity?

  Chapter 10, Contractarianism: Is Duty the Outcome of an Ideal Agreement?

While writing *A Guide,* I have learned a great deal from others. The reviewers of this book made many helpful suggestions. I am especially grateful to Dorothy L. Orzech, of Hartnell College, whose detailed comments led to many substantial improvements; I also thank Ronald Glass, University of Wisconsin–La Crosse; John Rowan, Purdue University Calumet; and David Schmidtz, University of Arizona. I would also like to thank Ken King at Mayfield Publishing for suggesting this project and for his patient advice and searching criticism during its various stages. Joan Pendleton did a great job copyediting the manuscript; Jennifer Westrick helped out in many ways. I thank them both.

Those who read *A Guide to Ethics* will no doubt have many ideas about ways in which it can be improved. I urge them to share their suggestions; I can be reached at sluper@trinity.edu or at the Philosophy Department at Trinity University in San Antonio.

Contents

A GUIDE TO ETHICS

1

Introduction
What Is Ethics?

We can begin to familiarize ourselves with ethics by considering the predicament of a remarkable young man who called himself "witty ticcy Ray." Oliver Sacks, a clinical neurologist, treated Ray for Tourette's syndrome, a condition that causes muscle spasms and involuntary outbursts of various sorts. Sacks describes his first encounter with Ray:

> He was 24 years old, and almost incapacitated by multiple tics of extreme violence coming in volleys every few seconds. He had been subject to these since the age of four and severely stigmatised by the attention they aroused, though his high intelligence, his wit, his strength of character and sense of reality, enabled him to pass successfully through school and college, and to be valued and loved by a few friends and his wife. Since leaving college, however, he had been fired from a dozen jobs—always because of tics, never for incompetence—was continually in crises of one sort and another, . . . and had found his marriage threatened by involuntary [vulgar] cries . . . which would burst from him at times of sexual excitement. He was (like many Touretters) remarkably musical, and could scarcely have survived—emotionally or economically—had he not been a weekend jazz drummer of real virtuosity. . . . The only time he was free from tics was in post-coital quiescence or in sleep; or when he swam or sang or worked; evenly and rhythmically, and found "a kinetic melody," a play, which was tension-free, tic-free and free.[1]

Although Ray seemed cheerful to people around him, he was "a man in despair" and had reached the age of twenty-four without even knowing that the name of his condition was "Tourette's syndrome." He persevered as best he could, for there was nothing else to be done, until he read a *Washington Post* article on tics that described Oliver Sacks's success "awakening" patients with a condition that is very much the opposite of Tourette's: sleepy-sickness

1

(*encephalitis lethargica*). Some of Sacks's patients were not only revived but also overstimulated; they erupted in excited, impulsive behavior that Sacks described as "Tourettism." The *Post* article discussed Tourette's, and when Ray read it he recognized his condition. He contacted Sacks, who confirmed Ray's self-diagnosis, and Sacks offered to treat Ray with the drug Haldol.

Ray accepted the offer, and eventually, Haldol entirely freed Ray from the effects of Tourette's. Surprisingly, however, Ray found that the disappearance of his disease was a mixed blessing. For two decades, he had shaped his identity under the influence of Tourette's; and, once relieved of its effects, he realized how inextricably those were bound up with who he was. Sadly, he told Sacks, "I consist of tics—there is nothing else."[2] Without Tourette's, he was no longer a virtuoso at music and, as Sacks says, "less sharp, less quick in repartee, no longer bubbling with witty tics or ticcy wit."

To bring back his "ticcing self," he had only to end his therapy. But life as his "Haldol self" was easier: He was stable at work, patient, and calm. Should he continue to take Haldol and live tic-free—or not?

Ray's decision raised three questions. First, what was good for Ray as an individual? That is, what would enhance his life? Would continued drug therapy be in Ray's best interest? Second, what was good for others? His choice had a bearing on the lives of others; he had to consider the ways his therapy and his ticcing affected his wife and friends. These first two questions are answered by applying one of the two main moral concepts: the concept of the *good,* which refers to what is *desirable.* The third question is a bit different: What must be done? Is there a way (or perhaps several ways) for Ray to meet all of his obligations? Here there are two possibilities: (1) The duties that apply to Ray dictate a single course of action, or (2) these duties eliminate some possibilities (or none), but leave Ray more than one permissible option. Here we apply the concept of the *right,* which is the other main moral concept. Typically, the term *right* can be equated with *obligatory,* but often it is used in a more inclusive sense. Sometimes when we say an action is right (or, better, all right) we mean it is *permissible*—that is, not wrong—rather than obligatory.[3]

The first question (What was good for Ray?) involves considering Ray's well-being. Well-being is a complicated matter; it is measured in terms of the extent to which our lives incorporate elements taken to be valuable in their own right. Virtually everyone agrees that a positive state of mind (what is sometimes called *happiness*) is one of these valuable things, but arguably there are others, such as success with our projects and personal relationships, a good character, and so on.

So what was good for Ray? No answer could be more instructive than his own. Ray decided that he did not want to be *solely* "witty ticcy Ray" *or* his "Haldol self." It was important for Ray to fit in smoothly with society, so he had good reasons to take Haldol, but it was also important for him to experience many of the effects of Tourette's. His very identity was at stake, for ticcing had become an integral part of who he was. So he had good reasons to discontinue his therapy. Fortunately, he did not have to choose either option. He split the difference (and himself!) and decided to take Haldol only on working days so that he could "let fly" on weekends. Given his background and situation, this double life really does seem to be the best life available to him. Were going on and off Haldol to become troublesome, he might eventually have to reinvent himself, letting go of "witty ticcy Ray" and cultivating his Haldol persona, but he was able to postpone that choice indefinitely.

How shall we answer the second question: What was best for Ray's family and friends? There were pluses and minuses in terms of their well-being, and it is difficult to say that the pluses outweighed the minuses to any appreciable degree. Life with the "Haldol Ray" was no doubt more predictable and less complicated: He drew less attention and was able to hold down a better job. On the other hand, his wife and friends had come to love "witty ticcy Ray" and would surely have missed this earlier Ray just as he himself did. Predictability and financial stability are not everything. Also, Tourette's is not life-threatening, so Ray's wife and friends were in no danger of losing him no matter how he chose. And Ray's own happiness was important to them: Given their love for him, it is reasonable to assume that they would not have wanted Ray to continue the treatment if it made him unhappy.

But was Ray's choice permissible—was it consistent with all of his obligations? It was indeed, especially when we recall that none of Ray's options would have significantly impaired the well-being of his wife and friends. The main impact was on Ray alone. Ray was morally permitted to abandon his drug therapy or to continue it if he chose; but, given his interests, splitting the difference was best.

Ray's case illustrates that in some situations we have several permissible options, so that in making our choice the concept of the good moves to center stage. In other cases the concept of the right is in the spotlight. Let's discuss a couple of these, starting with a simple illustration.

SIMPLE MORAL REASONING: THE CASE OF THE FRAUDULENT DOC

People tend to disguise what they are doing when they know full well that they are violating their obligations. A case in point involves a physician named William Summerlin. In the 1970s, he made a name for himself by attempting to discover ways to make tissue grafts more successful, and so facilitate organ transplantation. In 1974 Summerlin was immersing pieces of skin from mice in nutrient solutions, trying to wash them clean of identifying features that trigger immune responses and, as a result, rejection. He claimed that skin from one mouse could be cleansed and successfully grafted onto another mouse. One day Robert Good, Director of the Sloan-Kettering Institute, where Summerlin worked, wanted to see some successful grafts of skin from black mice onto white mice. Summerlin used a black felt-tip pen to darken the grafts on his white mice, making it appear that the grafts came from black mice.

An assistant noticed that the black coloring washed away with alcohol and turned Summerlin in. Good suspended Summerlin's research and set up a peer review committee to investigate the matter. The committee discovered that Summerlin not only had faked these results but also had been getting away with crude forgeries for years. People little suspected that a physician working at the prestigious Sloan-Kettering Institute would cheat. But perhaps the most remarkable thing about Summerlin was his attitude about his deception. When the story broke, he told the press that his

> error was not in knowingly promulgating false data, but rather in succumbing to extreme pressure placed on [him] by the Institute's director to publicize information . . . and to an unbearable clinical and experimental load which numbed [his] better judgment.[4]

Summerlin portrayed himself as a victim rather than a wrongdoer, a man destroyed by Good, an overly demanding boss. But was Good the bad guy? Certainly he should have done a better job of monitoring research he was charged to supervise. He might also have been more flexible in his demands on his employees (but note that jobs like Summerlin's are supposed to be highly competitive). Nonetheless, it was Summerlin's behavior that deserved criticism. In his desperation to excuse his conduct, Summerlin ignored the fact that he could have resigned from the position that was too demanding for him. He also ignored the effects his fraud had on the people around him. He betrayed the trust of his employer: As a result of the scandal, Good was forced out of his position. Journals had published Summerlin's fraudulent research papers, and scholars had relied on them. And money provided for life-saving research was completely wasted. Summerlin's behavior was wrong, and at some level he knew it—that is why he did it on the sly.

In straightforward cases like Summerlin's, moral reasoning is a matter of applying moral principles that are easily acknowledged and that express our obligations in the form of general rules. For example, it is an acknowledged moral principle that disseminating fraudulent data is wrong, since such data are harmful to others, often seriously so. Using this principle, Summerlin could have reasoned as follows:

1. Disseminating forged data is wrong.

2. Summerlin disseminated forged data.

3. So what he did was wrong.

Claims 1–3 constitute an *argument,* which is composed of one or more assertions, called *premises,* offered in support of another assertion, called a *conclusion.* In the argument against forging data, assertions 1 and 2 are premises, and 3 is the conclusion.

Simple moral reasoning such as this has four main elements:

1. *Logical considerations.* We must be able to tell when an argument is strong, at least to the extent that we can work out what a moral principle implies about our situation. For example, the argument concerning forged data is very strong indeed, for two reasons. First, it is deductively valid. A *valid* argument is one whose conclusion cannot possibly be false if its premises are true. Second, it is *sound,* which means that it is valid and its premises are in fact true. When an argument is sound, its conclusion must be true.

2. *Factual considerations.* We must accurately grasp the facts about our situation. For example, Summerlin had to recognize that at a certain point he pulled out a marker and colored the skin of a mouse.

3. *Evaluative (or normative) considerations.* We must evaluate our situation accurately. In elementary reasoning, we must be acquainted with moral principles whose relevance is easily recognized, and be able to tell which of them applies in our situation. *Evaluative,* or *normative,* considerations involve claims about good or bad, right or wrong. These contrast with factual, purely *descriptive* claims (such as "the sun is hot," and "few people desire to eat worms"), which are neutral from the standpoint of value.

4. *Conceptual considerations.* We must be clear about the concepts involved in our reasoning. For example, Summerlin would have to realize what forging data means and that publishing is a way of disseminating data.

Furthermore, success in even the most elementary moral reasoning requires that we be willing to apply relevant moral principles accurately and to size up our situation correctly. Anything that diminishes this readiness is an impediment to good moral reasoning. For example, anger, grief, and (as in the case of Summerlin) ambition can motivate us to turn a blind eye to what we are really doing. The example of William Summerlin shows how easily we can act badly even when the most elementary form of moral reasoning would counsel against it. In our eagerness to gain and maintain positions of prestige, we take shortcuts to what we want and spin a web of self-deception to excuse ourselves and to conceal what we are doing to people around us.

Often, however, elementary moral reasoning does not suffice. Events beyond our control sometimes thrust us into situations demanding complex moral reflection. In such cases we are not sure about applicable moral principles, perhaps because we cannot think of a relevant principle or perhaps because the principles we operate with prove too vague or seem mistaken. The principles themselves are at issue, and we need to identify and justify them, as our next examples illustrate.

｜ COMPLEX MORAL REASONING: TWO TRAGIC CASES

On January 11, 1983, a twenty-five-year-old woman named Nancy Cruzan was involved in an accident and thrown from her car. Paramedics restarted her breathing, but her brain had been deprived of oxygen for too long and her conscious life was ended. She was placed on a feeding tube. Four years later her parents asked Missouri authorities to remove the tube and let her die. The case went to trial in Missouri, and the court rejected Cruzan's parents' request, saying that there was not enough evidence that she would have refused continued treatment. The case then went before the U.S. Supreme Court in 1990, and it upheld the verdict of the lower court, yet stated clearly that patients have a right to refuse treatment. But when several people came forward to say that Cruzan had told them she would rather die than persist in a vegetative state, the Missouri court dropped its objection, and Cruzan's treatment was ended. Twelve days later – eight years after her tragic accident – Cruzan died.

Was the right thing done? The main argument in favor of removing Cruzan's feeding tube is this:

1. Competent people should be allowed to refuse medical treatment; if they later become incompetent, they may expect others to help carry out their wishes.

2. Before her accident, Cruzan decided that she would not want her body kept alive after her conscious life ended.

3. Under the circumstances, this earlier choice constituted a competent decision to refuse the use of a feeding tube.

4. So it was permissible for others to honor her decision by removing the feeding tube.

Is this argument sound? Premise 2 is a factual claim; it seems plausible enough, given the testimony of her friends. Premise 3, a conceptual claim, could be questioned on the grounds that Cruzan's earlier words were not specific enough to constitute a definite choice, but let us put this reservation aside. Premise 1 is a moral assertion, suggesting that people have the moral right to refuse treatment and may expect others to facilitate this refusal, so that imposing treatment is wrong. It must be distinguished from the claim that we have the legal right to refuse treatment—that interfering with our decision to refuse treatment is legally forbidden. Of course, moral rights should be protected by law, but there is no guarantee that all moral rights will be recognized by law.

Do we have the moral right to refuse treatment? A powerful case can be made in favor of it. Most of us think—with perhaps a few reservations—that competent people have the right to *self-determination:* We should be in charge of our own lives and free to make decisions about matters having little impact on anyone else. This principle of respect for self-determination directly supports the right to refuse treatment.

The right to refuse treatment can also be justified using a slightly more indirect route, for self-determination entails controlling what happens to our bodies (unless they are not separate from the bodies of others, as in Siamese twins and, perhaps, mothers and their fetuses): To say that we should be in charge of our lives is to say that we should be in charge of what happens to our bodies, as the *principle of bodily autonomy* asserts. That is, if the principle of respect for self-determination is true, then so is the principle of bodily autonomy—the former entails the latter. This is important, for the principle of bodily autonomy, in turn, requires our being free to turn down treatment. In other words, the principle of respect for self-determination entails the principle of bodily autonomy, and both support removing Cruzan's feeding tube. In fact, both principles were cited by the Supreme Court when it declared (in *Cruzan v. Director, Missouri Department of Health*) that there is a legal right to refuse treatment—a right protected by the Constitution. Using an arrow to indicate support, we can diagram our argument as follows:

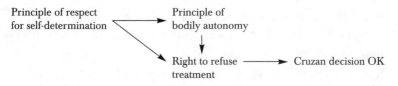

Nevertheless, some people object to Cruzan's treatment. The main argument is often put this way:

1.   Human life must be preserved at all costs.

2.   Preserving human life in the Cruzan case entailed leaving her feeding tube in place.

3.   So it was wrong to remove the tube.

Here the second premise is a very plausible factual claim; few would challenge it. The first premise might be called the *life-preservation principle*. Should we accept it?

Some might say that to deny the life-preservation principle is to betray a callous disregard for the immeasurable value of human life. But is it human life or is it conscious human flourishing that is valuable? Consider that after the brain dies, it is often possible to keep the rest of the body alive artificially. The suggestion that human life should be preserved at all costs has the consequence that all brain-dead bodies (and parts of brain-dead bodies) must be kept alive artificially as long as possible. Isn't this consequence implausible? It is true that some comatose people can recover if kept alive long enough. But we are not talking about comatose people. A comatose person's brain is *alive*. We are discussing the case of complete brain death, and here there is no chance of recovery. (Aren't there cases in which we cannot tell whether a brain has died completely? Perhaps, but for our purposes we can set these cases aside and assume we are dealing only with cases of true brain death. Here is the point: The life-preservation principle implies that bodies that are admittedly brain-dead, with no chance of regaining consciousness, should still be kept alive, which is an implausible proposition.)

These reservations about maintaining human life under any conditions suggest that what is truly valuable is something made possible primarily by a healthy brain: a flourishing conscious life. So the life-preservation principle is inaccurate, and the objection based on it is unconvincing.

A second objection to the removal of Cruzan's feeding tube uses the *slippery-slope* (or "opening wedge") *principle,* according to which we should disallow things when permitting them facilitates other things that are clearly objectionable. On the basis of this principle, one might oppose letting people or their bodies die for any reason. The argument is this:

The Slippery-Slope Argument for Preserving Human Life

1. When allowing something that is not clearly objectionable might lead to other things that are, we should not allow either (the slippery-slope principle).

2. If we permit the removal of feeding tubes, soon we will be saying that it is all right to kill people for objectionable reasons; for example, we will end up saying that it is all right to kill people because they are handicapped.

3. So we must draw the line and insist on the preservation of all human life.

When people use slippery-slope arguments, they are directing our attention to the fact that sometimes there is no sharp line between terrible behavior and unobjectionable behavior. They insist that we take out a bright red marker and draw a wide circle around the terrible behavior as well as conduct that might be confused with it and ban everything circled. This means that some unobjectionable things will be disallowed, but it is worth it to ensure that really awful things are not permitted.

Slippery-slope arguments are sometimes well-intentioned attempts to avoid disaster. And, indeed, we will want to reflect carefully before we adjust principles that have survived the test of time, making sure that the changes are genuine improvements. All too often, however, slippery-slope arguments are used in support of simplistic ethical views. They seem to justify our reluctance to do the moral reasoning it takes to respond to unforeseen, complex, or novel situations that demand more sophisticated moral principles. Take an extreme but analogous case: Suppose that an organization proposes to hold contests in which participants are allowed to fight bare-fisted, but a concerned official condemns the fights, citing, as grounds, the principle that any physical competition is wrong. The official's principle rules out fighting with bare fists, yet it is unreasonable because it also rules out legitimate competitive sports such as basketball. It is no good to draw a bright red circle around the objectionable if the circle includes the unobjectionable, and that is what slippery-slope arguments do. A better approach is to sharpen our drawing skills.

In view of these concerns about slippery-slope arguments, let us ask again whether it is reasonable to insist on the preservation of human life in all cases. Of course people should not be killed simply because they are handicapped and certainly not against their will. In fact, people rarely have legitimate grounds to kill others. But does the principle that competent people may refuse treatment endorse involuntary killings? Does it say we may kill people once we determine that they are handicapped? No, it does not, and so we may accept it without authorizing involuntary killings and killing based on handicap.

But should we accept all the consequences of allowing people to refuse treatment? Consider a second tragic case: While swimming, a ten-year-old boy named Kenneth Bergstedt suffered an accident that left him a quadriplegic. For twenty-one years, he lived on a respirator, under the care of his father, until his father became gravely ill. When confronted with the imminent death of his father, Bergstedt, then thirty-one, decided that he wanted his life-sustaining respirator removed. In his judgment, life restricted by his quadriplegia and without the loving care of his father would not be worthwhile. Reluctantly, his father agreed. Tests were done to ensure that Bergstedt was competent and understood his situation and that his quadriplegia was irreversible. The respirator was removed, and he died.[5]

Cruzan's objection was to continued life without consciousness; Bergstedt's was to continued consciousness without happiness. He refused further treatment because of the way he assessed the quality of his future life. But when people end treatment because they do not value their lives, aren't they committing suicide? If so, wasn't it wrong to remove Bergstedt's respirator, as the following argument suggests?

The Argument from Suicide

1. Like suicide itself, helping someone to commit suicide is wrong.
2. To remove Bergstedt's respirator is to help him commit suicide.
3. So it was wrong to remove the respirator.

If the argument from suicide succeeds, we will have to rethink what we said in the case of Cruzan. The principle saying we must allow competent people to refuse treatment does not rule out the possibility that their refusal will be based on assessments of the quality of their lives. Hence our grounds for allowing Cruzan to end her treatment commit us to allowing Bergstedt to end his. If suicide and assisting in suicide are wrong, yet permitted by an unqualified right to refuse treatment, we must restrict that right, and a restricted version might no longer apply to Cruzan.

Does the argument from suicide succeed? Its logical structure is beyond criticism, but we can still reject it if either of its two premises is false. Are both true?

Why grant the first premise? Well, there are two main ways to argue that suicide and assisting in suicide are always wrong (we will look at further grounds when we discuss Kantian ethics later). We might cite the life-preservation principle and say that life is too precious ever to be taken, but that principle has already proven to be unreasonable. Or we might cite a religious authority such as Augustine (354–430), who wrote

> It is not without significance, that in no passage of the holy canonical books there can be found either divine precept or permission to take away our own life. . . . Nay, the law, rightly interpreted, even prohibits suicide, where it says, "Thou shalt not kill."[6]

But Augustine also knew that in no passage is suicide explicitly forbidden, and he himself thought that the Sixth Commandment was not exceptionless: We may kill in self-defense. Couldn't suicide be another exception in some cases? As Augustine himself noted, an especially heroic case of suicide is mentioned in the Bible: that of Samson, who, with the explicit approval of God, sacrificed his own life in order to defeat his enemy. Why shouldn't we interpret this incident as endorsing some cases of suicide?

As these reflections indicate, it is not difficult to criticize the first premise of the argument from suicide. However, this is not the usual way people respond when they think about Bergstedt. Instead, they attack the second premise, hoping to show that Bergstedt did not in fact commit suicide. If they reject the second premise, they can maintain that removing Bergstedt's respirator was permissible regardless of whether suicide is wrong. We may settle the Bergstedt case even if we postpone our investigation of the morality of suicide.

How do they attack the second premise? By saying that when we contract a fatal disease or suffer a fatal injury, the illness or injury kills us; we do not kill ourselves, even if we do not combat the disease or injury. So ending treatment is not suicide even when the decision rests on concern about quality of life. And since its second premise is false, the argument from suicide fails, whether its first premise is correct or not. Since ending treatment is not suicide (and not assisted suicide), we can respect the right to end treatment without accepting suicide and justify withdrawing Cruzan and Bergstedt from life support. This is basically the view the courts have taken. In a recent decision, *Vacco v. Quill,* the Supreme Court ruled that while the right to refuse treatment is constitutionally protected, it does not follow that states must allow suicide. In other words, treatment can be stopped, but that doesn't mean physicians may deliberately end lives by administering fatal drugs.

Does this argument work? Can we postpone tackling the issue of suicide and still deal with the Bergstedt case? Let's review. First, we defended withdrawing life support from Cruzan and Bergstedt on the grounds that people have the right to refuse treatment. Then, faced with the charge that our reasoning is bad because it endorses Bergstedt's wrongfully suicidal choice, we responded by denying that he was suicidal. So even if suicide (and assisting in suicide) is wrong, the reasoning we are using to support Cruzan's and Bergstedt's choices is good, because our reasoning does not commit us to accepting suicide.

However, there is still a problem, since we based the right to refuse treatment on the principles of respect for self-determination and bodily autonomy. Here's the problem: The principles of respect for self-determination and bodily autonomy, individually and jointly, support allowing suicide. Perhaps letting people refuse treatment does not entail letting them end their lives. But we decided that people should be in charge of their treatment because we thought that they should be in charge of their lives and bodies, and now we see that being in charge of life and limb entails being free to decide how to die. If respect for people's self-determination and bodily autonomy leads us to acknowledge the right to refuse treatment, it is unreasonable not to acknowledge the right to suicide as well.

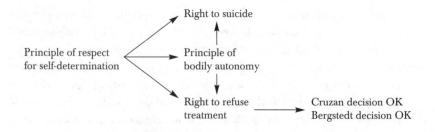

At this point we have two options. First, we could insist that suicide is always wrong and so is assisting in suicide. But we will also have to qualify (or abandon) the principles of bodily autonomy and respect for self-determination so that they do not support the right to suicide and make sure that the revised principles still endorse the right to refuse treatment, as exercised by Cruzan and Bergstedt. This is basically the route the courts seem to be taking.

However, our most straightforward option is our second one: to retain the principles of respect for self-determination and bodily autonomy and recognize that people should be permitted to refuse treatment and to commit suicide when they have made a competent, reasoned decision to do so after carefully assessing the quality of their lives and the impact their decision will have on others. This recognition does not leave us powerless to respond in compassionate ways to suicide attempts. We may try to dissuade people when their setbacks can be ameliorated with time or treatment (such as palliative care). We may also stop suicide attempts made by the mentally incompetent, or by people grieving over being jilted, and the like. When people are not thinking rationally, we are justified in helping them avoid throwing away an existence they will find worthwhile in time. But the tragic fact is that some people face incurable illnesses with intense pain that can be controlled only by blotting out consciousness; their decision to end their lives can be entirely rational. Isn't it unreasonable to stand in the way?

DEFENDING MORAL PRINCIPLES

We have moved very quickly beyond the lowest level of moral reasoning in which we do little more than apply principles to situations. Our discussion of Cruzan and Bergstedt has involved a higher level of moral reasoning in which we modify and evaluate moral principles themselves, selecting ones that forbid only what ought to be disallowed. Let us say a bit more about how moral principles are assessed by outlining a three-stage procedure:

1. *Determine whether our principles are consistent with our considered convictions about particular cases.* Here the idea is to use our confident views about

the proper way to handle specific situations to help us test general principles. For example, we might be confident in saying that it is right to let people with Tourette's decide whether to take Haldol and to let people with leg injuries decide whether to have surgery and so on. We can make sure that these judgments are consistent with our moral principles, such as the (relatively narrow) principle that we may refuse treatment or the (more general) principle of respect for self-determination. We want our deliberations to be guided by rules that apply generally, informing us about the acceptability of whole classes of behavior, but we also want these rules to square with our moral intuitions.

2. *Determine whether our principles are mutually consistent.* In defending moral principles, we need to make sure they are consistent with the other principles we accept. As we have seen, sometimes people adopt rules such as "people may do with their own lives whatever they wish" and "we must always preserve human life" only to discover that the combination is incoherent: Killing oneself is permitted by the first principle but forbidden by the second. When this happens, we must revise our principles so that the inconsistency disappears or else introduce a scheme for assigning higher priority to some principles over others. For example, we might say that the self-determination principle takes priority over the injunction to preserve life, or vice versa.

3. *Determine whether our principles square with an accurate comprehensive view of obligation.* Instead of stating what we must do piecemeal, in the form of several principles about limited types of cases, here the idea is to develop a *comprehensive statement* about how we must conduct ourselves in all situations and to assess our principles in light of that comprehensive formulation. For example, some say that each of us must bring about as much good as we can. Given this doctrine, assessing moral principles requires checking to see how well their acceptance would promote the aggregate good. Of course, it is not easy to formulate a comprehensive statement of what is required of us, and the views moral theorists have offered are different and not fully consistent with each other. In Chapters 7–10, we will examine several of these views.

Because different comprehensive doctrines compete for our allegiance, we must eventually compare and assess them. We will want to work out what each implies and see how well these consequences square with our considered judgments. This task need not lead to the conclusion that one is correct and the others wrong. Instead, we might decide that none is completely accurate and that only by combining insights expressed by each (or several) can we capture the truth.

How do we support comprehensive doctrines? This is a complicated matter. One approach is to invoke considerations of consistency. In working through our three-stage procedure for defending moral principles, we make sure that all of our moral claims, at whatever level of generality, are mutually consistent. We hope to find a mutual consistency among our judgments about particular cases (the lowest level of generality), our principles about types of cases (a higher level of generality), and our comprehensive statement about what we must do (the highest level). Finding such consistency indicates that we have found the truth on *all three* levels. A great deal of what ethicists do consists in constructing principles and comprehensive doctrines and testing for consistency.

METAETHICS

In addition to asking, What must we do? and making sure that all the things we say in answer to this question are consistent, there are other things we can do to buttress our confidence that we have the truth. We might ask three further questions:

1. What precisely do moral claims and moral terms such as "right" and "good" mean? (This is a *conceptual* question.)

2. What is the nature of moral properties such as goodness and rightness: In what sense, if any, are they real? (This is an *ontological* question, a query about the nature of reality.)

3. How do we get in touch with these properties; that is, how do we discover that they exist and that the claims we make about them are true? (This is an *epistemological* question – one that asks how we know things.)

The first question is closely related to the second, since one way to clarify a term's meaning is to describe the property it refers to. The second question invites us to compare moral properties to other kinds of properties. For example, we might ask whether *rightness,* a moral property, is part of the physical structure of the world, like the property of being two-legged or the property flatness. By characterizing moral properties and distinguishing them from other sorts of properties, we might be able to articulate how moral claims (which presumably refer to these properties) can be objectively true. When we look for moral properties, we might also find that they do not exist. The third question invites us to compare our knowledge of moral properties with our knowledge of other sorts of properties. We verify that a person has the property *two-leggedness* or that a tire has the property *flatness* through empirical observation; do we also verify that an action has *rightness* or that a person has the property *goodness* by observation? If so, then moral claims can be established through observation – once we are clear about the nature of the properties we are trying to detect.

Together, these three questions (conceptual, ontological, and epistemological) define a field of inquiry called *metaethics*. We will conduct some specifically metaethical inquiries in Chapters 2 – 4. Even when they are not at the forefront, these questions will always be somewhere in the background, for it is difficult to be confident that our moral claims are correct unless we have an idea about what they mean, what features of reality they are about, and how we know about moral reality.

ETHICS

Now we are ready to characterize the area of inquiry called *ethics,* or *moral philosophy,* which is the subject of this book. Ethics is the attempt to clarify how people ought to live. It elucidates the nature of the good person and the good life, telling us how to flourish or live well, and it characterizes the obligations we have, enabling us to identify what we must do. Ethics is the wide-ranging study of right and wrong, as well as good and bad, insofar as these pertain to conduct and character. It pays particular attention to clarifying the two most basic moral concepts – the concept of the good and the concept of the right – and figuring out how these two concepts are related to each other.

The distinction between metaethics and other sorts of ethical inquiry is quite flexible, but we can draw a line between the two. We can say that we are doing *normative ethics* when we provide answers to the questions, What must we do? and What makes a life as good as possible? We are also doing normative ethics when we justify our answers to these questions. In particular, the elementary form of reasoning in which we apply moral principles and the more complex form of reasoning summed up in the three-stage procedure for defending moral principles are forms of normative ethics. By contrast, we are doing metaethics when we investigate the ontological, conceptual, and epistemological assumptions we make in the course of doing normative ethics (that is, when we pursue any of the three questions that are definitive of metaethics). Ethics itself includes both normative ethics and metaethics.[7]

AN OVERVIEW OF NORMATIVE THEORIES

Starting in Chapter 5 we will examine the leading normative theories in some detail, but let's paint these in broad strokes now to anticipate what is to come. The theories can be divided into two groups, depending on whether they are addressed primarily to the question, What does it take to live as well as possible? or to the question, What must we do?

What Does It Take to Live as Well as Possible?

There are two main types of answers to this question. The first says that, fundamentally, some sort of positive state of mind, such as pleasure, is the only thing that is good for its own sake, and so the best life is one in which this state of mind predominates. We can call this view *value hedonism,* or *the hedonist theory of the good.* The second answer is that things other than subjective states are good in themselves; attaining each of these goods is a way of excelling or perfecting our lives, and so the best existence is the life rich in excellences or perfections. This is *the perfectionist theory of the good,* or *value perfectionism.* The hedonist theory will be our topic in Chapter 5; we take up the perfectionist theory in Chapter 6.

Value Hedonism   In order to explain value hedonism more fully, it is useful to distinguish between instrumental and non-instrumental value. Notice that some things are good (or valuable or desirable) merely as means—these things help bring about something else that is good. Their value is *instrumental.* Money is like this, and so is aspirin. Presumably, however, not all things have merely instrumental value. There are things whose value is *non-instrumental*—things that are good in themselves or good for their own sakes.[8] What has this kind of value? is one of the central questions in ethics. According to the hedonists, only one thing is good for its own sake: pleasure (or some other positive mental state), together with the absence of pain. Everything else can be valuable only in the instrumental sense.

A typical hedonist account is given by the ancient Greek philosopher Epicurus. According to him, my pleasure is good for me, while your pleasure is good for you, and so on. My good—what is good for me, or in my interest—is specified in terms of my own pleasure and the things that produce it, while yours is specified in terms of your pleasure. Hence Epicurus's account of the good is *agent-relative:* According to him, the question, Is such and such good? is incomplete as it stands; it must be considered shorthand for Is such and such good for ——? where we fill in the blank with "Fred" or "Mary" or the name of some other agent. The only possible exception is the case in which something is pleasant to an entire group of agents, or for each and every agent, in which case we may say that it is good for everyone (in the group).

While many hedonists follow Epicurus in offering an agent-relative account of the good, not all do. Some say that any agent's pleasure is good period, good in an *agent-neutral* sense. For such theorists, pleasure is objectively good. When you and I ask what things in the world are good, you ought to acknowledge that my pleasure is good, even if my pleasure does not pertain to your life (since, for example, it does not give you pleasure) and hence is not in this sense good for you. Similarly, I ought to acknowledge that your pleasure is good, even if it is not good for me. Hedonists in the utilitarian tradition (discussed in Chapter 8) tend to embrace agent-neutral accounts of the good.

Even though hedonists do not think that the question, What perfects life? is as basic as the question, What brings pleasure? they do encourage us to make our lives excellent, just as perfectionists do. Perfectionists recommend that we improve our conduct, characters, aspirations, and interpersonal relationships, and so do hedonists. Yet hedonists assign these matters a subordinate role in their value scheme. For hedonists, we are to arrange our conduct, characters, aspirations, and relationships so that our lives will be as pleasant in the long run as possible.

Value Perfectionism   Proponents of value perfectionism suppose there is an ideal human life that includes all final goods, all excellences or perfections. Perfectionists do value pleasure or some other positive subjective state and acknowledge that—as a rule—a good life is enjoyable. However, they think that things *other* than pleasure may be good in themselves, so perfectionists do not suppose that goodness is reducible to an agent's pleasure.

Most perfectionists think that there is a single human ideal—a single list of human goods—that applies to everyone. They mean to identify what is objectively good, and so they usually do not offer an agent-relative or subjective account of the good. Still, we certainly can imagine an agent-relative version of perfectionism. To do so, we might propose that we all are capable of inventing our own way of excelling and that achieving my ideal of excellence is good for me, while achieving your ideal of excellence is good for you, and so on.

Like hedonists, perfectionists say that some things are good for an agent, and thus in the agent's interest, but perfectionists do not accept the hedonists' limited vision of an agent's interests. They say that when we speak about something being "good for" us as individuals, we mean that it moves our life closer to the ideal. We mean it makes us or our life better—hence we are better *off*.

What Must We Do?

Five leading theories offer answers to the question, What must we do?

- *Virtue ethics.* A moral exemplar is someone whose character embodies certain excellences or perfections, and we ought to do whatever the moral exemplar would do.

- *Ethical egoism.* As individuals, we must do ourselves the most good (where "good" is defined narrowly, in terms of the individual's pleasure, safety, health, and so on).
- *Utilitarianism.* We must bring about the greatest aggregate good (taking all into account, not just ourselves).
- *Kantianism.* We must respect moral agency (or, We must act as reason dictates).
- *Contractarianism.* We must abide by rules that would be adopted by people who want their terms of association to be justifiable in a mutually agreeable way.

Let's compare these theories by seeing how each would answer a series of important questions.

1. *Do we have duties?*

Virtue ethics theory:	no
Ethical egoism:	yes
Utilitarianism:	yes
Kantianism:	yes
Contractarianism:	yes

When virtue ethicists in the ancient world (whom we discuss in Chapter 6) asked about how we *ought* to behave, they meant to distinguish exemplary conduct from base (ignoble) conduct, not conduct that is right from conduct that is wrong. Exemplary conduct, in turn, they explained in terms of good character: For them, character conceptually precedes conduct. Modern virtue ethicists, whom we will discuss in Chapter 11, follow the ancients in rejecting the modern notion of obligation and in treating character as preceding conduct. They continue to ask what we *ought* to do; but, like the ancients, when they speak of what we ought to do, they mean to indicate what is best or excellent, not what we *must* do. Other theorists accept the modern idea of obligation and treat conduct as prior to character: They assess character in terms of its propensity to produce proper conduct, turning the virtue ethics view on its head.[9]

2. *Is proper conduct separate from the individual's well-being?*

Virtue ethics theory:	no
Ethical egoism:	no
Utilitarianism:	yes
Kantianism:	yes
Contractarianism:	yes

Virtue ethicists and ethical egoists both claim that proper conduct is not fully separable from individual well-being: Proper conduct is good for the individual. For them, the question, Why do the right thing? does not arise or is easily answered by pointing out that the individual is better off after doing the right thing. But all the other theorists think duty and individual well-being are separate, and hence they have a much more difficult time explaining why we should conform to duty. Utilitarians, Kantians, and contractarians define duty independently from well-being and expect us to meet our obligations even if doing so is bad for us from the standpoint of our interests.

While ethical egoists and virtue ethicists both think of morality as, in large part, the enlightened pursuit of self-interest, they part company with each other over what *is* good for an individual. For the virtue ethicist, anything that makes one's life or character better is good for one. Yet acquiring an exemplary character may lead us to do things that are very damaging from the standpoint of our narrow interests, such as pleasure, comfort, and safety. Ethical egoism (at least as understood in the philosophical literature), by contrast, defines the individual's good narrowly and hence is critical of the ancient idea of the exemplary character.

3. *Is the good defined in terms of the right?*

Virtue ethics theory:	no
Ethical egoism:	no
Utilitarianism:	no
Kantianism:	yes
Contractarianism:	yes

On this issue, egoism, utilitarianism, and the virtue ethics approach all resemble each other more than they do Kantianism and contractarianism. Virtue ethics, egoism, and utilitarianism all account for what we "ought to do" in terms of what is good; egoism and utilitarianism analyze the notion of the right in terms of the good; while Kantianism and contractarianism proceed in exactly the opposite direction—analyzing the good in terms of the right.

Any theory that takes the notion of the good for granted and explains proper behavior in terms of the good can be called a *teleological* theory (from the Greek *telos,* or "end"). Virtue ethics, ethical egoism, and utilitarianism are all teleological views. Theories that say various ways of acting are right *in themselves* (as opposed to good in themselves) and that analyze proper behavior in terms of these duties can be called *deontological* theories (from the Greek *deon,* or "that which is binding"). Kantianism and contractarianism are deontological views: They say that something can be good only if it is the result of morally permissible behavior and that we must meet our duties whether we want to or not and regardless of whether doing so is good for us or anyone else. Utilitarianism is a hybrid view: it is teleological, but also deontological in saying that maximizing the good is right in itself.

This chart summarizes how the various normative theories are related to each other:

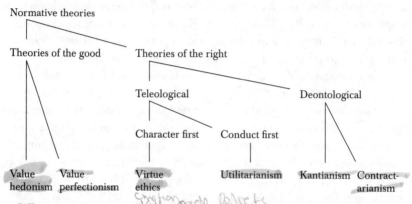

When we discuss normative theories that address the question, What must we do? our first topics will be the teleological theories: ethical egoism (discussed in Chapter 7) and utilitarianism (Chapter 8). Then we look at the deontological theories: Kantianism (Chapter 9) and contractarianism (Chapter 10). Finally, we consider some contemporary developments, including communitarianism, feminism, and the revival of virtue ethics (Chapter 11).

QUESTIONS FOR REFLECTION

1. Discussing the Summerlin case, we cited the principle that it is (always) wrong to disseminate forged data. Evaluate this principle. Is there a more general principle that we could adopt? Would it be reasonable to say, for example, that it is wrong to deceive others? (Can you think of cases in which deceiving others is acceptable?)

2. Suppose that A wants to marry B, who does not want to marry A. Does the right to self-determination entail that A may insist that B marry A? What does that right imply in this case?

3. Suppose that I have a deadly and highly infectious disease. It can be cured with an injection, but I refuse on religious grounds to receive the injection. Should others ignore my decision and compel me to receive the shot? Does the principle of self-determination entail that I may refuse?

4. Suppose it is right to let someone kill herself. It does not follow that it is right to help her do so. Can you think of situations in which suicide is allowable but assisting is not?

5. It is one thing to say that something is morally (im)permissible and another to say that it should be (il)legal. Suppose it is sometimes right to help patients kill themselves. In those cases should assisting in their suicide also be legal? Clarify. (Physician-assisted suicide has been legalized in only one state—Oregon, where the law went into effect in 1997. Under that law, only in about three dozen cases have people been given deadly drugs, and only in about half were the drugs used.)

FURTHER READINGS

Beauchamp, Tom. *Philosophical Ethics*. New York: McGraw-Hill, 2001.

Beauchamp, Tom, and Walters, LeRoy. *Contemporary Issues in Bioethics*. Belmont, Calif.: Wadsworth, 1994.

Nagel, Thomas. *The View from Nowhere*, Chapters 9–10. New York: Oxford University Press, 1986.

Rachels, James. *The Elements of Moral Philosophy*. New York: McGraw-Hill, 1999.

Rawls, John. *A Theory of Justice*, Section 9. Cambridge, Mass.: Harvard University Press, 1971.

Singer, Peter. *A Companion to Ethics*. Oxford: Blackwell, 1991.

Williams, Bernard. *Morality: An Introduction to Ethics*. New York: Harper Torchbooks, 1972.

NOTES

1. Oliver Sacks, *The Man Who Mistook His Wife for a Hat* (New York: Harper & Row, 1970), p. 97.

2. Sacks, p. 98.

3. Here is a quick summary of some moral terminology: The expressions in column A (1–6) are equivalent, and so are the expressions in column B (7–12), but each expression in B is weaker than the corresponding expression in A (7 is weaker than 1, 8 is weaker than 2, and so on).

A	B
1. Doing so and so is the right thing to do	7. Doing so and so is all right
2. I must do so and so	8. I may do so and so
3. I am obligated to do so and so	9. I am not obligated *not* to do so and so
4. I have a duty to do so and so	10. It is not my duty to not do so and so
5. It is wrong not to do so and so	11. Doing so and so is not wrong
6. Not doing so and so is not permissible	12. Doing so and so is permissible

4. Alexander Kohn, *False Prophets* (Oxford: Blackwell, 1986), p. 82. Facts about the Summerlin case are drawn from this book.

5. *McKay v. Bergstedt,* in 801 *Pacific Reporter,* 2d Series. 801 P.2d 617 (Nevada 1990).

6. Augustine *The City of God,* trans. Marcus Dods (New York: Random House, 1950), p. 26 (Book I, Sect. 20).

7. Some theorists describe the relationship between normative ethics and metaethics differently. They take it that normative ethics is ethics proper, so that metaethics is not a branch of ethics, but a separate domain of inquiry in its own right.

8. Some philosophers argue that we should separate the distinction between value as a means and as an end, on the one hand, from the distinction between extrinsic and intrinsic value, on the other. Something has *intrinsic value* when it derives its value from its own inner nature. Something has *extrinsic value* if its value is derived from something outside itself. Extrinsic value is closely related to instrumental value: If something's value is instrumental, it is extrinsic. For elaboration, see Christine Korsgaard, "Two Distinctions in Goodness," *Philosophical Review* 92 (1983): 27–49.

9. In his influential book *The Methods of Ethics,* Henry Sidgwick states that moderns emphasize *the right* while the ancients emphasize *the good* (Indianapolis: Hackett, 1981), Book I. First published 1874.

Subjectivism

Is Morality an Illusion?

Early one morning in July 1997, a burglar entered an Oregon slaughter-house that processed horse meat for export to Europe. The intruder brought along a device with a kitchen timer attached to flammable jelly and set it to explode into flames. The slaughterhouse was burned, leaving the horses unscathed. A few days later the authorities received a call from the Animal Liberation Front (ALF), claiming responsibility for the arson. ALF is a shadowy group of mostly college-aged activists opposed to the use of animals as experimental subjects and as food. It has smashed windows in butcher shops, released tens of thousands of animals from farms, destroyed several research facilities, and gained itself a place on the FBI's list of domestic terrorist organizations. Nonetheless, as its founder, Rod Coronado, points out, no one has been physically injured by its activities. It enjoys a degree of popularity, as is suggested by the fact that it is defended by the People for the Ethical Treatment of Animals (PETA), an animal rights organization that paid Coronado's legal fees.[1]

While most animal rights organizations do not destroy property, many, including the Humane Society of the United States and the Fund for Animals, agree with ALF's view that animals should not be used in medical research. In turn, other organizations such as Americans for Medical Progress (AMP) have sprung up to defend the merits of animal research. They point out that animal research has helped us improve our health in many ways. For example, polio used to strike down tens of thousands of children every year; the vaccine that prevents it was developed with the help of animal research. Animal experimentation is vital to finding cures for conditions such as cancer, heart disease, and AIDS.[2]

What prompted the creation of animal rights organizations like PETA was the increasingly widespread conviction that animals are not mere tools to be used as people see fit. They have interests that ought to be respected. But AMP and other critics reply that when human lives are at stake, it is acceptable to sacrifice animals. And many people would say something far more extreme: We may treat animals as we please. Where does the truth lie?

According to a perspective called *ethical subjectivism,* there is no objective truth to be discovered about the way we may treat animals or about any other ethical question, for that matter, since ethical judgments are purely matters of personal attitude. To make a value judgment is merely to register one's feelings. But if morality is simply a matter of feelings, isn't one moral opinion as good as another? Some subjectivists seem to think so; and, as a consequence, they tend to dismiss the arguments of others. Subjectivism is the ultimate conversation ender. To illustrate the attitude, imagine how a subjectivist who is also an animal researcher might respond to the criticisms of PETA members: "There are no facts about right and wrong. What PETA says makes it clear that its members disapprove of all animal research. I acknowledge their feelings, but so what? I happen to *approve* of conducting animal research that might save people, and that is what I am doing."

Is the subjectivist correct? Are ethical judgments nothing more than subjective responses? Is it really necessary to abandon the idea of objective moral truth? These are the questions we will consider in this chapter.

THE HUMEAN BEING

What is the basis for saying that ethical judgments are entirely subjective? For many people it is suggested by a view of moral motivation first spelled out by the eighteenth-century Scottish philosopher David Hume (1711–1776). Hume began by contrasting beliefs with desires: Beliefs purport to depict the world as it is, while desires represent the way we want the world to be. Then Hume asked whether beliefs or desires motivate us to do things. His answer, unsurprisingly, was that desires prompt action. To understand the role of desires in our lives, imagine that although I can see the contents of my office clearly enough and infer all sorts of things about it, I do not have any desires. Without them, I would be a zombie. If I wanted neither one thing nor another, nothing would make me sit at my desk or crawl inside it or stand on top of it. But with desires, I come alive—I have direction. Because I want to write this chapter, I sit and hammer away at the keyboard. Because I want to avoid pain, I don't slam my fingers in the drawer—and so on.

Beliefs, on the other hand, cannot prompt us to act in one way or another, not by themselves—not without borrowing force from desires. In many ways beliefs are like pictures that we store away so that we can retain information about our surroundings. Why would a depiction of some aspect of reality prompt us to take action? Right now I am sitting at my desk; I can see it in front of me, and if I close my eyes I can imagine it to myself. I have a picture, as it were, sitting on a shelf in my mind, but it is not capable of moving me one way or another.

Reasoning about beliefs is similarly powerless to cause us to act. In Hume's words, reason alone, or applied solely to beliefs, "can never produce any action, or give rise to volition." By applying reason to my beliefs, I can reach all sorts of conclusions. For example, from what I conjecture about my desk and its position, I might infer that if I were to bring my fist down hard, I would strike a hard object. But these conclusions are just more beliefs. By themselves, they do not make me want to move my hand – or do anything else.

None of this shows that beliefs and reasoning about beliefs have no effect whatever on my behavior, of course. Beliefs do not motivate, but they do facilitate. Hume put the point this way: "Reason is, and ought only to be the slave of the passions."[3] (Here "passions" is another word for desires.) According to Hume, our decisions are the product of both, but desires are definitely in the driver's seat. When we engage in rational deliberation about what to do, our desires interest us in some possible state of affairs, while our beliefs just tell us how to bring the world in line with our wishes. When the ALF people blew up the Oregon slaughterhouse, they did so because they *wanted* the consumption of animal flesh to cease and *believed* that destroying facilities was an effective means to that end.

But doesn't reasoning change our desires the way it changes our beliefs? Not really. Recall that beliefs represent the way the world is; since they might depict the world accurately or inaccurately, they can be true or false, and they can be criticized rationally, for the reasoning behind them may or may not be conducive to identifying the truth. Imagine, for example, that you ask me whether Exxon/Mobil has taken effective measures to prevent incidents like the March 1989 disaster in which 11 million gallons of crude oil leaked from the *Exxon Valdez,* only 3 – 4 percent of which was ever recovered from Prince William Sound. Suppose I answer "yes." But when you request the reason for my belief I tell you "I asked the company's public relations office." At that point you would be entitled to challenge my reasoning on the grounds that the source of my belief was not a disinterested party and hence unreliable.

In contrast, desires do not depict reality and cannot be true or false, so it is inappropriate to assess them for accuracy, the way we scrutinize our beliefs. From the critical standpoint, then, there is little to be done about our basic desires. We can try to make sure our scheme of desires is realistic and minimize the extent to which our goals clash with each other (so that we do not end up trying to achieve mutually incompatible goals). We might also disregard desires if we discover that their development has been facilitated by erroneous or irrational beliefs; for example, we might reassess a desire to drink ten quarts of prune juice a day when we discover that—contrary to our belief—massive quantities of prune juice do not prevent cancer.

All this might seem straightforward and unproblematic, but notice that Hume's account of psychology does not square with the ordinary conception of objective values. Ordinarily, we take objective values to be part of the fabric of reality. There are objective value *facts,* and if we grasp them—if we form accurate beliefs about them—these beliefs can impel us to act. Thus, we assume, beliefs about objective values provide us with the impetus to act rather than merely coaching us about how to satisfy preexisting desires. In other words, upon discovering an objective moral fact, such as that pointlessly harming animals is wrong, we come to believe in it; and this belief, in turn, has a compelling force on us when we decide how to behave toward animals. We expect that once people are convinced that a course of action is morally wrong, they will try to avoid it. That an action is wrong serves as a strong reason to avoid it, and when people have a strong reason to avoid something, they are moved to comply, even if they have to resist desires that pull in the other direction. Thus the ordinary view suggests that value facts influence the will through the beliefs they produce in us, but this idea clashes with the Humean understanding of our psychology—according to which beliefs cannot rationally compel us to desire anything, and desires, not beliefs, supply the impetus for our decisions. No beliefs can rationally compel us to decide to act in any particular way, and this holds for beliefs about moral facts as much as for any other sort. Even if the facts prompt me to believe that I have a duty not to harm animals, I will respond to that belief only if I want to act dutifully, and it is not irrational to lack that desire.

Because there is a clash between the plausible Humean view of psychology and the ordinary view of objective values, we might well begin to question the existence of objective values as they are often understood. All value-neutral facts seem to fit the Humean conception well enough. For example, facts about the food in front of me might prompt me to believe various things about it, but my beliefs cannot motivate me to eat in the absence of a desire for food. By contrast, an objectively good thing is thought to have "to-be-pursuedness somehow built into it," and a wrong action to have built-in "not-to-be-doneness," as the philosopher J. L. Mackie put the point.[4] Why should we think there is a special kind of fact called a value that is the only sort with motivational power? The more we think about them, the more we may come to believe that objective values are no more part of the real world than are fictional creations like unicorns, Anna Karenina, and Homer Simpson. Objective values are highly peculiar; as Mackie has suggested, "if there were objective values, then they would be entities or qualities or relations of a very strange sort, utterly different from anything else in the universe." According to Mackie's famous "argument from queerness," the extreme oddness of objective values constitutes reason to conclude that they do not exist.

SKEPTICISM

But if objective values are not real, our judgments about right and wrong, good and bad, are confused. How does the confusion arise? Hume supplies an answer. According to him, we encounter things in the world, and we have subjective responses to them—these are real enough. Objective values, however, are an illusion created when we project our subjective responses back onto the world, and we perpetuate the illusion in our moral judgments when we speak as if our responses are prompted by value properties that are part of the fabric of the world. Elaborating on Hume's points, Mackie defended a form of subjectivism called moral skepticism: He said that often when we make moral judgments we *intend* to attribute objective moral properties to things, but we are in error: "Although most people in making moral judgements implicitly claim, among other things, to be pointing to something objectively prescriptive, these claims are all false."[5]

If objective values are illusory, it is pointless to talk as if they are real, for then, as Mackie says, our evaluative claims will be mistaken. If we cannot evaluate things without implying that they have nonexistent objective moral properties, we might as well stop evaluating things and give up doing ethics.

However, even if objective values are not real, it does not follow that our evaluations are inevitably mistaken and hence pointless. For we might be able to make value judgments without intending to refer to objectively prescriptive properties, as subjectivists themselves have pointed out. In fact, subjectivists give us two possibilities to consider. According to some of them, evaluations attribute no properties to things; and according to others, evaluations refer to subjective properties. Either way, we avoid referring to objective properties. Hence subjectivists may, and usually do, resist Mackie-style skepticism. Let's examine these two subjectivist accounts of evaluation.

TWO FORMS OF SUBJECTIVISM

In the early twentieth century, a group of philosophers called *logical positivists* expressed grave doubts about the objectivist pretensions of evaluative judgments. Like Hume, whose views they refined, the positivists thought that some areas of inquiry should be abandoned—namely, areas whose claims cannot be verified using experience or mathematical or logical reasoning. The positivists' charge was that unverifiable claims are nonsense because they fail to assert anything at all. Among these unverifiable claims are ethical utterances. Hence, according to the positivists, ethical utterances are empty.

But even if they are empty, ethical utterances might still be useful, as positivists like the British philosopher A. J. Ayer soon noticed. One thing we can do with evaluative utterances is to express feelings, in much the same way as we evince pain by yelling "ouch!" In fact, Ayer and other so-called *emotivists* suggested that the role of ethical language is primarily to convey subjective responses. Suppose I say "You tortured animals," then add "and it was wrong." According to Ayer, "it was wrong," is not a statement of fact, "not even a statement about my own state of mind."[6] Instead, "it was wrong" expresses my feelings about your action. Adding it is like saying "You tortured animals!" in a special horrified tone, signaling a feeling of moral disapproval.

"It was wrong" can also carry the force of an imperative. Saying "it was wrong" is like giving the command, "Don't do that!" Other emotivists suggested further interpretations of the force of moral language. For example, according C. L. Stevenson, the best-known proponent of emotivism in the United States, saying "it is wrong to torture animals" is like saying "would that animal torture did not exist!"[7]

A second form of subjectivism bypasses Mackie's skepticism by saying that moral judgments describe our emotional responses and so refer to subjective properties. If to "you sacrificed an animal" I add "and it is wrong," what I am doing, according to this view, is saying that I feel disapproval of your sacrificing an animal. Contrary to what emotivists like Ayer suggest, I am not merely evincing my disapproval, but also reporting it.

SUBJECTIVISM AND ARGUMENTATION

Since our judgments may express or report our subjective feelings, moral valuations can be useful even if there are no objective values. But can we really salvage ethics if we understand moral judgments subjectively? The answer is controversial, but there are powerful grounds for skepticism about the idea of a workable subjectivist ethics, since subjectivists seem unable to explain the very activities that are central to ethics—namely, reasoning and arguing about moral issues.

Here's the problem. If moral judgments are merely expressions of emotion, they cannot be contradicted. Suppose I say, "You stabbed a dog to amuse yourself and it was wrong." What you did to the dog with your knife might not have been a case of stabbing—you and I can argue about that. We can also argue about whether you were trying to amuse yourself at the time. These are value-neutral factual matters. But we cannot have a genuine argument about whether this form of amusement is wrong, for there is no truth to the matter and hence nothing to argue about. And this is the way things are across the board, in the emotivist view: In moral disputes, there is never any assertion at stake. In effect, one of us is yelling, "Hooray for torturing animals!" while the other yells, "Boo for torturing animals!" So attempting to resolve purely moral disagreements makes no sense. Why would people try to do something that is clearly impossible?

The best reply the emotivist can offer is to suggest that the goal of moral argumentation is not what it appears to be; disputants seem to seek the truth, but what they really want is to cause others to share their attitudes, to disapprove of the same things. In other words, good argumentation is not about identifying the truth; a "good" argument is anything that aligns others' attitudes with our own. However, the process of influencing someone's attitudes can involve techniques that would be completely irrational and even immoral as judged by common sense. The most effective means might be persuasive but fallacious rhetoric or intimidation, conditioning, and brainwashing techniques, in which case emotivists must endorse these measures as good moral arguments.

Theorists who embrace the descriptive form of subjectivism fare no better in coming to terms with moral argumentation. In a sense, they do acknowledge that there are disputable moral facts. According to descriptive subjectivism, attitude reports are moral facts: When I say "it is not wrong to harm animals for fun," I am saying that I feel no disapproval of harming animals. But while these facts can be disputed, two points need to be considered: First, attitude reports are not in dispute during a typical moral argument. If to my statement that harming animals for fun is all right, you respond that harming animals for fun is wrong, we are not really disagreeing about anything. I am pointing out my attitude, and you are describing yours. Second, it would be silly to dispute such facts. I cannot be wrong about my sincere descriptions of my own emotions, so why deny them? Of course, someone might have reason to question my sincerity and insist that I do not really approve of gratuitously harming animals. A dispute along these lines could occur. But would it be plausible to say that moral disputes generally take this form? If you contradicted my claim about harming animals, would you really intend to question whether I approve of gratuitously harming animals? Or would you mean to say something that cannot be captured by a description of a particular person's state of mind: that harming animals is *wrong*?

OBJECTIVITY

We have seen that even if moral judgments are in no sense objective, evaluation can serve some purposes, such as expressing or describing attitudes. However, according to the subjectivist accounts of evaluation we have examined, it makes little sense to engage in the form of argumentation that lies at the heart of traditional ethics. So it seems impossible to salvage ethics unless we assume there are objective moral facts to be discovered and disputed. But how are we to understand moral objectivity? In what sense are value claims factual? In truth, these questions simply have not been settled. We could say that value properties are part of the mind-independent world and that a moral judgment is true when it accurately describes these properties. However, we have seen that this approach faces daunting challenges from Hume and Mackie. Rather than attempt to meet these objections, it is worth asking whether there are any other ways to understand moral objectivity. In fact, two alternatives seem especially promising.

According to the first, moral properties are not fully mind-independent, but not fully subjective either. John McDowell argues that they are real in the same way that color properties and other so-called secondary qualities are real.[8] John Locke introduced the term *secondary quality* in order to refer to features that give an object the power to affect observers in certain ways. Primary qualities, like size and shape, are, he said, independent of observers, but secondary qualities, such as color, are *powers to affect* observers in characteristic ways. The *appearance of redness* is in the head, so to speak, but *redness itself* is a special property of things in the world. It is the disposition or tendency some objects have to affect us in certain ways: Redness is the disposition to give the appearance of redness to unimpaired subjects in optimal viewing conditions. Perhaps moral properties can be thought of in the same way. Perhaps value properties are dispositional properties identified in terms of a characteristic reaction they cause in suitably receptive subjects in ideal conditions. If so, then moral properties are real even though they are only dispositional, and moral claims are as objective as claims about color.

A second promising view would define moral objectivity in terms of *reasonableness,* but only after distinguishing reasonableness from the limited form of *rationality* that Hume had in mind when he declared that "reason is . . . the slave of the passions." So let's clarify reasonableness and rationality before we examine how reasonableness defines objectivity.

Being rational is a matter of being reliably accurate in one's choice of beliefs and prudent in one's choice of actions. As for prudence, it is primarily a matter of selecting effective means to one's ends, but also a matter of balancing and revising ends to minimize clashes and wholly unrealistic expectations. Here is an illustration of prudence at work: Suppose that you and I want to begin a business of catching fish for resale, and we are discussing the terms for our association. If I am rational solely in the prudential sense, I might try to maneuver you into accepting as little of the profit as I can, even though we each will contribute the same resources. Perhaps your ability to sustain yourself depends on our joint endeavor, while I have many other outlets for making a living. Or maybe I can threaten you with force. In either case, I might exploit your situation so as to extract concessions from you and demand, say, 65 percent of the profits even though our contribution in terms of work and other things is the same. Because I have you over a barrel, you might reluctantly give in to my demands. However, you will also complain that I am being *unreasonable,* since I refuse to accept an equal division of the profits accruing from a joint endeavor in which each makes precisely the same contribution.[9]

More fully, reasonableness is marked by the willingness to interact with others according to terms acceptable to everyone involved, as long as the others are willing to do the same. To that end, reasonable persons are drawn into a dialogue with others in which all parties have an equal say and propose and discuss terms of association in a cooperative way.[10]

If reasonable people continued their deliberations long enough and had an accurate grasp of relevant morally neutral facts, such as information about psychology, perhaps they would reach a consensus of opinion about suitable terms for interacting with one another. The principles upon which they would converge, we might say, constitute the moral truth. *True moral principles,* according to this view, are those that would be accepted by reasonable people as suitable terms of association. These principles determine the right thing to do, the moral facts. If they leave a particular moral issue unresolved, we must conclude that the issue has no correct solution.

This account of objectivity avoids the suggestion that the world has moral properties with built-in compelling force. The people who find moral truths compelling are reasonable people, and that is because reasonable people are predisposed to respond to moral facts; for reasonable people want a specific sort of solution to conflict, and true moral principles are the solution they seek. We are not reasonable unless we have a characteristic attitude about solving conflict. In this way reasonableness contrasts with rationality, whose marks are the desires to be accurate and prudent.

EXPANDING THE CIRCLE

Let's return to our question about animals—which was, May we treat them as we please?—and see what answer reasonable people would offer. At the heart of the case against concern for animals is a fact about their ability to reciprocate any moral restraint we show them: Obviously, animals are not capable of appreciating the difference between right and wrong; therefore, it is absurd to expect them to act morally or to hold them to moral standards. This is the point to the fable of the frog that is asked by a scorpion to carry it to the other side of the river. At first the frog refuses, fearing that the scorpion will sting her. However, the scorpion reassures the frog, who then lets the scorpion climb onto her back. Yet, halfway across the river, the scorpion stings the frog. Greatly surprised, she asks, "Why did you sting me? Now we are both going to die!" "Because it is my nature," the scorpion replied. By nature, animals are not moral agents, so we cannot expect them to consider our interests. Why, then, should we consider theirs? Shouldn't we respond to animals the way we would respond to fellow human beings who are ready to attack us in a morally unconstrained way: by putting aside our normal scruples against violence and fighting back?

In its primary and central applications to reasonable people, morality does entitle us to expect reciprocity and mutual restraint. But should we accept the principle that we may do anything we wish to a creature that is not a moral agent? Presumably not, for infants, people with severe developmental disabilities, and those with gravely damaged brains are not moral agents, yet few of us would say that we may treat them as we please. We have duties toward these human beings even though they are not moral agents. Perhaps we owe animals consideration, too. After all, many animals have interests that matter to them in much the same way that our interests matter to us: Isn't this grounds to acknowledge that we have duties toward animals?

But how can we determine the objectively correct answer about the status of animals? Unfortunately, we cannot do so by imaginatively joining with other reasonable agents and working out the terms for our interactions. For animals would be left out, since they cannot deliberate about reasonable moral principles.

However, people can deliberate on behalf of animals, and we can extend our notion of reasonableness so that we can evaluate our behavior toward animals. Seeing that sentient animals have interests that matter to them, we can look for ways to accommodate those interests when they clash with ours. Identifying which accommodations are reasonable will not always be easy, because it is difficult to decide how much weight to give the interests of sentient animals as compared to the interests of people. Most of us would not say that each animal is the equal of each person, for then it would be wrong to save someone if we could do so only by killing an animal (or several of them). But as long as we can agree that the interests of sentient creatures do matter, we can also agree that everyone should show them consideration. In particular, we should go out of our way to avoid harming them.

This conclusion is a powerful one. If it is true, then medical research involving sentient animals should be carefully screened to ensure that its goal could not be achieved any other way, that its value for human beings is substantial, and that the animals involved will not suffer.

QUESTIONS FOR REFLECTION

1. Consider the following remark in David Hume's *Treatise:*

   When you pronounce any action or character to be vicious, you mean nothing, but that from the constitution of your nature you have a feeling or sentiment of blame from the contemplation of it. Vice and virtue, therefore, may be compared to sounds, colours, heat and cold, which, according to modern philosophy, are not qualities in objects, but perceptions in the mind.[11]

   Does this passage commit Hume to the descriptive form of subjectivism?

2. In a famous passage, Hume says, "Tis not contrary to reason to prefer the destruction of the whole world to the scratching of my finger."[12] Why would Hume say this? Is he correct?

3. In his *Principia Ethica,* G. E. Moore says that goodness is *simple* in the sense that it is not composed of other properties.[13] Moore goes on to say that goodness should not be mistaken for any natural property, such as pleasantness. He calls this error the naturalistic fallacy. Moore thinks that goodness cannot be a natural property because we can always sensibly doubt, regarding any natural property such as pleasantness, whether it is good; yet this doubt would not be sensible if goodness were the natural property at hand: If goodness were pleasantness, then the answer to "Is pleasantness good?" would be as obvious as the answer to "Is goodness good?" Is Moore correct? How might an emotivist respond? How might Mackie respond?

4. Some philosophers, such as W. D. Ross, have felt the need to posit the existence of a special faculty called "intuition" to explain our ability to detect goodness and rightness; this view is called *intuitionism.*[14] Can intuitionism be used in response to Mackie's skepticism about moral properties? (Or is positing a special faculty for detecting values just as problematic as positing "queer" moral properties?)

5. According to Roderick Firth, ethical judgments and properties can be analyzed in terms of the reactions of approval or disapproval of an ideal observer.[15] To say that an act is right is to say that a person with ideal attributes would approve of that act. These ideal attributes

include disinterestedness, dispassion, consistency, omniscience with respect to non-ethical facts, and the ability to fully imagine all relevant facts. Would Firth's theory be a form of subjectivism? How is an ideal observer related to a reasonable person?

6. In addition to his argument from queerness, Mackie offers the argument from relativity: The vast differences in moral beliefs among different groups of people provide evidence that there are no objective values. How strong is this argument from relativity? Why should we accept ethical subjectivism rather than cultural relativism (or vice versa)?

7. Suppose that no matter how long reasonable people continued their deliberations, they would converge on only some principles, but not all. What would follow about the nature of moral objectivity, defined in terms of reasonableness? Does what follows constitute a problem for the account of objectivity? Can you propose a better account?

8 Do we have duties toward any animals? Do our duties extend to all animals? Do our duties extend to plants? Should we refrain from eating animals?

9. Human overpopulation results in overcrowding and overconsumption of resources, which harm the interests of animals. Do we owe it to animals to reduce the human population by restricting the right to reproduce?

FURTHER READINGS

On Subjectivism

Ayer, A. J. *Language, Truth and Logic.* New York: Dover, 1952. First published 1936.

Copp, David, and Zimmerman, David, editors. *Morality, Reason and Truth: New Essays on the Foundations of Ethics.* Totowa, N.J.: Rowman & Allanheld, 1984.

Firth, Roderick. "Ethical Absolutism and the Ideal Observer." *Philosophy and Phenomenological Research* 12 (1952): 336–341.

Hare, R. M. *The Language of Morals.* Oxford: Oxford University Press, 1952.

Harman, Gilbert. *The Nature of Morality.* Oxford: Oxford University Press, 1977.

Honderich, Ted, editor. *Morality and Objectivity.* London: Routledge & Kegan Paul, 1985.

Hume, David. *A Treatise of Human Nature,* 2nd ed. Edited by L. A. Selby-Bigge. Oxford: Clarendon Press, 1978. First published 1739.

Mackie, J. L. *Ethics: Inventing Right and Wrong.* Harmondsworth, England: Penguin, 1977.

McDowell, John. "Values and Secondary Qualities." In *Morality and Objectivity,* edited by T. Honderich. London: Routledge & Kegan Paul, 1985, pp. 110–129.

Nagel, Thomas. *The View from Nowhere.* Oxford: Oxford University Press, 1986.

Rachels, James. *The Elements of Moral Philosophy.* New York: McGraw-Hill, 1999.

Rawls, John. *Political Liberalism.* New York: Columbia University Press, 1993.

Ross, W. D. *The Right and the Good.* Oxford: Clarendon Press, 1930.

Sayer-McCord, G., editor. *Essays on Moral Realism.* Ithaca: Cornell University Press, 1988.

Smith, Michael. "Realism." In *A Companion to Ethics,* edited by Peter Singer. London: Blackwell, 1991.

——. *The Moral Problem.* Oxford: Blackwell, 1994.

Stevenson, L. L. *Ethics and Language.* New Haven: Yale University Press, 1944.

On the Status of Animals

Frey, R. G. *Rights, Killing, and Suffering.* Oxford: Blackwell, 1983.

Gruen, Lori. "Animals." In *A Companion to Ethics,* edited by Peter Singer. London: Blackwell, 1991.

Midgley, Mary. *Animals and Why They Matter.* Harmondsworth, England: Penguin, 1983.

Regan, Tom, and Singer, Peter, editors. *Animal Rights and Human Obligations.* Englewood Cliffs, N.J.: Prentice-Hall, 1989.

Rollin, Bernard. *The Unheeded Cry.* Oxford: Oxford University Press, 1989.

Singer, Peter. "Animals and the Value of Life." In *Matters of Life and Death,* edited by Tom Regan. New York: Random House, 1980, pp. 218–260.

NOTES

1. Matt Bai, "Breaking the Cages," *Newsweek,* 29 September 1997, p. 66.

2. Heloisa Sabin, "Animal Research Saves Human Lives," *Wall Street Journal,* 18 October 1995.

3. David Hume, *A Treatise of Human Nature,* 2nd ed., ed. L. A. Selby-Bigge (Oxford: Clarendon Press, 1978), pp. 414–415. First published in 1739.

4. J. L. Mackie, *Ethics: Inventing Right and Wrong* (Harmondsworth, England: Penguin, 1977), p. 40.

5. Mackie, p. 35.

6. A. J. Ayer, *Language, Truth, and Logic* (New York: Dover, 1952), p. 107. First published in 1936.

7. C. L. Stevenson, *Ethics and Language* (New Haven: Yale University Press, 1945). The English philosopher J. L. Austin did more than anyone else to identify the many functions language can serve. Feeling generous, I might say "I give you this gold mine"; in doing so, I am not describing anything, I am making it

the case that you own the mine. At a marriage ceremony I might say "I do," thereby wedding another. Other *performative* expressions, as Austin called them, include "I promise ___" which binds me to do ___, or "I command," or "I prescribe or advise" and so on. None of these expressions is descriptive. See J. L. Austin, *How to Do Things with Words* (Cambridge, Mass.: Harvard University Press, 1962).

8. John McDowell, "Values and Secondary Qualities," in *Morality and Objectivity,* ed. T. Honderich (London: Routledge & Kegan Paul, 1985), pp. 110–129.

9. As John Rawls pointed out in his *Political Liberalism* (New York: Columbia University Press, 1993), p. 48, we contrast rationality and reasonableness in ordinary discourse when we say, for example, "Their proposal was perfectly rational given their strong bargaining position, but it was nevertheless highly unreasonable, even outrageous."

10. This account of the reasonable and the rational is drawn from Rawls's *Political Liberalism.* See especially pp. 48–54.

11. David Hume, *A Treatise of Human Nature,* pp. 468–469.

12. Hume, p. 416.

13. G. E. Moore, *Principia Ethica* (Cambridge: Cambridge University Press, 1903).

14. W. D. Ross, *The Right and the Good* (Oxford: Clarendon Press, 1930).

15. Roderick Firth, "Ethical Absolutism and the Ideal Observer," *Philosophy and Phenomenological Research* 12 (1952): pp. 336–341.

Cultural Relativism

Does Each Culture Invent Its Own Morality?

In 1987 a beautiful eighteen-year-old named Roop Kanwar put on her finest dress and led about five hundred of the villagers from Deorala, India, to the cremation site. Her husband had died suddenly from appendicitis, after only eight months of marriage. His body, wrapped in a white shroud with only his face showing, was placed onto the logs of a funeral pyre by his family. Brahman priests looked on, offering prayers. Kanwar then climbed onto the pyre next to her husband's body, laying his head onto her lap. She signaled a child—the brother of her husband—who lit the pyre, and she was burned to death, in keeping with the ancient regional custom called *suttee*. She is now regarded as a saint and a goddess.

Suttee has been the subject of violent controversy in India for well over a century. When the British ruled India, they were horrified at the practice; but when they attempted to ban it, people rioted. As a result, many British argued that it should be tolerated. Who were they to interfere with the customs and religious practices of others? No British person would encourage widows to burn themselves to death; measured by British standards, suttee was wrong. But was it right for the British to impose their views on the Indians? Didn't Indian customs determine what was right for Indians? In the end, however, this relativist argument did not prevail. In the mid–nineteenth century the British banned suttee, and it has remained illegal ever since. Nonetheless, it is still practiced in parts of India.

When it happened in Deorala, thirty-seven villagers were charged with burning Kanwar against her will. After ten years they were cleared of the charges (the verdict has been appealed), but it is still not entirely clear whether Kanwar participated in the ceremony voluntarily or not. Some say that her in-laws bullied her into it and dulled her senses with opium. One villager replied, "She was not forced. It is not a *suttee* if it is forced. When the fire was lit, she just sat there. . . . She seemed to feel no pain. When the gods want something, they can do anything." Another villager claimed that she tried to get off the pyre three times and was pushed back into the flames by the crowd.[1]

Are outsiders ever justified in criticizing the cultural practices of others? Many of us think there is a single true morality, one true view of the right, and perhaps one true view of the good as well, that applies both across cultures and within them and can be called upon to settle ethical disputes locally and globally. This position is called *ethical universalism.* (Sometimes it is called *absolutism,* a term we will define in Chapter 9.) As universalists we may suggest that it is wrong for anyone—including the villagers of Deorala—to urge or force grieving widows to burn themselves to death, and we may suspect that in practice suttee is not fully voluntary. And our moral objections to suttee might prompt us to ban it. But they might not; as we will see later, a universalist may condemn a practice and still tolerate it. Besides, universalism is not committed to the claim that the single true moral standard is so specific that it can be used to settle all possible disputes among people. It might be rather abstract, and too indefinite to solve all of the problems people might face. In theory, it might not apply to suttee. Moreover, even if there is a single true morality, it does not follow that we know what it is. Most of us will acknowledge that our views about moral truth are at least as fallible as our beliefs about, say, physics and chemistry. We may not be confident about our assessment of suttee, so we may be reluctant to condemn it.

Ethical relativists question the traditional universalist view. They say that no set of moral standards is universally binding—no single moral framework can be called upon to settle disputes within nations and across the world. Instead, moral judgments and accepted moral standards are fundamentally different across cultures or individuals, and what a given person should do must be assessed relative to his or her (individual or cultural) standards. So if we think our condemnation of suttee is based on the one true morality, we are mistaken. It is based on a standard we accept, and our standard is only one of many.

Different forms of ethical relativism are possible; we will describe some of the options. Then we will discuss a form of ethical relativism that enjoys wide support, especially in popular culture. We will call it *cultural relativism,* and it says that my actions can be accurately judged only by applying my own cultural standards, not by applying those of someone else's culture, which differ from mine.

ALTERNATIVES TO UNIVERSALISM

We can begin by describing some of the alternatives to universalism and locating ethical relativism with respect to these. This process will help us to understand exactly what ethical relativism says and how it is related to the universalist perspective it opposes.

There are two ways to deny the universalist view that there is one and only one true morality. One is to say that there is more than one true morality. This thesis can be labeled *pluralism*. The other is to say there is no true morality, which is a position called *nihilism*.

The most familiar nihilists are people who suggest that moral judgments such as "killing innocent people is wrong" are used to express the speaker's emotional reactions, not to make assertions. In this emotivist view of moral judgments, we treat the purported assertions in the first column below as we would the sentences in the second column.

It is wrong to kill innocent people.	Boo, killing innocent people! Hiss!
Love is good.	Yay, love! Hot doggie!
Harming your friends is bad.	Harming your friends! Ouch!

The sentences in the second column function only to express emotions about certain things. Since they do not say that anything is the case, they cannot be true (or false). If moral judgments merely function to express emotions, they, too, are incapable of being true. This emotivist view of moral judgments is one version of subjectivism, which we discussed in Chapter 2. Subjectivism says that moral judgments are merely expressions of emotion or reports about people's attitudes.

Emotivists can defend a view that might be classified as a form of ethical relativism. The view is that moral judgments are expressions of emotional reactions that vary across persons, groups, and time. However, emotivist relativism is not the only form of ethical relativism. Some ethical relativists are pluralists, and unlike emotivists and other nihilists, pluralists think that moral judgments are in some sense true.

Pluralists called *individual relativists* are inclined to think that we each have our own true morality. They say that the standards we accept determine what we should do, and these vary substantially from person to person. Other pluralists we may call *cultural relativists* maintain that moralities follow cultural lines: Each person's culture supplies the standards that determine what that person should do, and these differ fundamentally across cultures.

Here is a chart showing the various possibilities we have discussed:

Universalism	**Nihilism**			**Pluralism**	
There is one and only one true morality.	There is no true morality.			There is more than one true morality.	

	Emotivist relativism	**Individual relativism**	**Cultural relativism**
	Moral judgments are expressions of emotional reactions that vary across groups.	The standards a person accepts determine what she should do, and these vary across persons.	Each person's culture's standards determine what he should do, and these vary across cultures.

We will focus our attention on cultural relativism, the most widely accepted form of pluralism.

THE CASE FOR CULTURAL RELATIVISM

Cultural relativism seems to have two main sources of support. First, cultural diversity would seem to offer a powerful argument for cultural relativism. Second, its implications, especially its apparent toleration for the diversity of cultural practices, seem attractive.

The term *cultural diversity* can mean more than one thing, but supporters of relativism use it primarily to suggest that moral judgments and practices vary substantially from culture to culture. For this suggestion one can find many sources. For example, philosophers such as Michel de Montaigne (1533–1592) and relativist anthropologists such as Ruth Benedict (1887–1948) and William Graham Sumner (1840–1910) mention many practices that are favored in some societies yet condemned in others—among them, cannibalism, male prostitution, parricide, infanticide, and killing the elderly. On the strength of this diversity, they conclude that people in different cultures accept standards that are taken seriously by members of that culture only and that these standards are authoritative only in that culture. Sumner describes his own position as follows:

> The folkways are the "right" ways to satisfy all interests, because they are traditional, and exist in fact. . . . The "right" way is the way which the ancestors used and which has been handed down. The tradition is its own warrant. It is not held subject to verification by experience. The notion of right is in the folkways. . . . Therefore rights can never be "natural" or "God-given," or absolute in any sense. The morality of a group at a time

is the sum of the taboos and prescriptions in the folkways by which right conduct is defined.[2]

Many people seem willing to use observations about diversity in an argument in favor of cultural relativism. Here is one form the argument might take:

Argument from Diversity

1. Moral judgments vary along cultural lines (they are similar within cultures but fundamentally different across cultures).

2. So accepted moral standards vary fundamentally along cultural lines, and the standards of each individual's culture dictate what that individual should do.

Cultural relativism may also be defended on the grounds that it encourages us to acknowledge our own fallibility as judges of other cultures and to tolerate practices in other lands. Many of us know individuals who are quick to condemn ways of life that are different from their own. These judgmental people seem to think their own culture provides the final word on how everyone ought to act and may even want to forcibly impose their culture's practices on others. But cultural relativism seems incompatible with this narrow-minded view. Relativism *denies* that the standards of any one person's culture determine what people in other cultures should do. Hence it seems to provide a strong basis for condemning intolerance.

Does the argument from diversity justify the acceptance of cultural relativism? Are relativism's consequences as appealing as its proponents think? Let's discuss each of these questions.

ASSESSING THE ARGUMENT FROM DIVERSITY

One thing we must notice about the argument from diversity is that its conclusion consists of two separate claims, not one. The conclusion can be restated as

2a. Accepted moral standards vary fundamentally from one culture to another. (This might be called *descriptive* cultural relativism.)

2b. The standards of each individual's culture dictate what that individual should do. (Call this normative cultural relativism.)

Both of these claims are integral parts of the view we are calling cultural relativism, so both must be defended. Relativists will need to explain how the clustering of moral judgments referred to by premise 1 supports conclusions 2a and 2b. This will be difficult, for several reasons.

1. *Beliefs are problematic as support for facts.* The relativist seems to think that morality varies from culture to culture because people's *beliefs* about morality vary from culture to culture (as premise 1 says). But isn't this like arguing that the facts about God are different from one culture to another on the grounds that different cultures embrace different religious views? Imagine saying that when members of theistic cultures ask "Does God exist?" the answer is "yes," but when members of atheistic cultures ask the same question, the answer is "no"! Can a group of people make anything they like true simply by believing it is so?

2. *Descriptive claims are problematic as support for normative claims.* Notice that while premise 1 is a descriptive claim, conclusion 2b has normative implications. Yet as Scottish philosopher David Hume (1711–1776) pointed out in his *Treatise,* no set of merely descriptive claims entails a normative claim; "value" statements do not follow from "factual" statements; "ought" statements do not follow from "is" statements.[3]

3. *There is good reason to believe that all cultures share certain fundamental values,* which would mean that conclusion 2a, descriptive cultural relativism, is false. As many commentators have suggested, endorsing certain fundamental values is probably necessary for the existence of any continuing society.[4] For example, unless people valued having and caring for children, their society eventually would cease to exist, and their way of life would not survive to the next generation. Hence it is no surprise to see that every culture places a high value on the institution of the family. Of course, the value of families must not be exaggerated, either; it is critically important to balance the value of child rearing against other concerns, such as the grave problems created by overpopulation.

Other values must also play a role in a functioning society. For example, a society could not function if it did not condemn most forms of homicide. If people settled their disputes by killing their antagonists, the population would quickly dwindle to a vanishing point. And social cooperation would collapse if people freely lied and deceived each other whenever they thought it expedient to do so. Promises could not be made, because no one would expect them to be kept; and communication would be impeded because no one could rely on the spoken word of another.

4. *Even if moral judgments vary greatly across cultures, it is still entirely possible that all cultures accept the same fundamental moral standards,* which makes it difficult to see that the argument from diversity provides much support for descriptive cultural relativism. But wait: If all cultures accept the same ba-

sic moral standards, how could they possibly end up making very different moral judgments? Actually, several things could bring this about.

- *Moral complexity.* One possibility is that many judgments are inaccurate. Moral issues can be extremely complicated, so that any judgment is precarious. In Chapter 1, for example, we saw how complicated judgments about withdrawing medical treatment can be. Our best judgments may be only approximations of the truth, and it would not be surprising if people in different cultures accepted different approximations.

- *Varying circumstances.* The circumstances in which groups of people find themselves differ, and a standard might have to be implemented differently depending on the circumstances. Philosopher David Wong describes an example of this sort: Suppose that everyone in two societies accepts the general principle that women and men should have lifelong relationships with each other.[5] But in one society there are far more women than men or vice versa, while in another there are roughly equal numbers of each. Polygamy might well be considered acceptable in the first society and not in the second.

- *Differing beliefs (versus differing values).* People have different beliefs about things other than matters of right and wrong or good and bad, and these differences in opinion about value-independent facts could lead people who share the same fundamental moral standards to make very different judgments about what is right and good.

This last cause of diversity in moral judgments is probably the most significant of the three. To see how profoundly our factual beliefs can affect our value judgments, recall that during the Middle Ages inquisitors felt it necessary to torture people in horrible and often fatal ways. Today we accept the principle that it is wrong to harm innocent people, so we would condemn these acts of torture. But what accounts for our disagreement with the inquisitors? Did the inquisitors think that harming the innocent was all right? That is unlikely. They thought that satanic powers were at work on the earth, luring people away from salvation and into eternal torment. Using the threat of torture, the inquisitors hoped to compel people to practice the proper form of Christianity and thus avoid damnation. They thought they were helping people, not harming them, and the reason they thought so was because they believed a claim about value-neutral facts—namely, that torturing people is an effective way to save them from eternal torment. People in the modern era doubt this claim, and that is why we view the Inquisition with such horror.

Differences in belief rather than moral standards might also account for the fact that Westerners condemn suttee while many people in India do not. In modern Western cultures we consider it wrong to encourage self-immolation. If asked for justification, we would probably cite the principle that it is wrong to urge or force people to harm themselves, especially when they are not harming anyone else, and say that the widow is throwing her life away in a pointless and extraordinarily painful way. We might even raise the suspicion that suttee is a way to get rid of widows, who, by tradition, must be taken care of by their in-laws. But traditional Hindus have often recommended and praised suttee. Does that mean that they reject the principle that it is wrong to urge or force people to harm themselves? Isn't it possible that the Indians consider suttee beneficial to the widow, who becomes a goddess?

Consider the conservative religious justification behind suttee. Women are said to have so much energy that they cannot control it themselves and must submit to the direction of men or run amok (I'm not making this up). Women are said to be like power plants generating energy; when a man's wife dies, he loses his power plant and needs to find a replacement. But when a woman's husband dies, she is wild, uncontrollable, and dangerous; she should kill herself to avoid harming others. As one ancient document states: "After the death of her husband, [a widow] is especially dangerous and must shave her head, cake it with mud, sleep on a bed of stones. . . . If a widow is chaste and young, she is so infected with magic power that she must take her own life."[6] These opinions about unbridled feminine power are not moral judgments. They are beliefs about nonmoral facts. Because modern Westerners are not likely to share the beliefs, they condemn suttee.

What we have said so far is that cultural relativists must overcome some powerful obstacles if they are to explain to us why they think their argument from diversity supports relativism.[7] The argument is full of holes. Yet it is perhaps the chief source of support for relativism.

Still, people gravitate to relativism for another reason: They find its perceived consequences attractive. Let's examine these consequences and see how attractive they really are.

CONSEQUENCES OF CULTURAL RELATIVISM

As it turns out, the consequences of cultural relativism are disappointing. Consider a few reasons why this is so.

1.   *Cultural relativism cannot adjudicate cross-cultural disputes.* Imagine that a group of people we can call *protectors* are in a dispute with another group we

can call *whalers*. The protectors want to save the whales, but the whalers take the attitude expressed by a Japanese fisherman in a recent *New York Times* interview: "I don't think of whales as especially smart. . . . They're just like ordinary fish. We feel that they're just a big present from the sea."[8] The Japanese have taken whales for 2,000 years and continue to do so on the pretext that it is a form of scientific research. However, this research ends up on dinner tables in Japanese homes. Scientists using DNA sampling proved that many fish markets in Japan sell meat from endangered species of whales (for about $300 per pound).[9] Of course, the dispute over whaling is a complex matter, and there is a great deal of disagreement within Japan and other countries concerning what should be done. Instead of exploring it in its complexity, however, we will create a hypothetical case involving the fanciful protectors and whalers and approach it as the relativist might: by assuming that the moral standards of the whalers' culture are distinct from those of the protectors' culture. For simplicity, let us also suppose that the former standards unequivocally endorse killing whales until there are no more, while the latter prescribe saving whales (especially endangered species). Hence applying the two standards places the whalers and protectors in a deadlock. What should be done?

If we turn to cultural relativism to resolve the dispute, it turns its back on us. It says that for the protectors to defend the whales is "right for them" because by the standards of their culture they must preserve endangered species. However, cultural relativism also says that for the whalers to kill the endangered whales is "right for them." But if the protectors do what relativism endorses as "right for them," the whalers cannot do what it endorses as "right for them." The relativist is encouraging the two groups to pursue incompatible courses of action. What kind of resolution is that? The relativist concept of morality does not play the role most of us expect from the concept of the right: We want it to enable us to adjudicate disputes using reason rather than force. If cultural relativism were correct, then the concept of the right could not play this role.[10]

2. *Cultural relativism does not discourage intolerance.* At first glance it might seem possible for relativists to avoid recommending incompatible courses of action and exacerbating cross-cultural disputes. Some people think that cultural relativism supports a principle of tolerance, such as the following: When the cultural standards of others lead people to behave differently than we do, we should not interfere (or at least we should try to accommodate their ways). And if the protectors apply this principle, they will conclude that while they may do various things to help the whales, such as fishing for other things, they must not block the whalers.

However, there is still a problem. Whatever its merits, the principle of tolerance is a moral principle, and the relativist's credo is that *no* moral requirements are universally binding. People are bound only by their own cultural standards, and these are said to vary so greatly that no substantive moral principles are endorsed by all cultures. Presumably, then, the relativist would say that for members of many cultures the principle of tolerance is not binding. Relativists cannot call on the principle to solve the conflict between the whalers and protectors since that principle might be rejected by the cultural standards of either or both.

Can't the relativist reject intolerance without defending a principle of tolerance? If so, then perhaps the relativist could resolve cross-cultural disputes after all, by telling members of each culture not to interfere with the actions of others. But how would relativists go about criticizing intolerance? Well, they might try the suggestion that different peoples never have grounds for interfering with each other's culture-based practices. For example, isn't it obvious—relativists might ask—that the protectors could justify stopping the whalers only if it were *wrong* for the whalers to kill whales? But the hunts are *not wrong* "for the whalers," so the protectors cannot justify blocking them.

This attempt to rescue relativism will not work, either. It assumed that the only ground for stopping the whalers is that their hunts are "wrong for them." But this assumption is false. As relativists, the protectors could justify interference on the grounds that it is required by their cultural standards: By those standards, we have assumed, they must (it is "right for them" to) protect the whales; and since the only way they can protect whales is by stopping the whaling, they are justified in doing so. This reasoning does not assume that fishing is "wrong for the whalers"; rather, it appeals to the fact that halting the whaling is necessary if the protectors are to accomplish something that is "right for them." Certainly most of us would find it odd to say that it can be "right for me" to stop you from doing something that (I acknowledge) is "not wrong for you," but that is because most of us are not cultural relativists! We assume that one framework adjudicates morality for all disputants so that the very same requirements are binding on everyone, thus precluding the possibility that what is right for one of us clashes with what is right for another. Contrary to popular belief, interference with other cultures is entirely consistent with relativism.

3. *Cultural relativism bars all criticism of other cultures.* According to relativism, it makes no sense to criticize people for doing things that are sanctioned by the standards of their cultures. In fact, we must endorse what they do, at least in a qualified way, by saying that their actions are "right for them." In requiring this form of mutual endorsement, relativists seem to encourage

toleration; but, as we have seen, that impression is misleading, since relativism requires each of us to act strictly in accordance with our own cultural standards, which encourages intolerant peoples to remain intolerant.

While relativism does not encourage tolerance, it does force us to be nonjudgmental; isn't that a good thing? At first blush it might seem so. But it is one thing to be broad-minded about the peccadilloes of others and another to refrain from condemning horrifying practices that take place in other lands. When the Nazis came to power in Germany, they murdered Jews, Gypsies, and others in the name of fascist principles, and many of us in the rest of the world condemned what they did: Were we simply overlooking (or disputing) the fact that, after all, Nazis were a unified cultural group? Should we perhaps have qualified our condemnation and said that what they did was "right for them," even though it would not have been "right for us"? We want to say that what the Nazis did was wrong—period. But this condemnation makes no sense if cultural relativism is true, given that these actions were sanctioned by the cultural standards of the Nazis. If we are cultural relativists, the most we can say is that for us, the enemies of fascism, racial killing is wrong, and for us, it was right to fight the Nazis. But we must admit that it was right for the fascists to kill the Jews.

4.   *Cultural relativism implies that outside of shared cultures nothing is right or wrong.* If relativism is true, it follows that our cultural standards even determine whether there is a moral truth for us. If the people in a group failed to share cultural standards, nothing would be morally binding for them. They would exist in a state of moral anarchy. Killing, stealing, torture—such actions would be neither right nor wrong, and it would be impossible to argue that people should refrain from any form of behavior, no matter how brutal.

5.   *Cultural relativism implies that morality is arbitrary.* The relativist says that our cultural standards are decisive for us regardless of their origins. So, no matter why the members of a group adopt their standards—for convenience or money or under the threat of force or because they loathe other cultural groups or for the sake of novelty or for no reason whatever—those standards determine what is "right for them." In addition, members of a cultural group can change what is "right for them" by replacing their moral standards at any time and for any reason whatever. The result would never be standards that are morally superior to the old standards, however, since—according to relativism—it makes no sense to assess the standards themselves. So when Indians discouraged suttee and when Americans abandoned slavery, the result was not moral progress. Once a culture ceases to tolerate slavery, it is simply different, not better. Changing cultural standards changes

what is "right for future generations" without altering what was "right for past generations."

We have said enough to show that cultural relativism has seriously worrisome consequences. When we put this consideration together with the fact that large trucks can be driven through the holes in the argument from diversity, we find little reason to accept cultural relativism.

TOLERATION

Let's turn to a different matter. Many people think we should tolerate the practices and principles of other cultures. Some even go a step further and extol the importance of multiculturalism, by which we carve room within our society for practicing members of different cultures to live side by side. We have already said that cultural relativists themselves are in no position to defend toleration. But weren't they correct when they said that we should respect other cultures? If we give up relativism, can't we at least salvage the principle of toleration? And if so, how should we understand it?

Certainly toleration is important; however, we ought not accept all cultural practices uncritically, let alone endorse all culture-based practices, no matter how heinous. The form of toleration we should embrace is guarded: It allows for the fact that many practices are objectionable no matter how thorough their cultural backing. Consider fascists who justify their conduct by citing cultural traditions. Consider the people in African cultures who yearly force two million girls to undergo a form of genital mutilation involving the removal of the clitoris. And recall Kanwar, whose culture glorifies the immolation of widows. Resolving not to do these things ourselves is good, but we want to condemn them no matter who does them. Here we reject cultural relativism, which would force us to be supportive of offensive behavior, at least in a qualified way: If urging grief-stricken widows to burn themselves to death is traditional for certain people, then we must agree that it is right for them—so says the cultural relativist. But we do not agree.

Fortunately, we can recognize the importance of measured toleration if we are universalists. Toleration is a good idea for several reasons.

1. *People are fallible.* Merely believing that a practice is wrong does not make it so. I and my society are fallible, so I must give careful consideration to the possibility that my moral judgments are in error before I condemn the practices of other cultures. Upon reflection I may realize that I am entirely unable to back my condemnation with sound justification, in which

case I am in no position whatever to justify interfering with others who engage in the practice. I may also come to see that it is my own culture that needs criticizing.

2. *Different cultural practices might be morally optional.* It is entirely possible that superficially incompatible cultural practices are morally permissible. A trivial example is the British practice of driving on the left side of the road and the American practice of driving on the right: Either is entirely acceptable. Another example involves the rituals motivated by different religious faiths. An entire group might eschew modern technology, as the Amish do. Their way of life is permissible, but it can be very difficult for the Amish to interact with groups who help themselves to technology. Many cultural practices are acceptable even if incompatible with comparable practices in other cultures; here, toleration is in order.

3. *Interference would cause more harm than good.* Even when we conclude that another culture's practice is wrong, it can be a good idea to tolerate it simply because stopping it requires impermissible means or because it will do more harm than good. Whaling might be a case in point. Japan and a few other countries continue to allow their fishing industries to kill whales, and there is a good chance that these magnificent mammals will become extinct. But even if most people in the United States agreed that the hunting should be ended, it is by no means clear that there is a course of action available to us that would be both effective and permissible. It would be absurd to threaten Japan with war, for example. About all we can do is to attempt to persuade the Japanese to desist and sign international treaties to preserve the whale population. But we have already done these things. There is an international ban on whaling, and Japan is a signatory. Sometimes the only reasonable measures available to us are not good enough.

QUESTIONS FOR REFLECTION

1. Bernard Williams discusses a view he calls "vulgar relativism," which consists of three propositions: "that 'right' means . . . 'right for a given society'; that 'right for a given society' is to be understood in a functionalist sense [i.e., in terms of what helps the society to function]; and that (therefore) it is wrong for people in one society to condemn, interfere with, etc., the values of another society." He goes on to say that "the view is clearly inconsistent since it makes a claim in its third proposition, about what is right and wrong in one's dealings with other

societies, which uses a *nonrelative* sense of 'right' not allowed for in the first proposition."[11] Does cultural relativism as we have defined it succumb to a similar objection?

2. In the *Theaetetus* (179b) Plato said that the argument from diversity seems to presuppose that whenever several people disagree, each opinion has some sort of truth to it. But maybe most of the disputants have no expertise in the area and are simply wrong. Surely, Plato suggests, we should set their opinions aside and listen to the experts. Is he correct?

3. In Note 7, the claim is made that the argument from diversity does not support cultural relativism if the speaker-centered analysis of moral languages is correct. Is this claim correct? Why or why not?

4. The fact that the speaker-centered analysis does not support the version of cultural relativism we discussed does not entail that this analysis is false. But if we accept the speaker-centered analysis, we will have to adopt a version saying that each speaker's cultural standards dictate what *relative to the speaker* is good and right for an agent, and these standards vary from culture to culture. Should we accept the speaker-centered view and the new version of relativism?

5. Critically evaluate the following argument: Each individual makes moral assessments using, or "relative to," standards that that individual accepts. But these standards vary from individual to individual. Therefore, individual relativism is true: That is, the standards that determine the moral truth for a person are the standards that that person accepts.

6. Some ethical relativists say that it is wrong to judge others whose values are very different from ours, and it is wrong to make them conform to our values. Can the ethical relativist justify this claim? (Is it a universalist claim?) How? Is it true? Why or why not?

7. Notice that relativism could be applied to some moral standards and not others. For example, we could say that a single set of standards for assessing the right is universally binding, but no single set of standards for assessing the good is requisite. Contrast relativism as applied to (a) standards for assessing the right as well as standards for assessing the good, (b) standards for assessing the right only, and (c) standards for assessing the good only. Which form of relativism is most plausible? Why?

FURTHER READINGS

Benedict, Ruth. *Patterns of Culture*. New York: Pelican, 1946.

Brandt, Richard. "Ethical Relativism." In *The Encyclopedia of Philosophy*, edited by Paul Edwards. 75–78. New York: Macmillan, 1967.

———. *Ethical Theory*, chapters 5, 6, 11. Englewood Cliffs, N.J.: Prentice-Hall, 1959.

Harman, Gilbert, and Thomson, Judith J. *Moral Relativism and Moral Objectivity*. Cambridge, Mass.: Blackwell, 1996.

Krausz, Michael, and Meiland, Jack, editors. *Relativism: Cognitive and Moral*. Notre Dame, Ind.: University of Notre Dame Press, 1982.

Montaigne, Michel de. "Of Custom, and Not Easily Changing an Accepted Law." In *Complete Essays*, translated by Donald Frame. Stanford: Stanford University Press, 1973.

Moser, Paul, and Carson, Thomas, editors. *Moral Relativism: A Reader*. New York: Oxford University Press, 2001.

Nagel, Thomas. *The Last Word*. New York: Oxford University Press, 1997.

Plato. *Theaetetus*. In *Collected Dialogues of Plato*, translated by Edith Hamilton and Huntington Cairns. Princeton: Princeton University Press, 1961.

Rorty, Richard. "Solidarity or Objectivity?" In *Objectivity, Relativism, and Truth*. 21–45. Cambridge: Cambridge University Press, 1991.

Sumner, William G. *Folkways*. New York: New American Library, 1906.

Westermarck, Edward. *Ethical Relativity*, chapter 5. New York: Harcourt Brace, 1932.

Wong, David. "Relativism." In *A Companion to Ethics*, edited by Peter Singer. Cambridge, Mass.: Blackwell, 1993.

NOTES

1. William Dalrymple, "The Survival of Suttee," *World Press Review* 44 (1997): 16–17.

2. William Graham Sumner, *Folkways* (New York: New American Library, 1906), p. 41.

3. The relativist's argument is not only invalid, but is awkward for a further reason: If people across the world agree on anything, it is that cultural relativism is false! Does any culture in the world say that each person's cultural standards determine what that person should do? I know of none, and the vast majority of cultures are committed to universalism. (Of course, the mere fact that relativism is widely rejected does not show it is false, either.)

4. See, for example, Richard Brandt's seminal article "Ethical Relativism," in *The Encyclopedia of Philosophy*, ed. Paul Edwards (New York: Macmillan, 1967),

pp. 75–78; and Aberle, D. F., et al., "The Functional Prerequisites of a Society," *Ethics* 60 (1950): 100–111.

5. David Wong, "Relativism," in *A Companion to Ethics,* ed. Peter Singer (Cambridge, Mass.: Blackwell, 1993), p. 445.

6. Quoted by Dorothy Stein in "Burning Widows, Burning Brides: The Perils of Daughterhood in India," *Pacific Affairs* 61 (1988): 468.

7. One way to fill in the argument from diversity is to understand it as an inference to the best explanation: It is meant to explain judgment clustering–that is, the fact that people who share a culture make similar judgments, while people from distinct cultures make very different judgments–relying on the claim that accepted moral standards vary along cultural lines, together with an analysis of the meaning of moral assertions. Accordingly, the argument might look like this:

1. Moral judgments vary along cultural lines.

2. The best explanation is twofold:

    a. Accepted moral standards vary along cultural lines, and
    b. To claim that an agent should perform an action is to say that the action meets the agent's cultural standards.

3. So 2a and 2b are true (since as a joint hypothesis they are the best explanation of 1).

4. So cultural relativism is true (this follows from 3): Each agent's cultural standards dictate what is good and right for that individual, and these standards vary from culture to culture.

However, there are plenty of problems with this new argument. First, 2b equates "___ is right for a given person" with a descriptive claim–namely, "___ meets that person's cultural standards." How can a normative claim be equivalent to a descriptive claim? The second problem is more complex. According to 2b, when a speaker judges an agent, the speaker applies the standards of that agent's culture, not the standards of the speaker's culture. Instead, why not say that the speaker's standards are applied? That is,

2c. The claim that an item is good or right for an agent means that the item meets the standards of the speaker's culture.

For convenience, 2c might be called the *speaker-centered analysis* of moral language, to contrast it with 2b, which might be called the *agent-centered analysis.*

Isn't the speaker-centered analysis better? When we evaluate the actions of people in unfamiliar cultures, it seems unlikely that we judge relative to foreign standards rather than our own. Moreover, the speaker-centered analysis together with 2a would explain judgment clustering at least as well as the agent-centered analysis together with 2a.

But if the speaker-centered analysis is correct, cultural relativism as we have defined it is false. Read the first item in the next section, "Consequences of Cultural Relativism." According to the cultural relativist, the whalers and the protectors must both say that killing whales is right for the whalers, for both apply the agent's (the whalers') cultural standards. The speaker-centered account, on the other hand, gives us the following perplexing result: A protector must say that it is wrong for whalers to kill whales, while a whaler must say it is right for whalers to kill whales, *and both claims are correct.* Speaker-centered relativists not only judge their own actions by their cultural standards, but they also judge the actions of everyone else by these same speaker-centered standards. What is right for an agent is not dictated by that agent's cultural standards. Instead, it is determined by the standards of the person judging.

8. Nicholas Kristof, "Japan's Whalers Start to Take On a Hunted Look," *New York Times,* 24 June 1996.

9. Natalie Angier, "DNA Tests Find Meat of Endangered Whales for Sale in Japan," *New York Times,* 13 September 1994.

10. The problem is even worse for the individual relativist. At least cultural relativism would provide a basis for settling disputes among people who share a culture. But individual relativism says that the standards we accept determine the moral truth for us, and these standards vary even within a culture.

11. Bernard Williams, *Morality: An Introduction to Ethics* (New York: Harper & Row, 1972), pp. 20–21.

4

The Divine Command View
Is Morality God's Invention?

On July 25, 1978, Louise Brown, daughter of John and Lesley Brown, was born in Lancashire, England. Brown was no ordinary baby. She was the first human being conceived outside her mother's womb. Lesley Brown's fallopian tubes had been blocked, making the Browns an infertile couple; after two years of waiting, they gave up on adopting a child and visited fertility specialists Patrick Steptoe and Robert Edwards. Steptoe and Edwards took Mr. Brown's sperm and Ms. Brown's egg, used the one to fertilize the other *in vitro* (under glass—in a petri dish), and allowed an eight-celled embryo to develop. Then they placed the developing embryo into Ms. Brown's womb.[1] This first case of in vitro fertilization (IVF) stirred a great deal of concern by people who feared that the procedure might harm offspring. But more than 500,000 babies have been made possible by IVF, and the evidence does not demonstrate that IVF causes congenital birth defects.

In the decades following 1978, new reproductive technologies have proliferated, offering several possibilities beyond the simple approach used by the Browns. For example, eggs might be harvested from a donor, fertilized in vitro with the sperm of a second donor, and then inserted into the womb of a surrogate—a woman who is willing to bear the child. Eggs, sperm, and embryos can be frozen for use years later. And, of course, these procedures can be used to help homosexual couples and unmarried people. Furthermore, even more striking possibilities have emerged. We now know that it is possible to clone individuals, for a team of Scottish scientists led by Ian Wilmut cloned a sheep in July 1997; in theory, the same process could be applied to a human being. Wilmut replaced the nucleus of a cell set to grow with the nucleus from a cell of an adult sheep he wanted to duplicate. A third sheep carried the clone, named Dolly, to term. Will Wilmut's technique be applied to produce people any time soon? It seems unlikely. Cloning people was criminalized in the United Kingdom in 1990 and banned in the United States in 1998. However, on January 22, 2001, Britain moved to allow that human embryos be cloned to permit the harvesting of stem cells (which are enormously helpful in the treatment of many illnesses), as long as the embryos are then destroyed.

Some theorists reject all of these ways of assisting in human reproduction. And many other theorists oppose some of the new technologies. Far more concerns have been raised than we can discuss, but one is especially widespread in popular culture. As Daniel Callahan observes, "a common response to the announcement of the cloned sheep Dolly, opening the prospect of cloned human beings, was repugnance and recoil. It is a prospect that many speak of as 'unnatural,' and for that reason alone to be banned." Callahan adds that many people reacted similarly to the technology that made Louise Brown's birth possible: "While underground work on in vitro fertilization (IVF) was going on in the late 1960s and the 1970s, the aboveground discussion was filled with similar talk about the unnatural."[2] Callahan and others believe that the charge of unnaturalness is a powerful moral objection and suitable grounds for legal bans.[3]

In popular culture, the complaint against the unnatural (or against "playing God," as some prefer to say) seems to be based on two theistic assumptions. The first is called the *divine command theory*. It says God makes things good or bad, right or wrong; God's wanting something makes it right and good, and God's opposing something makes it wrong and bad. The second assumption is that God wants us to accept our nature. For, after all, God chose to make human nature as it is. These assumptions are thought to support the *injunction against unnaturalness,* as we might call the claim that people must not change or resist any aspect of human nature. And this injunction, in turn, is used to criticize acts, lifestyles, and technological innovations of many sorts. Not only has it been used against methods of reproduction that help couples like the Browns to have children, but it has also been wielded against allowing suicide or assisted suicide. Homosexuality, too, is often criticized on the grounds that it is not natural.

Those who accept the divine command theory often assume that it is required by a religious orientation. However, this is not true. In fact, a very different theory of morality has seemed more plausible to theists—namely, the *natural law view,* which says, roughly, that the moral law is prescribed by reason and willed by God *because* it is prescribed by reason. The divine command theory implies that morality would be a tissue of errors if God did not exist, but the natural law theory has no such implication. Unlike divine command theorists, natural law theorists need not suggest that the truth about ethical issues depends upon religious assumptions, about God's existence and what God wants, that are difficult to resolve.

In this chapter we will ask whether morality can be defined in terms of God's will. We will also examine some attempts to defend the injunction against unnaturalness, beginning with the argument basing it on the divine command theory.

THE DIVINE COMMAND THEORY AND HUMAN NATURE

Consider a popular argument based on the divine command theory:

Argument from Divinity

1. God makes things right and good by choosing them, wrong and bad by opposing them (the divine command theory).

2. God opposes our changing or acting in tension with any aspect of human nature.

3. So it is unacceptable for people to change or to act in tension with any aspect of human nature (the injunction against unnaturalness).

We need to examine both of the premises of this argument.

Is premise 2 defensible? The obstacles are substantial. For one thing, defending premise 2 requires finding evidence for God's existence. Another thing: The idea of an act that is in tension with human nature is not clear. Consider just two puzzles: First, if we can do something, why isn't it automatically consistent with our nature? Second, human beings are born with a sex drive; doesn't it follow that having sex is part of human nature, so that abstinence is contrary to human nature? Yet surely God does not oppose abstinence. But let us put these difficulties aside. Let us try, as best we can, to work with our intuitive understanding of "human nature." And let us ask why we should accept premise 2 if we assume that God exists.

One likely answer is this: Since God *chose* to make human nature as it is, God opposes modifying it or resisting any aspect of it. Is this answer convincing?

Not really. Why would God oppose our resisting or altering human nature as he created it? Surely there are aspects of our nature that are not perfect; yet by virtue of our ingenuity, which is another aspect of our nature, we are sometimes able to overcome these imperfections. If God gave us the means to eliminate imperfections, why wouldn't God want us to apply those means and improve ourselves? Indeed, how do we know that God did not plan for us to improve ourselves all along? Consider, for example, that we are subject to diseases and that our creativity and persistence have enabled us to cure many of them. Aren't both of these features—our susceptibility to illness as well as our ability to find cures—parts of our nature? Are we to stop all forms of medical treatment and, as they say, "let nature take its course"? Some people–the Marquis de Sade and Friedrich Nietzsche, for example–have even suggested that people are naturally cruel. Others might prefer the term "sinful." If the human being is a cruel animal, there is the possibility that harming others is natural for people. But so is our ability to suppress or redirect our cruelty. Don't such examples suggest that there are aspects of human nature that we should (and that God would want us to) overcome?

So far we have questioned the second premise of the argument from divinity. But what about the first premise, asserting the divine command theory? According to the divine command view, when we endorse an action as good or right, we are saying that God wills it. The words *this is right* are synonymous with the words *God wills this*– obeying God and acting morally are the same thing. Is this theory correct?

One problematic implication of the divine command theory is that if God does not exist, then ethics is a waste of time. In one famous passage from Dostoevsky's novel *The Brothers Karamazov,* a character cries, "All is permitted if God does not exist." This lament very nearly captures the implications of the divine command theory. In fact, however, the implications are even more bizarre; namely, if God does not exist, all moral claims are false, for according to the divine command theory, each moral claim says that God wills something or God opposes something, and all such claims are erroneous if God is not real. Thus it is false that acting naturally is right *and* false that acting naturally is wrong! We should hesitate before accepting a theory with such odd implications.

The divine command theory faces another powerful criticism. The objection was first suggested in the *Euthyphro,* where Plato asked a provocative question: Is something right (or "holy") because God wills it, or does God will it because it is right?[4] The second option implies that there is a moral standard independent of God's will and that God's choices are guided by and conform to this standard, which is inconsistent with the divine command theory. But according to the first option (which is the divine command theory itself), God simply chooses, and his choices are based on nothing. This means that had God directed us to torture children (or to do anything else we consider horrible), then torturing children would be right. It also means that when God chose whether or not torturing children was objectionable, he had nothing to go on; his choice here, as in all other value-creating decisions, was completely arbitrary. These consequences are hard to accept.

Perhaps we have been hasty. Isn't God the creator of the world and able to change it however he pleases? And wouldn't the moral facts be very different in a world unlike our own? Whether an action is reasonable depends on all sorts of things about the world: Hitting people with great force is objectionable, at least in part, because typically it causes them injury and pain. But God set things up that way and could have made a world in which people get a kick out of being attacked–a world in which we enjoy getting wounded and having our bones broken and benefit from it in the long run. So certain actions are unreasonable and wrong because of the way God made the world, but God could as easily make them reasonable and right by re-designing the world. Doesn't this show that the divine command theory is true?

No. The divine command theory implies that God could change the moral truth *without altering the world*. Simply by fiat and without changing the nature or consequences of our actions, he could make it right for us to do things that are unreasonable and harmful as things stand. To forestall misun-derstanding, let's put the point this way: Suppose that God has made this a world in which people who injure others are packed off to hell forever. Now suppose that in spite of these dire consequences, God declares that injuring others is morally obligatory. According to the divine command theory, injur-ing others would be obligatory–even though everyone who harms another faces eternal torment! Why accept such an implausible view?

Some people say that we ought to do anything God tells us to do: Doesn't this commit them to the divine command theory? No, it doesn't. Their obedience need not be based on the thought that God creates morality in the very act of issuing a command. Obedience might be prompted by at least two other lines of thought:

1. *Incentives.* Perhaps people obey God because they believe God will punish disobedience and reward obedience. This rationale is quite different from the idea that an option is morally required because God commands it. Threats and rewards are appeals to self-interest. These incentives can make it prudent to do what someone commands, but do they make obedience obligatory? Suppose a thief threatens to punch you or to shoot you in the leg unless you hand over your money: You now have a substantial prudential reason to comply, but are you duty-bound to obey the thief? Imagine that I threaten to punish you if you kill an innocent child: You are duty-bound not to murder the child, but is that because I have threatened you? People who base their conduct solely on the incentives God offers for obedience act in self-interest, not on moral grounds.

2. *Deference to authority.* Alternatively, people might obey God (and sa-cred texts, interpreted as well as possible) in the belief that God is an infalli-ble authority about morality and perfectly good–and so what God requires is invariably right. Hence we are never in a position to question God's re-quirements, even though God, like the rest of us, applies moral standards that

are not established by arbitrary fiat. Perhaps the idea that one should trust God's judgment (and recognize his omnipotence) was one of the points behind the story in Genesis 22:1–2, where God says to Abraham:

> Take now thy son, thine only son Isaac, whom thou lovest, and get thee
> into the land of Moriah; and offer him there for a burnt offering upon one
> of the mountains which I will tell thee of.

In response to this command, Abraham took his son to the designated mountain, and just as Abraham was about to plunge a knife into Isaac, he was stopped by an angel, who said "Lay not thine hand upon the lad . . . : for now I know that thou fearest God, seeing thou has not withheld thy son, thine only son from me." But suppose that God had not stopped Abraham. Would it have been morally permissible – or even praiseworthy – for Abraham to complete the sacrifice? Would God make the killing and burning of a child right by demanding it? Was there any need for God to stop Abraham at the last second if killing Isaac were not wrong?[5]

Perhaps we have said enough to indicate that the divine command theory is questionable. In fact, neither of the premises of the argument from divinity seems plausible, and so it lends little support to the injunction against unnaturalness. Is there a better way to defend this injunction?

THE NATURAL LAW THEORY

Historically, the view that has commanded the allegiance of most intellectual theists is not the divine command theory but rather the *natural law theory*. Let us describe this view and then see whether it might be used in support of the injunction against unnaturalness.

The natural law theory had its origins in ancient Greek and Roman thought. A core element of the theory – the idea of a divine law that is built into the structure of the universe – was conceived by ancient Stoics, who believed that the parts of the world function like parts of a body and together form an organism animated by divine reason. This organism is fated by divine law to develop in a preset way and then to be consumed in a cosmic conflagration, at which point the whole process is repeated from the beginning, over and over, in exact detail.

Later, Christian theorists such as Thomas Aquinas (1224–1274) refined the natural law theory. Aquinas's ethics was an attempt to combine Aristotelianism with Christianity. Aristotle had pictured the universe as an orderly whole in which most things have a function or purpose. To identify a thing's function, we must examine what it needs to develop fully and what it contributes to the overall pattern of the world. The good for each thing is to

perform its function. But while Aristotle thought that most things have a purpose, he did not assume that they were ascribed their purpose by themselves
or by any conscious being. Aristotle pictured the world as orderly and purposive but did not claim that the world was designed by an intelligent being.
In particular, no one gave human beings their function. Aquinas adopted Aristotle's teleological conception of the universe wholesale and added two key
ideas. First, God made the world as it is; and in ordering the world and its
inhabitants, God gave each thing the function that determines its good. Second, the world must conform to God's law: "All things subject to Divine prov-
idence are ruled and measured by [God's] eternal law."

But this law is not laid down by fiat. God wills his laws because he discov-
ers—using reason—that they are supported by reason. Here we have Aquinas's
answer to Plato's challenge in the *Euthyphro:* God's will is not arbitrary, since
God wills what reason dictates. (Not all natural law theorists have agreed with
Aquinas, however. Some of them—called *voluntarists*—accept the divine command view and maintain that natural laws are binding solely because God
wills them.)

Now, just as God is able to perceive the moral truth by reasoning it out,
in theory people are able to use their own reason to work out how they must
act, at least in broad outlines. This is because any rational creature "has a
share of the Eternal Reason, whereby it has a natural inclination to its proper
act and end" and "this participation of the eternal law in the rational creature
is called the natural law."[6] Our reason is an accurate guide—as far as it goes.
Only in one area is it blind: It cannot inform us of the existence of an afterlife, nor tell us what our comportment to the afterlife ought to be. According
to Aristotle, natural reason reveals that our end is happiness over a normal
life span, but Aquinas considered the Aristotelian picture of happiness incomplete. What natural reason cannot make evident to us is that we are "or-
dained to an end of eternal happiness."[7] Divine reason reveals this, and God
directs us to the end of eternal happiness. To mark off the component of divine law made evident to human beings through the use of our limited reasoning ability and powers of observation, Aquinas uses the term *natural law.*

A striking feature of Aristotle's view was that it did not develop the modern notion of duty or obligation—the idea of boundaries we may not cross.
The goal of ethics, according to many modern theorists, is to devise a framework of universal moral principles that lay out how reasonable persons must
act. This framework of rules will define *duties* that compel us to accommodate
the interest of others and *rights* that compel others to accommodate our interests. Aristotelianism contributed little to this task; in fact, there is almost
no discussion of individual rights in the ancient world, as several writers have
noted.[8] Aristotle described reason as a faculty that helps us to achieve the

good life, primarily by enabling us to identify and evaluate means to ends we have by nature. His ethics was expressed in terms of what it is good or best to do, not in terms of minimum standards we must meet. By contrast, natural law theorists such as Aquinas begin a transition to the modern notion of obligation. Reason issues a *law that we must not transgress,* and according to Aquinas this law is commanded by God because it is enjoined by reason. The first precept of natural law is that "good is to be done and ensued, and evil is to be avoided." Aquinas adds: "All other precepts of the natural law are based upon this: so that whatever practical reason naturally apprehends as man's good (or evil) belongs to the precepts of the natural law as something to be done or avoided."[9]

Notice that unlike the divine command theory, Aquinas's natural law view does not imply that ethical issues (aside from those that might concern the afterlife) depend upon controversial religious assumptions. Aquinas did say that God created the world and that God's commandments are binding. But he also said that moral truth has an objective basis independent of God's will. The commandments of reason are binding no matter who promulgates them, whether God or a mere mortal. Consequently, theists and atheists have a common basis for evaluating positions taken in moral disputes, even though they will not share a religious worldview, for both will find a position's *reasonableness* grounds to embrace it.

Let's take up the injunction against unnaturalness once more. Can this injunction be given a fresh justification if we appeal to Aquinas's natural law theory?

THE ARGUMENT FROM NATURAL LAW THEORY

If based on the natural law theory, the defense of the injunction against unnaturalness would take the following form:

Argument from Natural Law Theory

1. It is wrong to act contrary to reason. (It is wrong to act against the natural law that is dictated by reason and that God wills because it is enjoined by reason.)

2. It is contrary to reason to change or act in tension with human nature.

3. So it is unacceptable for people to change or to act in tension with human nature.

Is this argument persuasive?

The most vulnerable part of the argument is the second premise. Why should we consider altering human nature unreasonable? Aquinas's answer would begin with an assumption inspired by Aristotle: However human beings are predisposed by nature to develop or function, it is good for us to function or develop ourselves in those ways, and only in those ways, at least until we begin the afterlife. To this assumption Aquinas would add that it is contrary to reason not to live the best life we can, so reason (and God) requires us to embrace human nature as it is.

Should we accept the Aristotelian claim that the best way for us to develop ourselves is the natural way? Let us acknowledge that it surely embodies a grain of truth. Inevitably, any practical portrayal of the human good will model itself in part upon human nature. However, the fact that by nature we *do* develop or function in certain ways does not imply that developing in those ways and only in those ways is good. And there is no reason in principle why our portrayal of the ideal human life should look exactly like actual human life. As we mentioned earlier, there are many ways in which human beings are limited by nature; wouldn't overcoming some of these limitations make our lives better? Wouldn't it be good to develop a more robust constitution to forestall illness and to improve our intelligence and capacity for empathy?

For creatures such as us, whose capacities are not perfect, it helps to be able to improve ourselves. Why not say that this capacity is part of (perhaps even definitive of) human nature and that being self-enhancing beings is the best nature we could expect to have? And isn't it natural for us to take advantage of this capacity? The only way we can overcome one aspect of our nature is to make use of another, but it is hard to see why we should sanction one aspect as "natural" and not the other.

TEST TUBE BABIES AND CLONES

Neither the argument from divinity nor the argument from natural law theory provides a convincing basis for rejecting "unnatural" acts. Apparently, it is difficult to cite unnaturalness as a moral objection to anything. And if we do not condemn acts on these grounds, much of the suspicion surrounding many sorts of technological innovations will dissipate. In particular, it will be more difficult to sustain an effective attack on people like the Browns who use technology to overcome their inability to reproduce.

However, discrediting the charge from unnaturalness will not clear away the objections to all of the many uses of modern reproductive technologies. The issues are complex, and many of the considerations involved have nothing to do with worries about naturalness. We cannot resolve all of these issues here, but in closing let us mention some of them.

One area of controversy concerns unused fertilized eggs: Physicians who perform in vitro fertilization sometimes fertilize several eggs and store the embryos by freezing them. But what if the stored embryos are not needed? Is it acceptable to destroy them? If not, what is to be done with them? May surplus embryos be used in medical experimentation?

A second area of controversy concerns surrogate motherhood, which has been criticized on the grounds that it exploits women and provides a financial incentive for bearing children. Moreover, when combined with egg and sperm donation, surrogate motherhood introduces all sorts of confusing difficulties. Suppose, for example, that Mary, Tom, Betty, Bill, and Jill agree to the following plan: Mary's eggs will be fertilized with Tom's sperm then grown in Betty's womb so that Bill and Jill, who are both sterile, can raise the resulting child. But when the baby is born, all five decide they want to keep it. Who should have custody, Mary, who is the genetic mom, Tom, the genetic dad, Betty, the gestational mom, or Bill and Jill, who will be adoptive parents only if the others honor their agreement? (And what changes if Bill and Jill divorce?)

Perhaps the most heated controversy concerns human cloning. At this time it can be criticized on the grounds that it is not safe for any child that might be produced. The team in Scotland implanted twenty-nine cloned embryos before Dolly was born, and the long-term effects of the procedure are not yet known. But even if cloning proves to be safe, some people will question the motives of those who wish to raise their own clones: Aren't they narcissists who view the clones as a way to continue their own lives? If so, won't the parents of clones be overbearing and attempt to pattern their offspring after themselves? Perhaps would-be parents of clones will indeed be looking to continue their lives and identities by cloning themselves. However, don't many of the parents who reproduce the old-fashioned way have the same motive? Shall we ban them from reproducing too?

QUESTIONS FOR REFLECTION

1. Must we believe in God to live morally? Some say that unless I think that God will punish me for wrongdoing and reward me for good behavior, I do not have any incentive to be moral. God ensures that my moral behavior pays off and that my immoral behavior does not; hence if I do not believe in God, there is no point to being moral. Is this argument convincing? (Does the argument assume that self-interest is the only motive for moral behavior? Does it assume that something other than God—the government, for example—cannot provide the incentive to act well?)

2. Are we morally obligated to obey God? Consider the following argument: When others are experts about morality (or anything else) and we are not, we ought to do as they say. Hence we ought to do as God says because God's judgment is far more accurate than anyone else's. Is this argument any good? Does expertise alone entitle people to demand that others obey them? How would you answer the following response by Alasdair MacIntyre: "Although [God's moral expertise] provides us with a reason for doing what God commands, if we act only for this reason, we shall be in the position of taking God's advice rather than of being obedient to him." [10]

3. MacIntyre goes on to identify a reason to obey God that is connected to God's power rather than his goodness: "God makes it a condition of a favorable outcome for us that we obey him. . . . If God's goodness makes it reasonable to do what he commands, his power makes it reasonable to do this in a spirit of obedience." [11] In other words, God rewards people who follow his commands and punishes those who do not, which gives everyone a reason to obey him. Are these convincing grounds for obedience?

4. Some suggest that God is entitled to our obedience on the grounds that God created us, and when A creates B, B ought to obey A. Is this argument convincing? Suppose that in the year 2999 humanity will have become so technologically sophisticated that we are able to initiate a chain of events that result in the development of conscious, self-determining beings much like ourselves. Would it be reasonable for us to consider ourselves entitled to their obedience? Would it be acceptable to force them to submit to us—say, on the grounds that we may use force to gain what we are entitled to? Or is this sort of subordination of people slavery? (What would we say if we discovered that long ago clever aliens initiated processes that resulted in the development of human beings? Would we feel obligated to submit to the rule of the aliens when they returned?)

5. Should we accept the claim that it is good to function only as we are predisposed by nature to function? If not, how should we define the human good?

6. Why would it be objectionable for something to act contrary to its function? Suppose that a wrench's function is to turn nuts and that a good wrench can be defined as one that turns nuts well. Does it follow that it would be objectionable to use a wrench to dig with or to drive a nail?

7. Are there features of natural human development that are not good? It would appear that no matter how healthy people are, they are by nature mortal. Is that good?

8. According to Aquinas, we are obligated to act as reason dictates. But Aristotle said that we are best off if we consult reason. Whose view is more accurate?

9. Aquinas writes, "When Abraham consented to slay his son, he did not consent to murder, because his son was due to be slain by the command of God, Who is Lord of life and death: for He it is Who inflicts the punishment of death on all men, both godly and ungodly, on account of the sin of our first parent and if a man be the executor of that sentence of Divine authority, he will be no murderer any more than God would be." [12] In other words, because of original sin, everyone deserves to die, so God may kill anyone and may authorize others to kill. Is Aquinas correct? Is Aquinas saying that by God's command God makes it right for Abraham to kill his son (which would commit Aquinas to the divine command theory)? How might Aquinas respond to the following view: Since everyone deserves to die, anyone, and not just God, may kill anyone? (Aren't murderers executed by the state on the grounds that they deserve to die?)

10. Is it ever morally permissible to worsen our situation? Suppose that you would be better off if you were to exercise a lot more than you do and to watch less television, but you just do not want to. Isn't it all right for you to be a couch potato? Are we duty-bound not to smoke and drink even in moderation because they are not good for us?

11. Aside from the charge of unnaturalness and the concern that fertilized eggs might be sacrificed, what other objections might be raised to in vitro fertilization? Are any of these objections sufficient grounds for considering it morally wrong?

12. Suppose that cloning proves to be as safe as in vitro fertilization. Should it be considered morally impermissible? Why or why not?

FURTHER READINGS

On the Divine Command Theory

Helm, Paul, editor. *Divine Commands and Morality.* Oxford: Oxford University Press, 1981.

Kierkegaard, Søren. *Works of Love,* translated by Howard Hong and Edna Hong. New York: Harper, 1964.

Outka, G., and Reeder, J. P., editors. *Religion and Morality.* Garden City, N.Y.: Anchor, 1973.

Phillips, D. Z., editor. *Religion and Morality.* London: Macmillan, 1996.

Plato. *Euthyphro.* In *Plato: The Collected Dialogues,* edited by Edith Hamilton and Huntington Cairns. Princeton: Princeton University Press, 1961.

On the Natural Law Theory

Aquinas, Thomas. *Synopsis of Theology.* Translated by T. Gilby. 60 vols. New York: McGraw-Hill, 1963–1973. Original date 1266–1273.

Finnis, John. "Natural Law." In *Routledge Encyclopedia of Philosophy,* edited by Edward Craig. London: Routledge, 1998.

——. *Natural Law and Natural Rights.* Oxford: Clarendon Press, 1980.

On the Ethics of Reproductive Technology

Bayles, Michael. *Reproductive Ethics.* Englewood Cliffs, N.J.: Prentice-Hall, 1984.

Catholic Church, Congregation for the Doctrine of the Faith. "Instruction on Respect for Human Life in Its Origin and on the Dignity of Procreation." *Origins* 16 (1987): 698–711.

Robertson, John A. *Children of Choice: Freedom and the New Reproductive Technologies.* Princeton: Princeton University Press, 1994.

Snowden, R., et al. *Artificial Reproduction: A Social Investigation.* Boston: Allen & Unwin, 1983.

United States Congress, Office of Technology Assessment. *Infertility: Medical and Social Choices.* Washington, D.C.: Government Printing Office, 1988.

Wertheimer, Alan. "Two Questions about Surrogacy and Exploitation." *Philosophy and Public Affairs* 21 (1992): 211–239.

NOTES

1. Peter Gwynne, "Was the Birth of Louise Brown Only a Happy Accident?" *Science Digest,* October 1978, 7–12.

2. Daniel Callahan, "What's Natural?" *Commonweal* 126, no. 13 (1999): 7–8.

3. In his "The Wisdom of Repugnance: Why We Should Ban the Cloning of Humans," *The New Republic,* 2 June 1997, Leon Kass criticizes cloning on the grounds that it "shows itself to be a major alteration, indeed, a major violation, of our given nature as embodied, gendered and engendering beings—and of the social relations built on this natural ground."

4. See *Euthyphro,* 10a: "Is what is holy holy because the gods approve it, or do they approve it because it is holy?" In *Plato: The Collected Dialogues,* ed. Edith Hamilton and Huntington Cairns (Princeton: Princeton University Press, 1961), p. 178.

5. For a probing discussion of the Abraham story, see Søren Kierkegaard's *Fear and Trembling,* trans. Howard Hong and Edna Hong (Princeton: Princeton University Press, 1983).

6. Thomas Aquinas, *Treatise on Law,* question 91, second article, in *Social Ideals and Policies,* ed. Steven Luper (Mountain View, Calif.: Mayfield, 1999), p. 203.

7. Aquinas, *Treatise on Law,* question 91, fourth article, p. 203.

8. For example, Isaiah Berlin, "Two Concepts of Liberty," in *Social Ideals and Policies,* ed. Steven Luper (Mountain View, Calif.: Mayfield, 1999), p. 446. Berlin credits Condorcet.

9. Aquinas, *Treatise on Law,* question 94, second article, p. 204.

10. Alasdair MacIntyre, *A Short History of Ethics* (New York: Macmillan, 1966), p. 113.

11. MacIntyre, p. 113.

12. Thomas Aquinas, *Summa Theologica* I–II, question 100, article 8.

5

Hedonism
Is the Pleasant Life the Best Life?

The movie *Matrix* presents a future world where machines have enslaved human beings to be used as sources of energy. The humans are unaware of the horrifying situation they live in, since they are hooked together with elaborate machinery that creates an illusory world called the "Matrix." However, a rogue group of people has found a way to penetrate to the reality behind the appearance. They give the hero of the movie a choice. He can take a blue pill, which will allow him to remain in the illusory life he has always known and erase the memory of his decision. Or he can take a red pill, which will awaken him so that he can perceive the real but enormously unpleasant world and join the effort to overthrow the machines.

Put in the hero's place, some of us might be so horrified that we would take the blue pill and return to ignorance. What, after all, is important in life? Isn't it being as happy as possible as long as we can, where happiness is understood to be a pleasant state of mind? And isn't it far more likely that we (and everyone else) would spend our time more pleasantly in the Matrix than in a harrowing battle with murderous futuristic machines? Those who think this way might be drawn to a view we shall label *value hedonism*. According to this view, the only thing that is good for its own sake (rather than as a means to something valued independently) is some positive subjective state, such as pleasure, together with the absence of suffering; and the best form of existence is a life that overflows with this positive subjective state and with things that produce it.

But most of us would not react this way to the *Matrix* scenario. We would find the hero's own choice more congenial: He chose the red pill and did battle against the machines! For us, pleasure is well and good, but it is not the only thing that matters. Perhaps, however, we are the ones who are deceived: Maybe the hedonists are correct, and our aversion to being blissfully (but totally) cut off from reality is the product of confusion. In this chapter, we wiln try to decide whether the hedonist theory of the good is correct or not.

Value hedonism is usually defended on the basis of a claim about human motivation. Our first order of business will be to examine this defense. Then we will consider some arguments against value hedonism. Finally, we will discuss the work of two historically influential hedonist thinkers, who make quite extraordinary claims about their approach to life: the Greek thinker Epicurus (341–271 B.C.) and the Indian prince Gautama (c. 563–483 B.C.), called the Buddha ("Enlightened One").

VALUE HEDONISM DEFENDED

How do we decide what is good in itself? We might ask whether there are things that human psychology *prompts* us to seek. Suppose we find that A–Z are the only things desired for their own sakes and that this attraction to A–Z can be attributed to human nature. Then it seems reasonable to suppose that A–Z are the only things that are good in themselves. If all of us naturally value wisdom, for example, then wisdom is intrinsically valuable; if each of us naturally values only our own wisdom, then for each of us only our own wisdom is valuable.

If we accept this strategy, then the next step is to figure out what people seek by nature. Suppose we decide that, due to human nature, pleasure is the only thing that we seek for its own sake—this view is called *psychological hedonism.* Then we might well think that pleasure is the only good. And this is precisely the way some hedonists seem to reason. They think that since by nature you and I want to enjoy ourselves as much as possible (and to suffer as little as possible), then our pleasure is good for us. Since by nature our pleasure (and the absence of pain) is ultimately the only thing we want, it is our only good. Thus their argument boils down to this:

Argument from Psychological Necessity

1. By nature each of us seeks one and only one thing for its own sake: our own pleasure (and the absence of pain). (psychological hedonism)

2. The things we seek naturally (and for their own sakes) are the things that are good in themselves.

3. So for each of us one and only one thing is intrinsically valuable: our own pleasure.[1] (value hedonism)

Is this argument plausible? Of course, it is only as strong as its premises. Let's consider these in turn, starting with the second premise, and then working our way back to the first.

tive statements do not entail normative statements, we would
~~the~~ second premise if it said that we may deduce what is desir-
~~~~ ~~it~~ is desired. However, there is a more charitable interpretation:
Premise 2 is itself a value claim that is taken to be plausible on its face. In the
ancient world, claims like 2 were considered obvious. It was assumed that the
things we are attracted to naturally are the things that are good. If we want to
know what is really good, we have only to consult nature.

But is premise 2 true? No doubt we will want to qualify it in various ways,
but there are reasons to accept it. The main point is this: While the human
good is an ideal, it is a version of what human beings can be; otherwise, it
makes little sense to speak of it as being the *human* good. Moreover, it is a version of what we are naturally drawn to; otherwise, it is odd to describe it as
the human *good*. Hence if human nature prompts us to shape our lives in certain ways—say, by making certain activities attractive—it is plausible to assume, at least initially, that it is good to shape our lives in those ways and only
in those ways. On further reflection, we might have to change our account of
the good, but our revision will not be something wholly new; it will not point
us to a life that we have no natural attraction to or aptitude for whatsoever.

These points certainly do not show that the second premise of the argument from psychological necessity is true. However, they suffice to show
that it is not entirely misguided. So let us move on to the first premise, which
claims that psychological hedonism is true.

PSYCHOLOGICAL HEDONISM

Assessing psychological hedonism will take some work. Let's start by considering two arguments for psychological hedonism. Then we can develop an
argument against it.

First Defense: The Argument by Extended Satisfaction

We might be led to adopt psychological hedonism because we conflate (run
together) certain ideas that are really distinct. Thus one route to hedonism
involves failing to distinguish between "satisfying our desires" (that is, "pleas-
ing ourselves") and "seeking pleasure." For once we run these ideas together,
we might succumb to the following:

Argument by Extended Satisfaction

1. Acting voluntarily is trying to satisfy our desires.

2. Trying to satisfy our desires is trying to get pleasure.

3. So acting voluntarily is trying to get pleasure.

At first, this argument seems quite plausible, but if we look at it carefully we soon detect flaws.

Note, first, that even if the argument by extended satisfaction were sound, it would not support the hedonist claim that we seek nothing for its own sake except pleasure and the absence of pain. The trouble is that the argument stretches the idea of pleasure seeking so much that we are said to "seek pleasure" no matter what motivates our behavior, and so premises 1 and 2 do not support any view about our motivation, including the hedonist's view. To make the problem vivid, suppose that my motivation is just the opposite of the way hedonists portray it: Suppose that the only thing I want for its own sake is pain and the absence of pleasure. As a result, I throw myself against walls, smash my toes with rocks, and spend my life trying to satisfy my desire to avoid pleasure. If we insist on labeling this effort an "attempt to get pleasure," we end up saying that my attempt to satisfy my desire not to have pleasure is an attempt to get pleasure! We can speak this way if we like; but the fact is that in the example at hand I seek pain, not pleasure, a motivation the hedonist means to rule out.

And, in fact, we should not speak this way because the second premise of the argument by extended satisfaction is false. Seeking pleasure is not the same thing as doing what we want, as Joseph Butler (1692–1752) suggested in his *Sermons.*[2] The difference is easily overlooked, because doing what we want is usually pleasant. If we want to dive into a pool, and we do it, we will probably enjoy ourselves. But even if satisfying a particular desire is pleasant, it does not follow that pleasure was *what* we desired. Pleasure can result from our getting what we want without itself being what we want, just as pain can result from reaching a goal without itself being the goal.

To make this clear, we need to distinguish between the object of a desire, on the one hand, and the consequences of satisfying a desire, on the other. If I desire ___, then ___ is the object of my desire. If I desire to write a novel, the object of my desire is writing a novel: Writing my novel satisfies my desire. And completing my task might have all sorts of consequences. Perhaps scenes in it will inspire someone to appreciate a mother's love for the first time. Probably another consequence will be that I feel pleased about writing the novel. But these are consequences of my desire, not its object. Again, satisfying a desire is usually enjoyable. But it does not follow that pleasure is the objective.

Second Defense: The Appeal to Introspection

It is unlikely that all proponents of psychological hedonism have blurred distinctions in the way the argument by extended satisfaction does. However, it is hard to find another argument, unless we count an appeal to introspection, as offered by Epicurus. Epicurus said that ultimately we rank options using our own pleasure as our standard. I rank alternatives on the basis of how much pleasure I expect to get from each option, while you rank options on the basis of how much you expect to enjoy them, and so on. Epicurus appeared to think that we can confirm his claim through introspection: We can pay careful attention to the choices we make and see for ourselves that while we choose some things for the sake of others, pleasure is the only thing we choose for its own sake.

But he will have to do better than that. It is true that sometimes we want things because they are pleasant—eating candy, watching comedy shows, and vacationing are all things we do because we enjoy them. But if we help a friend or save someone from a fire, it is likely that any pleasure we get is merely an unsought side effect, not the object of our choice. Isn't that what introspection tells you?

Counterargument: The Hedonistic Paradox

Paradoxically, if we aim solely at achieving as much pleasure as possible, we are likely to end up with less than we might otherwise have managed; and when we think through why this is, difficulties arise for the psychological hedonist. In a moving confession, John Stuart Mill (1806–1873), the most famous proponent of the view that happiness or pleasure is the sole good, describes what it is like to be caught up in this predicament:

> I was in a dull state of nerves, such as everybody is occasionally liable
> to. . . . In this frame of mind it occurred to me to put the question directly
> to myself: "Suppose that all your objects in life were realized: . . . would
> this be a great joy and happiness to you?" And an irrepressible self-
> consciousness distinctly answered, "No!" . . .
>
> I never . . . wavered in the conviction that happiness is the test of
> all rules of conduct, and the end of life. But I now thought that this end
> was only to be attained by not making it the direct end. Those only are
> happy . . . who have their minds fixed on some object other than their own
> happiness; on the happiness of others, on the improvement of mankind,
> even on some art or pursuit, followed not as a means, but as itself an ideal
> end. Aiming thus at something else, they find happiness by the way. The en-
> joyments of life . . . are sufficient to make it a pleasant thing, when they are
> taken en passant, without being made a principal object. Once make them
> so, and they are immediately felt to be insufficient. . . . The only chance is
> to treat, not happiness, but some end external to it, as the purpose of life.[3]

To explain what Mill has in mind, we will need to distinguish between getting pleasure directly versus getting pleasure indirectly. We get pleasure indirectly when it results from our attaining something other than pleasure that we regard as worth having for its own sake. For example, suppose I desire to understand the theory of relativity for its own sake, and I satisfy my desire; as a result, I am pleased. My pleasure is indirect. By contrast, when it results from satisfying my desire for pleasure, or my desire for something that is a means to my pleasure, I get pleasure directly. There is no doubt that we can get *some* pleasure directly: We do so when we watch comedy, or when we take aspirin. But what happens if we try to get all of our pleasure this way?

The problem for the psychological hedonist is that two claims Mill makes about himself seem true of most people. First, if we try to get all of our pleasure directly and never indirectly, thereby abandoning the idea that anything other than pleasure matters in its own right, pleasure eludes us. All we can do is take pills, watch films, and so on, activities that quickly prove to be unsatisfying, and we are left with greatly impoverished lives. By contrast, when we take the indirect route, we have little trouble. We put the thought of pleasure aside and pursue things we consider valuable in themselves. In pursuing these, we make ourselves cheerful as a side effect, simply because it is enjoyable to achieve what we think is worthwhile. If these claims are true of us, we cannot avoid the conclusion that we get much of our pleasure indirectly. But psychological hedonism implies that we cannot get pleasure indirectly. Apparently, it is mistaken.

Is there a way for psychological hedonists to respond to our criticism? Suppose they admitted that

1. We pursue things other than pleasure for their own sakes, thereby getting pleasure indirectly,

but also insisted that

2. We would abandon these indirect pursuits if they stopped being pleasant or if we believed that we could get more pleasure some other way.

Could psychological hedonism be rescued in this way, given that statements 1 and 2 are both true? Mill may have thought so.[4] But the attempt fails. By definition, psychological hedonism says that only pleasure is sought for its own sake, and this claim is incompatible with 1.

Anyone who thinks that claims 1 and 2 rescue psychological hedonism is probably confusing it with a different view—namely, that pleasure is our highest priority (though not necessarily the only thing we seek for its own sake); it outweighs all other things. Let us call this position *dominant-end psychological hedonism,* and for clarity let us call psychological hedonism as it is traditionally understood *exclusive-end psychological hedonism.*[5] It is easy to confuse these two doctrines, because exclusive-end hedonism *entails* dominant-end hedonism: If the only thing you care about is pleasure, then (vacuously) you care about pleasure more than anything else. But they are not the same: Dominant-end hedonism does not entail exclusive-end hedonism. And while 1 and 2 support dominant-end hedonism, they do not support exclusive-end hedonism.[6]

THE ELECTRONIC VOLUPTUARY

We have been criticizing the main defense of value hedonism—the argument from psychological necessity—by attacking an assumption on which it rests, namely psychological hedonism. But now it is time to consider a direct attack on value hedonism: the well-known case of the electronic voluptuary.

In the 1950s some experimenters inserted electrodes into the pleasure centers of the brains of rats, enabling the rats to stimulate themselves electrically by depressing a lever. They ignored food and stimulated themselves for hours on end.[7] After reading about these experiments, it did not take philosophers long to develop scenarios in which people take the place of the rats and get even more elaborate treatment. For example, imagine machinery that we could (painlessly) attach to our brains that would give us experiences that are perfectly lifelike, as well as enormously pleasant, and that would last a lifetime. We might even add an option: Once we attach ourselves to the machinery, we forget all about doing so. If presented the opportunity, would we permanently abandon real life so as to become electronic voluptuaries? (Notice that, in a way, the flip side of this question is broached by the movie *Matrix*. We are asking whether it is better to maintain contact with the familiar real world or break it off to enter a blissful but illusory world, while *Matrix* asks whether it is better to abandon a familiar illusory world and establish contact with a real but quite horrendous world.) Would we say that life as an electronic voluptuary is better?

Some might, but most of us recoil from the idea, and this fact counts against both value hedonism and psychological hedonism. The voluptuary is guaranteed a lifetime of bliss, while ordinary existence is a rocky road that brings far less pleasure. If our only concern were pleasure, we would become voluptuaries. Since we would not choose to do so, we must care about things other than pleasure. We think that having real friends matters for its own sake, that it is important to have a real impact on the world, and so on. Being drawn to meaningful deeds and relationships, we choose real life over an illusory substitute that gives us only the appearance of friends or the appearance of accomplishments. But if we conclude that things other than pleasure are good for their own sakes, we must also conclude that value hedonism is false. Moreover, if we care about things other than pleasure, psychological hedonism has to be false.

GAUTAMA AND EPICURUS: NEGATIVE HAPPINESS

Let us end our discussion of value hedonism by considering a remarkable claim made by Gautama and Epicurus. They promise (with some qualifications) that if we adopt the values of the hedonist and follow certain practical advice, we can achieve an invulnerable form of happiness. We can become happy regardless of our circumstances and remain happy no matter what happens to us. A promise like that is worth taking seriously!

Epicurus and Gautama develop an approach to happiness that is largely overlooked in the contemporary Western world. Roughly speaking, our approach is to take our desires for granted and strive to accumulate the power and knowledge necessary to shape the world as we want it to be. In pursuing this strategy, we become hostages to fate, for all too often the world refuses to give way to our demands. The alternative approach, pursued by Epicureans and Buddhists, is to work in the other direction: Instead of conforming the world to our desires, we could conform our desires—and our conception of happiness itself—to the world. Epicureans and Buddhists equate living well with happiness, but characterize happiness almost entirely in a negative way. That is, they portray it in terms of what it excludes, rather than in terms of what it includes: Essentially, it is the absence of suffering, the absence of any form of mental turmoil.

Given this negative hedonist understanding of happiness, how can we achieve an invulnerable form of happiness? Doing so involves cultivating a virtuous character, but the main strategy is to pare down our desires so that they are easily met in the world as it is. We abandon any desire whose satisfaction is beyond our control. In particular, we cultivate indifference concerning wealth, beauty, fame, honor, and even our own survival. Concerns like these set us up for disappointment and make our happiness precarious. If we want only what is in our control, we will be virtually self-sufficient, and our happiness will be invulnerable.

Epicurus puts his view this way: The goal is to achieve *ataraxia,* which is a secure state of tranquility, a pleasant state of not desiring (not wanting, not needing). *Ataraxia* is a passive or static pleasure, according to Epicurus; it does not include active pleasures, which are gained from satisfying desires. The way we achieve *ataraxia* is, roughly, to limit ourselves to desires that are "necessary" in the sense that without them we will suffer:

> All such desires as lead to no pain when they remain ungratified are unnecessary, and the longing is easily got rid of, when the thing desired is difficult to procure or when the desires seem likely to produce harm.[8]

We ought to retain the desire to eat when hungry, for example, since starvation is painful. However, it is best to be content with food that is cheap and plentiful. Those accustomed to lobster from Maine and caviar from the Black Sea must struggle for money to purchase these rare delicacies and will consider anything else a poor substitute. Given his reservations about the life of the gourmet, it is an irony of history that the term "epicure" derives from Epicurus's name.

Gautama expresses views that are much like Epicurus's. He suggests that we suffer because we want elusive things, especially perpetual life, and because "it is a suffering not to get what is desired."[9] But by eliminating our attachment to our existence and ridding ourselves of the desires that draw us to life, we can end our suffering. We can achieve *nirvana,* which means "extinguished," as when a flame is put out. There is pleasure in nirvana, but it is the pleasure of tranquil aloofness and of the secure knowledge that we need never suffer again.

Knowing that fear of death is a chief cause of unhappiness, Epicurus and Gautama offer distinctive ways to cope. In fact, the help their approach offers us in dealing with mortality is one of its chief virtues, in their view. Let us take a moment to explain.

Epicurus on Death

Epicurus advises us to assess the value of things in accordance with a hedonistic formulation according to which passive pleasure (or, as he usually says, the absence of pain) is the only good and pain the only bad—so that what brings us neither is a matter of indifference. Yet death, thought of, as Epicurus did, as our complete annihilation, is painless. In utterly ceasing to be, we are no longer able to experience anything at all.

> Death . . . , the most awful of evils, is nothing to us, seeing that, when we are, death is not come, and, when death is come, we are not. It is nothing, then, either to the living or to the dead, for with the living it is not and the dead exist no longer.[10]

So the fact that we will die is of no concern. It is true that death deprives us of the ability to experience pleasure, but Epicurus says we feel the need for pleasure only "when we are pained because of the absence of pleasure."[11] The dead experience no such need. It is also true that some people are fearful when they anticipate death, but they are being irrational: Why concern ourselves with matters of indifference? As Epicurus says, "Whatsoever causes no annoyance when it is present, causes only a groundless pain in the expectation."[12] Epicurus admits that painful diseases often bring about death and that these are bad precisely because they make us suffer. However, he makes the extraordinary claim that they are not as bad as people think:

Continuous pain does not last long in the flesh; on the contrary, pain, if extreme, is present a very short time. . . . Illnesses of long duration even permit of an excess of pleasure over pain in the flesh.[13]

Gautama on Death: The No-Self Doctrine

Gautama's approach to death is a bit harder to grasp than Epicurus's. Gautama questioned the commonsense idea that the world is populated by substances. A fish is an example of a substance; one of its attributes is the property *sliminess*. Ordinarily, substances are understood to be unchanging objects that persist over time and serve as substrates for changing attributes. As Western philosophers (such as John Locke) came to see, we have no clear idea of such substances, for any time we try to describe what they are, we find ourselves mentioning properties, which are supposed to *inhere* in substances and which, therefore, must be distinct from them. The idea of a substance is confused, so we must give it up. Reasoning much like this led Gautama to reject the belief in persisting substances. But doing so means giving up the commonsense idea of the self as well, since it too is thought to be a substance. For Gautama, rejecting the belief in substances means adopting the *no-self doctrine,* which advises abandoning the notion of the self.

Taking this advice will have a powerful impact on those who deplore death. For if we give up the notion of the self, we cannot say that death is a bad thing. We will reject the very idea that we die. The idea of dying is itself confused, for if there are no selves, there is no one who might or might not cease to exist. Thus in one Buddhist document, the story is told about a monk named Yamaka, who defended the "pernicious" view that enlightened people, "at the break up of the body, will be annihilated, will be destroyed."[14] Yamaka is set straight by his peers: It is false to say that the self is annihilated. But it is also false to say that the self is not annihilated. There are no selves. Compare Epicurus's view: While there are selves, their survival is unimportant.

However, the no-self doctrine has a further consequence that will concern those who seek relief from suffering. Suppose people pare down their desires in the way Gautama suggests and gradually achieve tranquility, but continue to regard suffering as a bad thing. What will happen when they give up the idea of the self? Without the distinction between *self* and *other,* the fact that suffering is their own ceases to be important. No matter where suffering occurs — whether experienced by a human being near or far away or by some other creature — it will trouble them. Their orientation toward suffering is neither selfless (more concerned about others than themselves) nor self-seeking, but impartial.[15]

Negative Hedonism Assessed

Through Epicureanism or Buddhism, we can, at least in theory, make ourselves self-sufficient, a considerable advantage in a world, like Epicurus's or Gautama's, that is apt to disappoint. But is it really desirable to become self-contained in this way? Where does the truth lie?

Unfortunately, complete invulnerability comes at a high price. If we disentangle ourselves from the world around us, and adopt the negative notion of happiness, our happiness is little more than the absence of unhappiness. If we give up all concerns that lead us to think that dying is bad, we find ourselves with no reason for thinking that living is good. Living well cannot require ridding ourselves of our reasons to exist. Can it?

If not taken to an extreme, however, it is good advice to reappraise our expectations and ask if they are realistic. There is nothing wrong with having unattainable dreams, of course. But insofar as the notion of happiness is malleable, we should define it so that it is within our reach, even if our wishes and dreams are beyond us, enticing us to do still more with our lives than is required for simple happiness.

QUESTIONS FOR REFLECTION

1. If you were in the situation dramatized by *Matrix,* would you take the red pill or the blue one? Why? What would the psychological hedonist do? What would the value hedonist do? How would you respond?

2. Which is correct: (a) the reason it is important for us to do something (such as helping a friend) is that it is pleasurable; (b) the reason something is pleasurable is that doing it is important? How does this bear on whether or not psychological hedonism is correct?

3. Critically discuss the following passage from Butler's *Sermons,* in which he questions psychological hedonism:

   That all particular appetites and passions are towards external things themselves, distinct from the pleasure arising from them, is manifested from hence; that there could not be this pleasure, were it not for that prior suitableness between the object and the passion.[16]

   When Butler refers to "appetites and passions," he means desires. Is he right when he says that we never desire pleasure directly and that whatever pleasure we experience is a consequence of satisfying desires whose objects are things other than pleasure? If not, can his criticism of psychological hedonism be rescued?

4. Which view is more plausible, dominant-end hedonism or exclusive-end hedonism? Is either view correct?

5. Is pleasure the only thing that proves unsatisfying if pursued directly? Suppose we aim at loving relationships or knowledge or other things for their own sakes. Will our effort undermine itself, somewhat in the way of the hedonistic paradox? If not, what does this suggest about psychological hedonism?

6. Consider the view that pleasure is one of several things that are equally important. Does the case of the electronic voluptuary refute this view? Is the view true?

7. Elliott Sober tries to rescue psychological hedonism from the sort of criticism we offered using the case of the electronic voluptuary. According to Sober, those who choose not to become electronic voluptuaries need not really care about anything but pleasure. Their decision can be given an alternative explanation: The thought of abandoning ordinary life to become a voluptuary is distressing.[17] It starts hurting us while we are trying to reach our decision and will continue to do so until we actually become a voluptuary or decide not to. So to stop the pain, we give up on becoming a voluptuary. Is this response successful? (Why do people find the prospect of becoming voluptuaries distressing? Is it because their attachment to real life or to things — other than pleasure — involving real-life matters to them so much that they would not trade it for an existence whose only virtue is that it is blissful?)

8. Is Gautama giving us good advice when he tells us to abandon the notion of the self? Must we give up all desires if we give up the notion of the self? Can we abandon the desires that are incompatible with our achieving nirvana without giving up the notion of the self?

9. Is Epicurus correct when he assures us that death is nothing to us? Is it possible to hold that death is insignificant while also holding that life is worth living?

10. Epicurus says that pleasure is important to us only insofar as its absence is painful. Is he correct?

11. Critically assess the following argument given by Epicurus in his *Letter to Menoeceus:*

> [What produces] a pleasant life . . . is sober reasoning, searching out the grounds of every choice and avoidance. . . . Of all this the beginning and the greatest good is prudence. . . . From [prudence] spring all the other virtues, for it teaches that we cannot lead a life of pleasure which

is not also a life of prudence, honor, and justice; nor lead a life of prudence, honor, and justice, which is not also a life of pleasure. For the
virtues have grown into one with a pleasant life.

12. In Chapter II of *Utilitarianism,* John Stuart Mill says that "pleasure, and
freedom from pain, are the only things desirable as ends," but he acknowledges that this supposition that "life has . . . no higher end than
pleasure" strikes many people as "utterly mean and groveling; as a doctrine worthy only of swine." Mill adds that "when thus attacked, the
Epicureans have always answered that it is not they but their accusers,
who represent human nature in a degrading light; since the accusation
supposes human beings to be capable of no pleasures except those of
which swine are capable." Yet "human beings have faculties more elevated than the animal appetites, and when once made conscious of
them, do not regard anything as happiness which does not include
their gratification." Is it fair to say that the Epicurean doctrine is worthy
only of swine? If not, is Mill's response the best one?

FURTHER READINGS

Epicureanism

Epicurus. *The Epicurus Reader: Selected Writings and Testimonia.* Translated by Brad In-
wood and L. P. Gerson. Indianapolis: Hackett, 1994.

Lucretius. *On the Nature of Things.* Translated by W. H. D. Rouse. Cambridge, Mass.:
Harvard University Press, 1975.

Luper, Steven. *Invulnerability: On Securing Happiness.* Chicago: Open Court Press, 1996.

Mitsis, Phillip. *Epicurus' Ethical Theory.* Ithaca, N.Y.: Cornell University Press, 1988.

Sedley, David. "Epicureanism." In *Routledge Encyclopedia of Philosophy,* edited by Edward Craig. London: Routledge, 1998.

Buddhism

Kalupahana, David. "Buddhist Moral Philosophy." In *Living Well,* edited by Steven
Luper. Fort Worth: Harcourt Brace, 2000.

——. *Ethics in Early Buddhism.* Honolulu: University of Hawaii Press, 1995.

Radhakrishnan, S., and Moore, Charles, editors. *A Sourcebook in Indian Philosophy.*
Princeton: Princeton University Press, 1957.

Williams, P. *Mahayana Buddhism: The Doctrinal Foundations.* London: Routledge, 1989.

Hedonism

Butler, Joseph. *Fifteen Sermons upon Human Nature.* In *British Moralists,* vol. 1, edited by
L. A. Selby-Bigge. New York: Dover, 1965. Originally published 1726.

Good, I. J. "A Problem for the Hedonist." In *The Scientist Speculates,* edited by I. J.
Good. London: Heinemann, 1962.

Mill, J. S. *Autobiography.* New York: Columbia University Press, 1924.

——. *Utilitarianism,* edited by Oskar Piest. Indianapolis: Bobbs-Merrill, 1957. First published 1861.

Nozick, Robert. "The Experience Machine." In *Anarchy, State and Utopia.* New York: Basic Books, 1974.

Smart, J. J. C., and Williams, Bernard. *Utilitarianism: For and Against.* Cambridge: Cambridge University Press, 1973.

Sober, Elliott. "Psychological Egoism." In *The Blackwell Guide to Ethical Theory,* edited by Hugh LaFollette. 137–140. Oxford: Blackwell, 2000.

NOTES

1. Epicurus defended (agent-relative) value hedonism using this kind of argument in the following excerpt from his *Letter to Menoeceus:*

    > Pleasure is our first and kindred good. It is the starting point of every choice and of every aversion, and to it we come back, inasmuch as we make feeling the rule by which to judge of every good thing. (In *Greek and Roman Philosophy after Aristotle,* ed. Jason Saunders [New York: Free Press, 1966], p. 51.)

    In this passage he suggests that pleasure is our ("first and kindred") good because by nature ultimately we rank options by applying the standard of pleasure. His explicit reasoning is as follows:

    a. Pleasure is the one thing that each person desires for its own sake.

    b. So pleasure is the good.

    Of course, b does not follow from a, but there is little doubt that Epicurus is relying on the assumption that human motivation is (largely) decisive from the moral point of view. Stated fully, then, his argument is this:

    1. By nature each individual desires one and only one thing for its own sake: his or her pleasure.

    2. The things we seek naturally (and for their own sakes) are the things that are good in themselves.

    3. So for each individual one and only one thing is intrinsically valuable: his or her pleasure.

2. Joseph Butler, *Fifteen Sermons upon Human Nature.* In *British Moralists,* vol. 1, ed. L. A. Selby-Bigge (New York: Dover Books, 1965).

3. John Stuart Mill, *Autobiography* (New York: Columbia University Press, 1924), 93ff.

4. See chapter IV of *Utilitarianism.*

5. Similar distinctions are available to the psychological egoist: *Dominant-end egoism,* naming the self as one's highest priority, can be distinguished from *exclusive-end egoism,* naming the self as one's only non-instrumental concern.

6. Of course, claims 1 and 2 will support dominant-end hedonism only if they are true. Is 2 true? Not if what we say about the electronic voluptuary in the next section is right. If pleasure mattered more to us than anything else, we would become voluptuaries if we could. Yet most of us are repelled by the idea.

7. James Olds and Peter Milner, "Positive Reinforcement Produced by Electrical Stimulation of the Septal Area and Other Regions of the Rat Brain," *Journal of Comparative and Physiological Psychology* 47 (1954): 419–427. These results have been used in criticism of hedonism by several people, including I. J. Good in "A Problem for the Hedonist," in *The Scientist Speculates,* ed. I. J. Good (London: Heinemann, 1962); J. J. C. Smart, "An Outline of a System of Utilitarian Ethics," in *Utilitarianism: For and Against,* by J. J. C. Smart and Bernard Williams (Cambridge: Cambridge University Press, 1973); and Robert Nozick, "The Experience Machine," in *Anarchy, State and Utopia* (New York: Basic Books, 1974), pp. 42–45.

8. Epicurus, *Principal Doctrines,* Doctrine 26, in *Greek and Roman Philosophy after Aristotle,* ed. Jason Saunders (New York: Free Press, 1966), p. 55.

9. "The Synopsis of Truth," in *A Sourcebook in Indian Philosophy,* ed. S. Radhakrishnan and C. Moore (Princeton: Princeton University Press, 1957), p. 276.

10. Epicurus, "Letter to Menoeceus," in *Greek and Roman Philosophy after Aristotle,* p. 50.

11. Epicurus, "Letter," p. 51.

12. Epicurus, "Letter," p. 50.

13. Epicurus, *Principal Doctrines,* Doctrine 4, p. 53.

14. "Yamaka," translated by David Kalupahana, in *Living Well,* ed. Steven Luper (Fort Worth: Harcourt Brace, 2000), p. 238.

15. In Chapter 7 we discuss a view called *ethical egoism,* which claims that we ought to pursue only our own interests, and in Chapter 8 we consider a position called *utilitarianism,* which claims that we ought to pursue the interests of all sentient beings impartially. People who want to eliminate their own suffering tend to shift to a utilitarian stance (and agent-neutral hedonism) if they adopt the no-self doctrine. More precisely, they tend to adopt a form of utilitarianism that says to reduce suffering as much as possible, treating the suffering of each creature impartially (combining negative hedonism with utilitarianism). Contrast Epicureanism, which supports a form of ethical egoism (more precisely, ethical hedonism): We are each to minimize our own suffering.

16. Joseph Butler, in *British Moralists,* vol. 1, ed. L. A. Selby-Bigge (New York: Dover, 1965), p. 227.

17. Elliott Sober, "Psychological Egoism," in *The Blackwell Guide to Ethical Theory,* ed. Hugh LaFollette (Oxford: Blackwell, 2000), pp. 137–140.

6

Perfectionism
Do We Live Best When We Excel?

> The Governor of She in conversation with Confucius said, "In our village there is someone called 'True Person.' When his father took a sheep on the sly, he reported him to the authorities." Confucius replied, "Those who are true in my village conduct themselves differently. A father covers for his son, and a son covers for his father. And being true lies in this." [1]

Taken from the *Analects,* which record the views of the Chinese sage Confucius (551–479 B.C.), this passage reports a conversation that will surprise many readers from the West. At least initially, we balk at the idea that telling lies to "cover for" thieves is acceptable, let alone a way of being "true." But what if the thief is one's father? Confucius realized that honesty is important; but because one's family plays a central role in the good life, family comes first.

What does it take to live well? As we saw in the last chapter, theorists called value hedonists think that the best life is solely a matter of achieving some positive state of mind, such as pleasure, contentment, or tranquility. But other theorists disagree. They think there are things other than pleasure that are good in themselves. *Perfectionists* portray the best life as one that is as rich as possible in these excellences or perfections—in the things that are good in themselves. Each good has its own essential nature, and the ideal life is carefully crafted so that each good can be achieved.

How might the perfectionist proposal be defended? If life has elements that are good in themselves, it is quite plausible to say that the best life embraces these goods. So in large part the defense of perfectionism comes down to producing a plausible list of goods not limited to pleasure. But how can we tell if something is good for its own sake? Perfectionists have offered two related suggestions:

1.   The *self-realization theory* assumes that, fundamentally, a human be-ing's good consists in developing or realizing his or her identity, and things become good in themselves by being essential to identity. According to this view, we can identify goods by spelling out what is essential to an identity. Confucius, for example, thought that we derive an identity from certain re-lationships and social roles and claimed that the best life is one in which we cultivate these as thoroughly as possible. In the modern era, it is common to find theorists such as Friedrich Nietzsche emphasizing more individualistic goods, such as creative contributions.

2.   The *nature-based account* says that the good consists in developing hu-man nature well, and things become good in themselves by being essential to (or part of) the development of human nature. Usually this view is spelled out by appealing to the idea of a *function*. The idea is that human beings are con-structed to function in certain ways; that, fundamentally, their good consists in performing their function (or functions) well; and that things become good in themselves by being essential to (or part of) the human function. Starting in the fifth century B.C., Socrates (470–399 B.C.), Plato (428–347 B.C.), and Aristotle (384–322 B.C.) developed the nature-based approach, and their views have dominated Western moral theory for over a thousand years. With-out too much distortion, we can also attribute this approach to Confucian-ism's main rival in ancient China, namely Daoism, which is often attributed to an old man name Laozi.

How successful are the two strategies? Let us explore them by discussing the views of theorists who were among their most influential advocates.

CONFUCIUS AND THE SELF-REALIZATION THEORY OF THE GOOD

In ancient China, sages tried to clarify something they called the *dao* (some-times spelled *tao*). This term means "way," so their question was, What is the way? or What enables us to live well? Confucius answered this question by replacing it with another: What is it to be *ren?* The term *ren* refers to becom-ing a person, and so in effect Confucius was asking what it takes to develop as a person in the fullest way.

Becoming a Person

Sometimes Confucius offers a succinct answer to his question—namely, the golden rule, which he usually states negatively: "Do not do unto others as you would not have them do unto you."[2] But Confucius gives a more elaborate answer as well: *Ren* is a matter of being shaped by *li*, or human conventions of all sorts—laws, rules of etiquette, customs, traditions, rites, and so on. In other words, conventions make possible the distinctively human way of being. In large part, this is because they constitute the fabric of the common life we share with others in our community. According to Confucius's image, conventions provide the steps for an elaborate ceremony in which all participate.[3] People in the Confucian community take part in a vast ritual whose elements are given by sacred traditions passed down by their ancient forebears. When we play our part, our activities are mutually supporting, and our interests are linked. We are brought together into a closely knit community with which we identify; thereby, we extend the narrow boundaries of the individual self, embracing generations in the past, present, and distant future.

Roles and Relationships

The most important threads in the social fabric are roles and relationships that bind people together. These are the hearts of a person's identity: I am the son of my mother and father, and you are the student of your teacher. These are also the keys to exemplary conduct, which is usually explained as a matter of exercising virtues such as filial piety and respect that enable our relationships to flourish. For Confucius, the most important relationships are those that bind people into families, and the familial virtues of "filial and fraternal responsibility" are "the root" of becoming *ren*.[4] Other roles in society are modeled after an extended family; for example, teachers and rulers are considered parental figures, which gives them an elevated status indeed. To get an idea of how Confucius expects us to behave toward our parents, consider two passages in which he explains filial conduct.

First, "Give your mother and father nothing to worry about beyond your physical well-being."[5] Our comportment should be so upright that our parents know it will never reflect badly on them; we might become ill due to circumstances beyond our control, but that should be their sole concern about us—this is what proper respect for parents requires.

Second, "Those today who are filial are considered so because they are able to provide for their parents. But even dogs and horses are given that much care. If you do not respect your parents, what is the difference?"[6] We should take care of our parents in their old age—that goes without saying. What needs emphasizing is that we should do so out of loving reverence for these people who gave us so much.

It is not difficult to see why the family is at the heart of Confucian society. Our parents are our first teachers. We learn by observing them, and they have the responsibility for setting us an example of exemplary conduct. They must also gain our love and respect. Our filial piety is then carried over into respect for the traditions our parents revere, enabling us to identify with the community as a whole.

The idea that we are extensions of our ancestors and families gives Confucianism a distinctly spiritual dimension: We have a meaning that transcends the individual life. But this is a secular form of spirituality. Confucius had little interest in or patience for otherworldly concerns. When asked about the afterlife, he dismissed the question and advised focusing on the life we know:

> Zilu asked how to serve the spirits and the gods. The Master replied, "Not yet being able to serve other people, how would you be able to serve the spirits?" Zilu said, "May I ask about death?" The Master replied, "Not yet understanding life, how could you understand death?"[7]

Reservations and Alternatives

While the Confucian approach has considerable plausibility, it is still subject to criticism. Especially worrisome is that Confucius's deeply conservative view is resistant to change, whereas traditions sometimes need changing. What if we are part of a society whose traditions are antithetical to the interests of people in other societies? What if our society's traditions denigrate some of its own members? What if we find ourselves in a role that subordinates us to others? We will then be expected to identify with roles and traditions we might well find repugnant. Consider that Confucius himself endorsed a traditional hierarchy of authority in which elders are respected but males are given pride of place. For example, while younger brothers are to submit to the authority of elder brothers, there is no suggestion that brothers are to submit to the authority of elder sisters.

Some ways of responding to this sort of worry are compatible with Confucianism, and others are not. Defenders of Confucianism can try to convince us that changing society's traditions is almost always a bad idea, so it counts in favor of Confucianism that it resists such changes. Revising traditions, they might say, is a serious and dangerous business; a great deal is at stake, since inherited values and ways shape who we are. They form us into families with distinctive identities: For the members of each family, the word *we* comes naturally and calls to mind a perspective quite distinct from the point of view summoned by the word *I*. By the same token, members of many families take on a common identity through their mutual respect for the ways of their community. If we abruptly and completely abandon the values and traditions of our forebears, we cease to be who we are, at least in part. We commit a kind of suicide and sever ties to our grandparents and great grandparents – people we once revered.

A second response concedes that people must gradually change their ways as their circumstances change. But Confucius realized this, his defender might say, and he left open the door to the revision of traditional ways. His suggestion was that in making these revisions we strive to conserve the heart of the ancient ways. As Herbert Fingarette puts the point, Confucius's idea is

> to seek inspiration in one's own traditions in such a way as to reveal a humanizing and harmonizing interpretation for the conflictful present. "He who by reanimating the Old can gain knowledge of the New is indeed fit to be called a teacher" (2:11).[8]

Confucianism is a profoundly human-centered vision according to which the human community, acting as a whole and over generations, establishes what is required for people to flourish and revises its ideals as it goes. No passage in the *Analects* is more characteristic of Confucianism than chapter 29 of Book 15, where Confucius says, "it is humanity that broadens the *dao,* not the *dao* that broadens humanity."

Another way to defend Confucianism involves subordinating the self-realization account to the nature-based account of the good. That is, we might argue that self-realization is fundamentally a matter of developing our nature. We might then clarify the goods attained in natural development and use our account as an objective basis for deciding how to revise traditions. The plausibility of this defense depends on the plausibility of the nature-based theory of the good, which we will examine in a moment. (Arguably, Confucius's own followers soon began to look to human nature for clues about the good. In the fourth century B.C., Confucius's most illustrious follower, Mencius, suggested that people are born with a predilection to behave well. As evidence, Mencius cited the fact that anyone who sees a child standing dangerously near the edge of a well will spontaneously react with alarm and concern.)[9]

A final response to the fact that some traditions and traditional roles are repugnant is to say that this is a problem for Confucianism, not for the self-realization account itself. The self-realization account does not imply that identity is given to us by our society. It does not say what accounts for a person's identity. Perhaps we each invent our own identity, as existentialist philosophers say. If so, then, arguably, we each make our life worthwhile by realizing the identity we invent, and this identity might lead us to reject traditional roles we do not accept.

THE NATURE-BASED ACCOUNT OF THE GOOD

Consider now the nature-based account, which says that things become good in themselves by being essential to (or part of) the development of human nature, and so the key to living well is to develop our nature. An extreme version of this account was developed in the third century B.C. by Chinese sages called Daoists whose views are expressed in the *Daodejing* (or *Tao-te Ching*). A more moderate version was developed by Aristotle.

Daoism and Spontaneity

As Daoists use it, the term *dao* refers to the aspects of nature by which all things are brought into being and organized into an orderly cosmos. It is also used normatively, for the way things are naturally is the best way for them to be, according to Daoists. Human beings are just one small part of the order created by the *dao,* no less than other creatures and no more. All is well when we move in the well-worn ways carved out for us by the *dao;* our lives are then a splendid part of the natural order. But when we try to improve ourselves and make our own way—formulating higher ideals and prescribing better ways to act—our efforts backfire. The Daoist idea is to work with nature, not against it, like a cook named Ting who appears in the *Zhuangzi* (or *Chuang Tzu*), another Daoist classic:

> Cook Ting was cutting up an ox for Lord Wen-hui. At every touch of his hand, every heave of his shoulder, every move of his feet, every thrust of his knee—zip! zoop! He slithered the knife along with a zing, and all was in perfect rhythm, as though he were performing [a] dance. . . .
>
> "Ah, this is marvelous!" said Lord Wen-hui. "Imagine skill reaching such heights!"
>
> Cook Ting laid down his knife and replied, "What I care about is the Way, which goes beyond skill. When I first began cutting up oxen, all I could see was the ox itself. After three years I no longer saw the whole ox. And now—now I go at it by spirit and don't look with my eyes. Perception and understanding have come to a stop and spirit moves where it wants. I go along with the natural makeup, strike in the big hollows, . . . and follow things as they are. . . .
>
> "There are spaces between the joints. . . . If you insert [the knife] into such spaces, then there's plenty of room. . . . That's why after nineteen years the blade of my knife is still as good as when it first came from the grindstone. . . ."
>
> "Excellent!" said Lord Wen-hui. "I have heard the words of Cook Ting and learned how to care for life!" [10]

The *dao* enables us to live well, fitting us seamlessly into the fabric of nature, by making proper behavior instinctual. To flourish, we need only tap into these inner resources. However, we can also turn against our instincts and act in artificial ways. Unfortunately, this is what humanity has done. We no longer respond to the inner promptings by which our ancestors led simple lives that kept them close to nature. Our civilization views these instincts with contempt, calling them primitive and unrefined, and replaces them with desires that make us anxiously self-conscious, competitive, and discontent. Our values are the artifacts of socialization. We must have the latest fashions in clothing and housing, and more than others have of everything others crave. We want to rise in the social hierarchy, attaining positions that carry high status, precisely because others covet those positions. Civilized people can no longer tell what they need, because their lives are staked on satisfying wholly artificial desires: They want what they do because others want those things. Humanity has cut itself off from its own roots.

The problem cannot be solved by developing theories about morality and the good life. Daoists are skeptical about creating accounts of the *dao* to steer ourselves by. We cannot make ourselves better through philosophizing or reading books about ethics. The very first passage of the *Daodejing* warns us that "the way that can be spoken is not the way." Moreover, the text offers advice that sounds paradoxical: It tells us that the *dao* never acts, yet nothing is left undone, implying that we are to behave in a similar way.[11] But isn't it impossible to leave nothing undone unless we act? Not if we understand "acting" as calculated behavior prompted by a theory about the *dao*. All such theories are bound to be misleading and simplistic, according to Daoists, and cannot substitute for our own instincts. To be in accord with the *dao* is to live spontaneously, responding to inner promptings that know how to ensure that nothing is left undone. The *Daodejing* contrasts sages, who display true virtue in their spontaneous behavior, with would-be sages, who try to be virtuous (and to make others virtuous) by devising recipes for living well. Among those criticized are advocates of the Confucian idea that living well involves following the rites:

> Those of highest virtue do not keep to virtue and so they have it.
> Those of lowest virtue never stray from virtue and so they lack it.
> The former never act yet leave nothing undone.
> The latter act but leave things undone.
> . . . Those who have mastered the rites act, but if others do not respond,
> they roll up their sleeves and resort to force.[12]

Sitting in their air-conditioned rooms and listening to their favorite CDs while they scan the pages of this book, modern readers will be skeptical about the Daoist's claim that we cannot improve on nature. However, some of us will respond favorably to elements of the Daoist vision. Perhaps we would be better off if we thought of ourselves as part of the natural order, rather than viewing it merely as a resource to exploit. If we recognized the beauty and mystery of our world and of the ways it has ordered itself, perhaps we would attempt to live in harmony with that order—for example, by limiting the human population, eliminating pollution, and conserving areas of the world containing a rich diversity of living things.[13] However, Daoism has an element of anti-intellectualism that makes its proponents resist explicitly spelling out the nature-based account of the good life. For that, we will have to turn to the work of other theorists, such as Aristotle.

Aristotle and Human Flourishing

Aristotle begins his account of the human good by explaining a basic assumption he will make—namely, that if people have an ultimate end, then it is the human good. He thinks we will find this assumption agreeable, once he explains what he means by an ultimate end. Something is an ultimate end, he says, if it has three defining features:

1. It is sought for its own sake.

2. It is not sought for the sake of anything else.

3. It is the reason all other things are sought.

Surely, Aristotle says, if something meets these three conditions, we will want to take it as the human good:

> Suppose . . . that (a) there is some end of the things we pursue in our actions which we wish for because of itself, and because of which we wish for the other things; and (b) we do not choose everything because of something else, since (c) if we do, it will go on without limit, making desire empty and futile; then clearly (d) this end will be the good, i.e. the best good.[14]

But is there such a thing? Aristotle thinks there is, and he thinks it is called *eudaimonia.* This term means human flourishing, or well-being, or—if we use the term to imply "doing well" and not just "feeling good"—happiness. But calling the ultimate end happiness does not get us very far. To get clear about the good, we need to figure out what our ultimate end is, not what it is called. How can we do that?

One way is to ask ourselves what is desired for its own sake and not for the sake of other things. For Aristotle (at least in one interpretation), it will turn out that no one item is the ultimate end; rather, a bundle of things is the ultimate end. We arrive at this idea as follows. First, we sort through our goals and clarify their teleological or purposive organization, separating what we want for its own sake from what we want as a mere means to other things. After doing so, however, we find that several things are desired for their own sakes. According to Aristotle these goods are pleasure, honor, knowledge, friendship, and virtue – all of these over the course of a whole life. But no *one* of these goods is our ultimate end all by itself, and hence no one of them constitutes happiness. In fact, even though pleasure, honor, knowledge, virtue, and long life are each sought for their own sakes, each is also sought for the sake of something else as well. The desire for pleasure, for honor, for knowledge, and so on – each is partially instrumental, and hence not truly ultimate, because we seek each of these goods in order to attain the combination of them all. We have one goal (and only one) that is truly ultimate in the sense that it is not even partially instrumental: the desire for the combination of all of the things we seek for their own sakes. This is the ultimate end that Aristotle identifies with *eudaimonia*. Anything less would be incomplete; it would fall short of the best life.

To signal the fact that the human good includes everything pertaining to life that is worthy of our choosing, Aristotle calls the human good *self-sufficient*. Even gifts of fortune, such as wealth and beauty, are parts of the best life, although they are not good in themselves, because they are the indispensable means to things that are good in themselves. However, in saying that the human good is self-sufficient, Aristotle does not imply that we can be happy all by ourselves and maintain our happiness entirely through our own efforts. Although having a virtuous character enables us to become happy in favorable circumstances, the element of luck cannot be eliminated in our quest for the best life. Here Aristotle's view contrasts sharply with Epicurus's. Epicurus calls the happy person self-sufficient, and in doing so he does imply that attaining and maintaining happiness is entirely within the individual's reach.

Aristotle uses a second strategy to help identify the good. It involves the assumption that flawless specimens of humanity are so constructed that they function well when they act in certain ways and that acting in these ways is good for them. (Regrettably, Aristotle considers women and "natural slaves" defective.) Something similar can be said for things other than human beings as well. Generally speaking, a good ___ is a ___ that performs its function well. A good lamp, for example, excels at its definitive function of illumination. Cats, too, are constituted to function in certain ways; their good is flawless feline functioning. Accordingly, a study of proper human functioning will help reveal what activities are goods.

What are the human ways of functioning? Aristotle picks out two as especially significant. The first Aristotle considers most important since no other creatures (save the gods) function in quite the same way: We reason and are able to shape our activities by applying the critical standpoint of reason. We function well only when we live rationally. Second, humans are social creatures in the sense that we do well only when we form a society and establish various sorts of relationships with others. To flourish is to live well with others. Here Aristotle is in agreement with Confucius. For both philosophers the good life involves relationships that bind people together as well as attributes of character that enable these relationships to flourish. However, insofar as Aristotle portrays the good life in terms of behavior prompted by human nature, his view overlaps with Daoism.

To function well is, Aristotle adds, to display *arete*—virtue or excellence. In fact, there are two main forms of excellence, corresponding to two parts of the psyche. One part of the psyche is rational, while the other is not; and while the first part displays what Aristotle calls the *intellectual virtues,* the second displays *virtues of character.* When we philosophize or contemplate the way things are, we are using theoretical reason; and if we excel in thinking ability, we will display intellectual virtues, the most important of which is wisdom or good judgment (*phronesis*). The nonrational part of the psyche is the seat of appetites or desires. It cannot reason, but it can be shaped or influenced by reason, so to some extent our characters can be molded by reason. As Aristotle puts the point, "the faculty of appetite or of desire in general . . . is rational . . . in the sense in which we speak of rational obedience to father or friends, not in the sense in which we speak of rational apprehension of mathematical truths." [15] Ideally, we want to create a harmony between the two parts of our psyche so that we are drawn only to things deemed desirable by reason.

Aristotle also says that each virtue of character is a mean between two extremes of action or emotion, and he calls each of the extremes a vice; but this so-called *doctrine of the mean* is not intended to give us a clear procedure for identifying virtues of character. We cannot identify virtues by locating points midway between two extremes, and we cannot discover vices by locating the two extremes. Caspar Milquetoast, a bland and emotionally lukewarm cartoon character, is not Aristotle's moral exemplar. Virtuous behavior does involve moderation, but it is moderate in the sense that we must apply good judgment and take all relevant factors into consideration before we act:

> [Virtues of character] must aim at the mean. . . . For instance, it is possible to feel fear, confidence, desire, anger, pity, and generally to be affected pleasantly and painfully, either too much or too little, in either case wrongly; but to be thus affected at the right times, and on the right occasions, and towards the right persons, and with the right object, and in the right fashion, is the mean course and the best course, and these are characteristics of virtue.
>
> . . . Virtue, then, is a kind of moderation . . . , inasmuch as it aims at the mean or moderate amount. [16]

Will grasping Aristotle's account of good character make us better people? Perhaps, but Aristotle believes characters are difficult to transform.

We can acquire the virtues of character only by habituation, or conditioning, which in practice means being brought up properly by people who themselves are good. Our parents might, for example, reward us when we act bravely and punish us when we act cowardly, and gradually we form a habit or disposition of courage. Later, as our intellectual lives mature, we come to recognize the importance of acting in certain ways. It is at this time that studying Aristotle's ethics can help. Then our reason can guide our actions, allowing us to refine the good responses we are already habituated to make. In time our behavior may become truly excellent. Because of its guiding role in conduct, *phronesis,* or good judgment, underlies all of the virtues, helping to give them a certain unity.

Reservations

Despite its attractions, the nature-based account of the good faces difficulties. Some might think to challenge it on Humean grounds: Merely descriptive statements, no matter how detailed or numerous, cannot entail normative statements. However, it is best to understand the nature-based account as resting on a plausible value claim—that the things we seek naturally (and for their own sakes) are the things that are good in themselves—rather than the assertion that claims about the good follow from observations about our in-built motivation.

Another criticism is that human nature seems far more malleable to modern theorists than it did to ancient sages. It is far from clear what we are naturally attracted to or what natural development comes to. And what if it turns out that human beings have natural desires that are repugnant? Suppose, for example, we are naturally cruel and drawn to the suffering of others?

Aristotle might respond to the first of these criticisms in a conciliatory way. Perhaps human nature is quite malleable, he might say, and in that case we will simply have to conclude that the objective truth about the best life is a very sketchy truth. For Aristotle to make such a concession is very much in the spirit of his work. In fact, his preface to *Nicomachean Ethics* signaled his awareness that his subject matter was imprecise: "We must be content if we can attain to so much precision in our statement as the subject before us admits of. We must be content if we can indicate the truth roughly and in outline." [17]

As for the concern that human nature might include unsavory motivations such as cruelty, Aristotle might do well to consider a suggestion by Friedrich Nietzsche. Nietzsche thought that our psychic makeup does include elements we condemn as well as elements we embrace. But, he says, we should embrace all of our basic motivations and find an appropriate outlet for each. After all, it is not as if we could make a desire that is truly in-built go away just by condemning it and refusing to take it into our identity. It will still exist and find ways to affect our behavior.

PERFECTIONISM AND EXEMPLARY CONDUCT

Let us put aside any doubts we might have about the perfectionist idea of the good life and pose a question that marks a transition from our discussion of the good here in Chapters 5 and 6 to a discussion of the right, which we undertake in earnest in the remainder of the book. Here's the question: What is the best way to conduct ourselves once we have a list of things pertaining to life that are good in themselves? Suppose, for example, that we agree on Aristotle's list—pleasure, friendship, honor, knowledge, virtue, and long life—perhaps updated with items that are not explicitly on his list. (Karl Marx thought that creative work is one of life's prime goods, and while Aristotle might have classified the contemplative activities of the knowledge seeker as a kind of work, it is not the only form of creative self-expression we would consider good. So we may wish to add creative work to the list of life's goods. In addition, loving relationships are goods most of us seek, and not all such relationships fit neatly under Aristotle's category of friendship.) Once we have a list, what is the next step?

It might seem as if the answer is simple. Once we have our list of things that are good in themselves, won't it be obvious what to do—namely, whatever makes it possible to attain those goods or whatever makes it possible to attain as many of them as we can, thus making our lives as good as possible? Actually, it might be quite difficult to decide how to conduct ourselves. Even with our list, we will face two difficulties. First, each good has complexities we need to grasp. Unless we master the nature of a good such as friendship, which is demanding and easily misunderstood, we will not know how to achieve it or what conduct is consistent with maintaining it. Second, even if we know what things are good, it is by no means clearly appropriate to do whatever it takes to achieve them as closely as possible. For surely some actions, such as killing innocent people or robbing people in dark alleys, are inappropriate even if they do help us to attain goods. Aren't they?

But what do we mean when we say an action is inappropriate? Well, modern ethicists tend to put the point this way: An action that helps us to achieve a good might nonetheless be morally wrong—it might violate our obligations. But ancient ethicists would put the point differently, for they did not really have the modern concept of an obligation—or at least many modern theorists have suggested as much (the matter is controversial). Instead of classifying conduct as right or wrong, ancient ethicists classified conduct as exemplary or not exemplary, as noble or ignoble. And exemplary conduct, in turn, they explained in terms of good character. In their view, character is conceptually prior to conduct: In order to understand good conduct, we must first understand good character, for the former derives from the latter. This is a distinctive feature of the ancient approach; in the modern era, any ethical system that has this feature is called a *virtue ethics*. Let us see if we can clarify this approach to ethics a bit more.

Virtue Ethics

According to the virtue ethicist, whether ancient or modern, in the final analysis the best choice just is the one a good person would opt for. It is the moral exemplar—the person with the virtues of character—who defines exemplary conduct. And having good character constrains our behavior in significant ways, for the exemplary person will consider some ways of acting as base or ignoble (and in that sense inappropriate) and will avoid them even if those actions are the means to other goods, such as pleasure.

One might have thought it was the other way around—that exemplary conduct is best consulted in order to define the moral exemplar. And certainly this is closer to the dominant view in the modern era. Nowadays we tend to think that we can specify our moral duties in the form of rules or principles—Do not lie, for example—and then understand a good character as a set of attributes that incline one to act dutifully. This view suggests that becoming a good person is first and foremost a matter of recognizing which moral principles are binding on us and then shaping our priorities and habits—or characters—so that we always meet our obligations. But ancient virtue ethicists did not accept any part of this view, and modern virtue ethicists are inclined to agree with them. Their approach contrasts with the dominant modern view in three main ways.

First, as we said before, ethicists in the ancient world were not really asking what our obligations are. They thought that if we could identify the excellences of character, we could strive to acquire these perfections; and if we succeeded, our behavior would be the natural outflow of our character. As for the excellences of character, these, in turn, were understood to be good in themselves and thus desirable elements of the best life, alongside other things that are good for their own sakes. We want to become exemplary persons because it is good for us, not because we must—not because we have a duty to perform, and having a good character enables us to perform it. Having a good character is the best way to be, and it is part of the best life we can live. But what if, in our circumstances, we cannot achieve all of the goods that make up the best life, and ignoble behavior would bring us as close as we can come? Why not act badly, if doing so is the most effective way to make our lives as good as possible? The ancients did not give us a complete answer to this kind of question. Instead, they had a profound confidence that we can achieve each good in a way that also allows us (and others) to achieve the next, so that it is never best for us to act badly.

Second, ancient virtue ethicists would have rejected the idea that we can first recognize the appropriateness of a way of acting and then shape a good character by working out which dispositions will tend to make us act in that way. According to the ancients, only people with good characters can fully understand why one way of acting is good and another is bad, and only they can reliably make good choices. In large part, they can recognize the best option because it is the choice their good characters draw them to. It is love and respect, for example, that enable virtuous people to see how objectionable it would be to send their fathers to jail for petty crimes.

And third, ancient virtue ethicists thought that even the wise and virtuous cannot devise rules that are applicable in all situations. Aristotle would have said that an effort should be made; for good rules can be made into law, and the best state is governed by laws designed to establish and perpetuate the good life. Unlike Confucius, he believed that the best state is governed by the rule of law, not people. However, no rules, however sophisticated, can handle all situations properly, so sometimes a bad outcome will result when rules are applied. Dealing with cases in which the rules fail requires the wisdom and finesse of good judges.

True Person, True Friend

To see how difficult it can be to devise universally applicable rules, consider the passage about "True Person" at the beginning of this chapter. Clearly, Confucius thought that loyalty to and respect for one's father is important enough to outweigh absolute, abstract, and bloodless principles such as "Never tell lies." Turning him in for petty theft is objectionable – especially when we go out of our way to do so and expect to be praised. And once Confucius's point is put that way, it rings true. It would be terrible to learn our father is a petty thief, yet our situation is only made worse if we are the instruments through which his iniquity becomes widely known. Severing the bond between a child and a parent is one of life's greatest calamities. It is therefore deeply objectionable for a father to put this bond in danger by stealing. His act of theft is likely to diminish him in the eyes of those whom he loves and it will place them in the agonizing position of having to decide how to respond. On the other hand, his children should carefully weigh the consequences of turning him in and pursue alternatives, such as replacing the stolen item anonymously. As well, they should give him the benefit of any doubt: Perhaps he stole because otherwise his family would have starved to death.

But can we point to a principle that the zealous son violated, one that always guides people well in such situations? Confucius does not offer one (unless we count the golden rule itself) and doubtless would have said that loyalty cannot be summed up in a convenient formula. Nevertheless, let us investigate whether a reliable principle can be provided. We may do so by discussing one plausible candidate: Never be the instrument through which the people you care about are apprehended by legal authorities.

Unfortunately, there are situations in which this principle is a poor guide, as a recent event illustrates. In 1997 two eighteen-year-old high school buddies named David Cash and Jeremy Strohmeyer went to a resort in Nevada, and Strohmeyer started playing with a seven-year-old girl named Sherrice Iverson. They tossed paper at each other for a while, then she ran into a rest room, and Strohmeyer followed. Abruptly, he ceased being playful and forced her into a stall. Meanwhile, Strohmeyer's friend Cash peered over from an adjoining stall, saw the two struggling, and after asking Strohmeyer to stop, walked out of the bathroom. After Cash left, Strohmeyer molested Sherrice, murdered her, and stuffed her in the toilet. Rejoining Cash a half hour later, Strohmeyer confessed what he had done. Cash kept the confession to himself. Nonetheless, Strohmeyer had been filmed by a surveillance camera and was arrested. He pled guilty and was sentenced to life without parole. Cash himself was never sentenced, and to this day Cash believes his behavior to be beyond reproach. After entering Berkeley to study nuclear engineering, he was interviewed on a Los Angeles talk show and said, "It's a tragic event, okay. But the simple fact remains that I do not know this girl. The only person I knew in this event was Jeremy Strohmeyer. . . . I didn't want to be the one that took away my best friend's last days." He told the *Los Angeles Times* that he was not going to "lose sleep over somebody else's problems."[18] He even bragged to his roommates about the incident, as if it were something to be proud of. His comments made him unwelcome on the Berkeley campus, where he became a pariah. Strangers spit at him, and he needed to be escorted by a campus security guard.

If Cash knew that Strohmeyer was going to harm Sherrice, which Cash himself denies, then he might have been able to stop him (and then the involvement of the authorities would not have been necessary). And it is worth noting that stopping him was important for Strohmeyer's sake. Even better would have been to help him become the sort of person who would not rape and kill, for that would have made Strohmeyer a better person; and as perfectionists say, to be a better person is to be better off. Strohmeyer is now a convicted rapist and murderer. As he sits in prison, no doubt he wishes he had had a friend with the courage to stop him.

On the other hand, if Cash did not realize what Strohmeyer was planning, then he could not have prevented the crime; and in refusing to turn Strohmeyer in, he might well claim to have acted from a principled determination not to help authorities apprehend a friend. If, after the crime, he turned his friend in, he would be "the one that took away [his] best friend's last days."

But what should we think about covering for friends who murder? As Confucius and Aristotle thought, friendship is one of the chief goods available in life. If you and I truly are friends, I care about you for your sake, and vice versa. Moreover, I want you to be successful in your projects, and I look to protect your interests – and you reciprocate my good will. So strong is the bond of true friendship that it merges our lives and welds our very identities together. However, let us recognize what Cash's continued loyalty to Strohmeyer implies. Precisely because the identities of friends overlap, what friends do reflects on us; we take pride in our friends' accomplishments, and we feel shame at their misdeeds. Hence we cannot count as friends people who engage in behavior we find profoundly repugnant, as Confucius himself seemed to think: "Regard loyalty and good faith as your main concern. Do not make friends of those who are not up to your own standard. If you commit a fault, do not shrink from correcting it." [19]

To this day Cash considers himself Strohmeyer's friend. Doesn't this suggest that he does not condemn Strohmeyer for murdering Sherrice? Friends share in each other's projects; does Cash's continued loyalty signal that he would help with crimes Strohmeyer might commit in the future or at least turn a blind eye to them? Surely we should break our ties to friends who are murderers and turn them in. So we cannot always abide by a principle that forbids bringing our friends to the attention of the police. Yet exactly when is a wrongful act serious enough to warrant breaking with people we care about? It is difficult to say and harder to express in the form of a rule.

QUESTIONS FOR REFLECTION

1. In *Confucius – The Secular as Sacred*, p. 57, Herbert Fingarette says that Confucius assumes that "there is one *li*" and "this *li* is the *li* of the land in which he lives (other lands being barbarian)" and "the Ancients of his tradition lived this *li*." But Confucius's assumptions are questionable when we take into account cultural diversity. How might Confucius respond? Would his answer be adequate?

2. Suppose Daoists are correct when they say that the *dao* shapes everything in the world. Doesn't it follow that the *dao* shaped humanity? How, then, are human beings able to act contrary to the *dao?* What sort of response might Daoists make to this question?

3. Is there a unity underlying the virtues? Compare and contrast Aristotle's view that *phronesis* underlies the virtues with Confucius's view of the virtues.

4. Critically assess the position Aristotle takes in the following passage in *Nicomachean Ethics:*

   Suppose . . . that (a) there is some end of the things we pursue in our actions which we wish for because of itself, and because of which we wish for the other things; and (b) we do not choose everything because of something else, since (c) if we do, it will go on without limit, making desire empty and futile; then clearly (d) this end will be the good, i.e. the best good.

5. According to Aristotle, A and B are true friends only if A considers the well-being of B good for its own sake and B returns that attitude. What, according to Epicurus, should our attitude be toward friends? Whose account is more plausible, Aristotle's or Epicurus's?

6. Is it possible to attain and maintain happiness entirely through our own efforts? Compare and contrast the views of Aristotle and Epicurus. Whose view is more plausible?

7. Is it possible to base an account of the good on claims about human nature? If so, how can this be done? If not, what is the alternative?

FURTHER READINGS

Aristotelianism

Annas, Julia. *The Morality of Happiness.* Oxford: Oxford University Press, 1993.

Cooper, John. *Reason and Human Good in Aristotle.* Cambridge, Mass.: Harvard University Press, 1975.

Heil, John F. "Aristotelianism." In *Living Well,* edited by Steven Luper. Fort Worth: Harcourt Brace, 2000.

Nussbaum, Martha. *The Fragility of Goodness.* Cambridge, Mass.: Harvard University Press, 1986.

Rorty, Amelia. *Essays on Aristotle's Ethics.* Berkeley: University of California Press, 1980.

Confucianism

Confucius. *Analects*. In *The Analects of Confucius: A Philosophical Translation*, translated by Roger Ames and Henry Rosemont. New York: Ballantine, 1998.

Fingarette, Herbert. *Confucius – The Secular as Sacred*. New York: Harper Torchbooks, 1972.

——. "Following the 'One Thread' of the Analects." *Journal of the American Academy of Religion*, 47, no. 3 (1980): 373–405. Thematic Issue S.

Lau, D. C., and Ames, Roger T. "Confucius." In *Routledge Encyclopedia of Philosophy*, edited by Edward Craig. London: Routledge, 1998.

Rosemont, Henry, Jr., "Confucius and the Analects." In *Living Well*, edited by Steven Luper. Fort Worth: Harcourt Brace, 2000.

Daoism

Chan, Wing-tsit. *The Way of Lao Tzu*. Chicago: University of Chicago Press, 1963.

Graham, Angus. *Disputers of the Tao: Philosophical Argument in Ancient China*. La Salle, Ill.: Open Court Press, 1989.

Hall, David, and Ames, Roger. *Anticipating China: Thinking Through the Narratives of Chinese and Western Culture*. Albany: State University of New York Press, 1995.

——. "Daoism." In *Routledge Encyclopedia of Philosophy*, edited by Howard Craig. London: Routledge, 1998.

Ivanhoe, P. J. "Daoism." In *Living Well*, edited by S. Luper. Fort Worth: Harcourt Brace, 2000.

Laozi. *Daodejing*, translated by D. C. Lau. Hong Kong: The Chinese University Press, 1982.

Zhuangzi. *Basic Writings*, translated by Burton Watson. New York: Columbia University Press, 1964.

NOTES

1. *Analects*, 13.18, in *The Analects of Confucius: A Philosophical Translation*, trans. Roger T. Ames and Henry Rosemont, Jr. (New York: Ballantine, 1998).
2. *Analects*, 12.2 and 15.24, trans. Ames and Rosemont. As Herbert Fingarette noted in "Following the 'One Thread' of the Analects," *Journal of the American Academy of Religion*, 47, no. 3 (1980): pp. 373–405, Thematic Issue S, the rule is expressed in a positive way at 6:28: "As for *ren*–you yourself desire rank and standing; then help others to get rank and standing. You want to advance; then help others to advance. In fact, to manage from yourself to take the Analogy–that is where *ren* is."
3. As Herbert Fingarette emphasized in *Confucius – the Secular as Sacred* (New York: Harper Torchbooks, 1972).
4. *Analects*, 1.2, trans. Ames and Rosemont.
5. *Analects*, 2.6, trans. Ames and Rosemont.

6. *Analects,* 2.7, trans. Ames and Rosemont.

7. *Analects,* 11.12, trans. Ames and Rosemont.

8. Fingarette, *Confucius – The Secular as Sacred,* p. 68.

9. Mencius, *Mengzi,* 2A6.

10. *Chuang Tzu: Basic Writings,* trans. Burton Watson (New York: Columbia University Press, 1964), pp. 465 – 467. I thank my colleague Ewing Chinn for recommending the use of this passage.

11. *Daodejing,* chapter 37, trans. P. J. Ivanhoe, in *Living Well,* ed. Steven Luper (Fort Worth: Harcourt Brace, 2000).

12. *Daodejing,* chapter 38, p. 89.

13. Consider some of the ugly consequences of the American way of life. According to the Environmental Protection Agency, people in cities in the United States generate well over 200 million tons of solid waste every year – per capita, we generate more than four pounds of solid garbage a day. Only about a quarter of this waste is recycled; most of it goes into landfills or incinerators. We also generate about 280 million tons of hazardous waste yearly. Every day, billions of gallons of wastewater are generated by homes and commercial operations in cities. This water contains many toxic compounds, and while most of it is treated to varying degrees, much of it overflows antiquated treatment plants; and so raw sewage, together with treated wastewater, is discharged into rivers, estuaries, and oceans. Industrial facilities produce billions more gallons of wastewater every day. Further sources of pollution are acids draining from mines, runoff from animal feeding operations, and storm waters that wash chemicals from farms and other areas. (See the publications of the Environmental Protection Agency, such as "Characterization of Municipal Solid Waste in the United States: 1997 Update," U.S. Environmental Protection Agency Report No. EPA 530-R-98-007. Much information is available at http://www.epa.gov.)

14. Aristotle, *Nicomachean Ethics,* trans. Terence Irwin (Indianapolis: Hackett, 1985), p. 2 (1094a18 – 22). John Stuart Mill makes a similar assumption. Writing in *Utilitarianism,* Mill says: "The only proof capable of being given that an object is visible is that people actually see it. The only proof that a sound is audible is that people hear it; and so of the other sources of our experience. In like manner, I apprehend, the sole evidence it is possible to produce that anything is desirable is that people do actually desire it." (*Utilitarianism,* in *Social Ideals and Policies: Readings in Social and Political Philosophy,* ed. Steven Luper. [Mountain View, Calif.: Mayfield, 1999], p. 145.)

15. Aristotle, *Nicomachean Ethics,* book 1, chapter 13, in *Social Ideals and Policies,* p. 117.

16. Aristotle, *Nicomachean Ethics,* book 2, chapter 6, in *Social Ideals and Policies,* p. 120. As virtues of character, Aristotle includes the following (together with corresponding vices in parentheses): courage (cowardice, foolhardiness), temperance (self-indulgence, insensibility), generosity (prodigality, meanness),

magnificence (vulgarity, niggardliness), magnanimity (vanity, pusillanimity), friendliness (obsequiousness, churlishness), truthfulness (boastfulness, false modesty), mildness (irascibility, impassivity), wit (buffoonery, boorishness), and justice (injustice).

17. Aristotle, *Nicomachean Ethics,* book 1, chapter 3, in *Social Ideals and Policies,* p. 114.

18. Cathy Booth, "The Bad Samaritan," *Time,* 7 September 1998, pp. 59–60.

19. *Analects,* 9.25, trans. Raymond Dawson (Oxford: Oxford University Press, 1993).

7

Ethical Egoism

Is Duty a Matter of
Self-Enhancement?

At approximately 11:00 A.M. on April 20, 1999, at Columbine High School in Littleton, Colorado, two masked students named Eric Harris and Dylan Klebold began shooting people. Before they were done, they had killed twelve students, one teacher, and themselves. At the scene one panicked student told reporters about her encounter with the gunmen. "Everyone around me got shot. I begged him for 10 minutes not to shoot me. He just put the gun in my face and there was bleeding everywhere and he started laughing and was saying that it was all because people had been mean to him last year." Understandably, most of the people in the school rushed out in terror. But some put their own lives in jeopardy to assist others. A teacher named Dave Sanders did his best to help students and teachers to escape. "Mr. Sanders was taking bullets for people," according to a student named Stephanie Lohrenz. When the gunmen approached the school cafeteria, Sanders "ran into the cafeteria and warned everybody," according to English teacher Cheryl Lucas. Then he moved off to warn others and was shot. Before help arrived, Sanders died. Frank DeAngelis, the principal, described Sanders as "so unselfish, someone who brought out the best in people."[1]

What Sanders did seemed to involve acts of supererogation: He went beyond the call of duty, gravely risking—in fact, losing—his life, which is more than his students and fellow teachers could reasonably have demanded. His example suggests that human beings are able to make extraordinary sacrifices on behalf of others. But should we? Or ought we to avoid personal sacrifices and try to do the best we can for ourselves in all circumstances? According to a view called *ethical egoism,* it is good and right to be entirely self-serving. It defines our *interests* or our *good* in terms of the self, as follows.

For Each Individual

- That individual's self is good for its own sake.

- Nothing else is good for its own sake.

Then it defines rightful conduct as the pursuit of the good, as follows:

- Each individual should do just what is in that individual's greatest interest.

Notice that the egoist's accounts of the good and the right are *agent-relative*: They define what is right for me and what is right for you, not what is right period, unlike an *agent-neutral* account.

In this chapter, we will consider arguments for and against ethical egoism. Along the way, we will examine a view we must carefully distinguish from ethical egoism—namely, *psychological egoism*, which says that, despite the behavior of people like Sanders, we care about ourselves for our own sakes and are unable to care about anything else for its sake. Our mental and physical conditions are aspects of the self, and egoists emphasize that we tend to want to enjoy ourselves and be healthy and safe. But other things—money, acquaintances, and so on—are merely useful tools at best. Ethical egoism is a normative view: It endorses self-serving behavior. Psychological egoism, by contrast, is descriptive: It makes no suggestion whatever concerning how people should be motivated but describes how people are motivated and what they seek. Psychological egoism does not even say that we always act in our own interest. Indeed—unlike ethical egoism, which defines an individual's good as what enhances the individual's self—psychological egoism takes no stand on the matter of what truly is in our interest. Instead, it says we always do what we think will enhance the self.

THE INCAPACITY DEFENSE

Ethical egoists might take psychological egoism and their analysis of the good for granted in order to defend their analysis of the right. Together, these assumptions seem to support ethical egoism, for they imply that the individual's self-enhancement is the one and only good the individual seeks. The idea is this: If we cannot help but pursue our own good and it is the only good we can pursue, isn't self-seeking behavior right?

What, after all, is the alternative? Suppose someone tells you that you really ought to realize others' good as best you can—and not simply to the extent that it is in your interest. If your own good is the only thing you can seek for its own sake, it is pointless to tell you to act otherwise: You cannot do so. Surely we can be required to do only what we can do, and we cannot be required to avoid options we choose by necessity: *ought* implies *can,* and *ought not* implies *can avoid*. In sum, then, the *incapacity defense* of the egoist's account of the right is as follows:

Incapacity Defense

1. Psychological egoism is true, so we cannot stop trying to enhance ourselves, and we cannot seek anything else.

2. The ethical egoist's account of the good is correct, so the individual's self-enhancement is the individual's only good.

3. So our self-enhancement is the one and only good we can pursue, and we do so inevitably.

4. It cannot be right to do what we cannot, nor wrong to do what we must.

5. So it is right for each of us to act in self-interest.

Initial Difficulties

One problem with this argument is that it seems pointless to tell us that it is right to do things we will do by psychological necessity. In fact, it seems confused: Doesn't the claim that we are obligated to behave in a certain way imply that we are free not to behave in that way? In response, egoists might weaken their conclusion; instead of saying that (a) acting in self-interest is morally required, they might say that (b) acting in self-interest is not morally wrong (there cannot be moral objections to acting in self-interest). This response has a significant virtue: Conclusion (b) is supported by the incapacity argument although conclusion (a) is not. However, there is a problem: Conclusion a, not b, is what it takes to support ethical egoism as we have defined it.

Another problem with the incapacity defense is that premise 2 eventually will need justification,[2] but let us focus on the heart of the argument, which is premise 1, asserting the truth of psychological egoism. Is this view defensible?

Main Difficulty: Psychological Egoism

There are three main arguments for psychological egoism; let us consider them one by one.

1. *The hedonistic defense.* One way to defend psychological egoism is to base it on psychological hedonism, which we discussed earlier. Psychological egoism is compatible with people caring about *any* aspect of the self, while psychological hedonism says that we care only about experiencing pleasure, which is *one* aspect of the self. If we care only about our own pleasure, we care only about an aspect of the self. Thus psychological hedonism

entails psychological egoism (but psychological egoism does not entail psychological hedonism), so by establishing the truth of the hedonist's view, it would be possible to support psychological egoism.

Unfortunately, however, we cannot defend psychological egoism on the basis of psychological hedonism, for the latter is in just as much need of justification as the former, as we saw in Chapter 5.

2. *The hidden motives argument.* Another defense says that whenever people seem to act from genuine concern for the well-being of others, they are really acting from a self-serving motive that remains concealed in the background. Many people appear to put their well-being aside for others: The teacher Dave Sanders is a case in point. War heroes apparently sacrifice their lives to save their comrades-in-arms. People like Mother Teresa devote their lives to helping the poor; before she died in 1997, she spent fifty years helping lepers and other extremely unfortunate people in Calcutta. However, the psychological egoist will be quick to find self-centeredness behind the appearance of altruism: Perhaps Mother Teresa wanted to earn herself a place in heaven, or maybe she wanted fame and publicity. She may have been tormented by feelings of guilt, which she eased by helping others.

But why should we give credence to this attempt to explain away apparent acts of altruism? The fact that apparently altruistic actions might have been prompted by less generous intentions does not show that these actions really were self-seeking. Psychological egoists cannot rest their case on the grounds that we cannot decisively refute the possibility of hidden motives, especially when the most straightforward view is that in cases like Sanders's no such motives existed. Offering the hidden motives argument is like showing that an imperceptible man is standing in the corner of the room by inviting us to prove otherwise. It is difficult to meet that challenge, but why should we try when given no grounds whatever for the suspicion that prompted it and when the suspicion lacks plausibility on its face?

3. *The argument by extended self-interest.* A final defense of psychological egoism unfolds as follows:

Argument by Extended Self-Interest

a. Acting voluntarily is attempting to do what we want.

b. Attempting to do what we want is trying to act in self-interest.

c. So acting voluntarily is trying to act in self-interest.

The conclusion here, claim c, looks to be just another way to express psychological egoism, so this argument seems to provide strong support for psychological egoism. But does it?

One minor objection to the argument by extended self-interest concerns premise a. Doesn't duty sometimes prompt us to do things we don't want to do? For example, suppose that a child pays me too much for a toy I am selling, and I want to keep the extra money, but I give it back, because I believe keeping it would be wrong. Then it would be appropriate to say that I have voluntarily done something I did not want to do. Although persuasive, this objection will not deter people who are seduced by the extended-self-interest argument. They will retort that we allow duty to override other considerations only when we want to do our duty!

But what about premise b? Is it acceptable? The reasoning in its favor is probably this: Whatever we desire we consider an interest of ours and vice versa. For example, if I desire to eat, I consider eating to be in my interest. So when we do what we want, we pursue our interests. And the pursuit of our interests is the same thing as the pursuit of self-interest. However, tempting as it is, this reasoning is bad, since it involves equating the following notions:

i.   Doing what we want

ii. Pursuing interests of the self

iii. Pursuing self-interest

The thought is that notion *i* is the same as *ii*, while *ii* is the same as *iii*, so *i* must be the same as *iii*. However, this reasoning fails, because *ii* is ambiguous—it has two different meanings. When we refer to *interests of the self,* we might mean either of the following, and we often conflate (fail to distinguish) the two:

* Things the self wants (or desires)
* Things that are in the self's interest

Things the self wants need not be things that are in the self's interest. Only things that enhance the self are in the self's interest. But the self might want all sorts of things, including things that are harmful to it. Now, if we are going to refer to interests of the self in an argument, we must use it in one sense or the other, not both at the same time. However, we failed to do so. When we equated notion *i* with *ii*, we used *interests of the self* to mean *things the self wants.* And when we equated *ii* with *iii*, we used *interests of the self* to mean *things that are in the self's interest.*

Why not accept premise b even though our reasoning for it was no good? Suppose we simply stipulate that when we refer to *acting in our own interest,* we mean *doing what we want.* Can't we rescue the argument for psychological egoism this way? No, we cannot, for the argument by extended self-interest will not show what the egoist needs to show—namely, that people are always self-seeking. The argument is compatible with our wanting anything, yet psychological egoism says there are things we *can't* want. If we use the words "act in self-interest" to refer to the same thing as the words "do what we want," then very little is implied by the claim that we always "act in self-interest." In particular, it will not imply that we care only about the self. It will not imply that we want only what we take to enhance the self. In fact, it is entirely compatible with the suggestion that people like Sanders have a motive that is supposed to be ruled out by the egoist: profound concern for the welfare of others for the others' sake.

All things considered, it looks as if we will have to abandon the incapacity defense of ethical egoism, since it is based on psychological egoism, which itself rests on shaky grounds.

Let's move on to a second argument for ethical egoism.

THE CONSEQUENTIALIST DEFENSE

Why do we consider moral restrictions necessary? Is it because collectively people are best off under these restrictions? If so, then perhaps egoists can defend themselves by arguing that accepting ethical egoism will result in the greatest aggregate good.

Would they be right? The answer is not obvious. Ethical egoists might press their case by asking a series of questions. Is anyone more motivated to further your well-being than you? Is anyone more familiar with your goals or better able to work out the best ways to reach them? Won't everyone do best if we each take responsibility for our own well-being? And isn't a policy that makes each person best off also one that maximizes the aggregate good? If we answer yes to these questions, we seem to have a decent argument for accepting ethical egoism.

However, the argument is far from decisive. Ethical egoism doesn't stop at encouraging us to take responsibility for our own well-being. It also tells us it would be all right to harm others if doing so were in our interest (although ethical egoists typically will deny that harming people ever is in our interest). When we consider this side of egoism, we will be less confident that the egoist way is the best way.

In any case, there is a more pressing objection: As stated, it is based on *consequentialism,* which is the requirement that we maximize the aggregate good. Consequentialism does not specify what is good; it is neutral on that point. It presupposes that we have identified what is good in itself and tells us to bring about as much good as we can. To make it clear that the egoist's second argument is based on consequentialism, let us review it:

Argument from Consequentialism

1. It is right to bring about the most good.

2. We will bring about the most good if everyone accepts the ethical egoist account of the right.

3. So everyone ought to accept the ethical egoist account of the right.

Obviously, the first premise is a statement of consequentialism.

But what is wrong with that? Here's the problem: Consequentialism says that we must maximize the aggregate good, not just our own. Egoists have no business accepting this claim, since their view is precisely that one's own good is the only good. The aggregate good is a matter of indifference to egoists, so it is bizarre for them to defend their doctrine on the grounds that it maximizes the aggregate good.

Still, nothing stops ethical egoists from using consequentialism against itself reasoning as follows: "You consequentialists assume that we must produce as much good as we can. For the sake of argument, we will grant this. But the fact is that as a whole people are best off when they accept ethical egoism. So consequentialism is self-defeating: In effect, it tells us to reject consequentialism and become egoists!"

In brief, the second defense is worrisome because, unlike consequentialists, ethical egoists are indifferent about the aggregate good. However, if consequentialism supports the adoption of ethical egoism, then ethical egoists will have a partial defense of their view, because they will have silenced one of their critics.

THE RECONCILIATION DEFENSE
AND THE PRISONER'S DILEMMA

Ethical egoists might try to argue that their account explains commonsense ethical principles such as "killing and robbing innocent people is wrong." They could suggest that a proper understanding of ethical egoism would lead us to accept virtually the same moral principles as common sense offers us. If their theory explains commonsense judgments, then common sense supports their theory, and it will be reasonable to conclude that egoists have captured the truth about morality after all.

To align their account with common sense, ethical egoists such as Epicurus and Hobbes begin with two assumptions about commonsense morality. One is that moral requirements are *conventions,* meaning by this that we conform to these requirements in the expectation that others will too. We are willing to play by the rules, but only because we expect that others will do the same. Still, not every convention we can imagine would be an acceptable moral rule. (Imagine a convention directing us to steal whenever possible.) Why are some potential conventions accepted as moral rules, while others are not? This brings us to the second assumption: We adopt conventions when doing so makes each and every person better off. Each person is better off (or at least no worse off) with the convention than without it; the conventions are, as we might say, *collectively advantageous.* In brief, then, commonsense morality consists in conforming to social conventions that are collectively advantageous.

Epicurus reflects this conception of rightful conduct (or justice) in the following passage:

> Natural justice is a symbol or expression of expediency, to prevent one man from harming or being harmed by another. . . . There never was an absolute justice, but only an agreement made in reciprocal inter-course . . . , providing against the infliction or suffering of harm.[3]

Consider, for example, the convention of honoring promises, which ordinarily is judged morally requisite by common sense. The egoist can easily explain why breaking a promise is wrong. If all of us keep our word, each is much better off, and so normally we keep our promises in the expectation that others will do likewise. Many of the things that improve the human condition are possible only through complex, coordinated tasks that people undertake with the understanding that others will do their part.

Having aligned commonsense rightful conduct with adherence to social conventions that are collectively advantageous, ethical egoists then suggest that conforming to collectively advantageous social conventions is always in our interest. This claim seems plausible, since a convention can be collectively advantageous only if it is in each person's interest. And now the egoists' case is complete: If the enlightened pursuit of self-interest is the same as adherence to collectively advantageous social conventions, and adherence to these conventions is rightful conduct as judged by common sense, then morally proper conduct as judged by ethical egoism coincides with morally proper conduct as judged by common sense. Here is a summary of the argument:

Reconciliation Argument

1. The conduct endorsed by common sense is simply conformity to social conventions that are collectively advantageous.
2. Rightful conduct as judged by ethical egoism is conformity to social conventions that are collectively advantageous.

3. So rightful conduct as judged by ethical egoism is the same as rightful conduct as judged by common sense.

Is this reconciliation argument a sound defense of ethical egoism?

Some will urge that its second premise is false, since there are circumstances in which individuals will violate collectively advantageous conventions if they follow the ethical egoist's policy of always doing what is in their greatest interest. To see why, consider a puzzle called the Prisoner's Dilemma. Imagine two (or more) people – say, Bill and Jill – who always try to get what is best for themselves. Suppose that they plan to set up some sort of cooperative arrangement, such as the practice of helping each other harvest their crops every year. As an ethical egoist, Bill will think through the possible outcomes of his interaction with Jill and rank those outcomes as follows (giving preference to 1, then 2, and so on):

1. Bill does not cooperate, but Jill does. (That is, Jill helps Bill, but Bill does not reciprocate.)

2. Both cooperate.

3. Neither cooperates.

4. Bill cooperates, but Jill does not.

		Bill	
		Cooperates	Doesn't Cooperate
Jill	Cooperates	2nd best for both	Bill's best, Jill's worst
	Doesn't Cooperate	Jill's best, Bill's worst	3rd best for both

Bill prefers 1 above all other outcomes because it allows him to receive Jill's help without doing anything in return. Bill ranks 4 below all other outcomes because it puts him through the ordeal of helping Jill without gaining anything in return. He ranks 3 over 4 because he wants to avoid the ordeal of helping Jill. And he ranks 2 over 3 because he can harvest more of his crop in cooperation with Jill than he can alone. Jill will think through the possible outcomes of her interaction with Bill and rank the outcomes in an analogous way (interchanging 1 and 4). But now Jill realizes that Bill prefers 1 over 2 and predicts that he will refuse to help her harvest her crops after she helps him. And Bill realizes that Jill will refuse to help him. So neither will help the other, because each is afraid of ending up with his or her worst outcome. Instead, they end up with their second-worst outcome, outcome 3.

The upshot seems to be that ethical egoists cannot act cooperatively. They cannot conform to social conventions such as promise keeping even though for each and every person the situation in which everyone conforms is better than the situation in which no one does. The problem is that the best situation for a given egoist is the one in which everyone except him or her conforms, and egoists will try to put themselves in the situation that is best for them. Paradoxically, by attempting to put themselves in the best situation, egoists prevent themselves from reaching even their second-best situation, the one in which everyone cooperates. Contrary to premise 2, the pursuit of self-interest backfires and prevents us from conforming to collectively advantageous social arrangements.

In response, egoists might deny that it is rational to exploit cooperative arrangements. The very fact that universal cheating prevents anyone from cooperating with others is itself reason enough for us not to cheat. The prisoner's dilemma does not show that the universal pursuit of self-interest backfires; instead, it shows that universal cheating backfires, and the rational response is therefore universal cooperation.

But this reply is too quick, since universal cooperation and universal cheating are not the only options. Why not cheat only on rare occasions when I can do so without detection and a great deal is at stake? Of course, leading ethical egoists, such as Epicurus (341–270 B.C.) and Thomas Hobbes (1588–1679), will say that a policy of selective cheating is irrational and that a policy of not cheating is rationally preferable, since I am likely to get caught cheating, whereupon I will be punished in a wholly unacceptable way and will acquire a reputation that will lead others to shun me. Epicurus makes this point succinctly in the following passage:

> It is impossible for the man who secretly violates any article of the social compact to feel confident that he will remain undiscovered, even if he has already escaped ten thousand times.[4]

And Hobbes develops a similar view:

> He . . . that breaks his covenant, and consequently declares that he thinks he may with reason do so, cannot be received into any society, that unite themselves for peace and defense, but by the error of them that receive him; nor when he is received, be retained in it, without seeing the danger of their error; which errors a man cannot reasonably reckon upon as the means of his security.[5]

But are Epicurus and Hobbes correct? No; unfortunately, we can imagine circumstances in which selective cheating would be rational. In his *Republic,* Plato described a magical ring that can make people invisible. Wearing this ring—the ring of Gyges, it is called—you could walk into a bank in broad daylight and make off with a billion dollars, and no one could stop you. If you owned the ring of Gyges, it would be absurd to argue that you should refrain from stealing a billion dollars on the grounds that you might be caught and punished. (Perhaps there is some other reason to avoid theft, but punishment is easily avoided by wearers of the ring.)[6]

So why not have our cake and eat it too? When we stand to gain a great deal and the chances of detection are low, isn't it in our interest to violate practices that are in the collective interest? If so, then premise 2 of the reconciliation argument is false, and ethical egoism as we have defined it implies that on some occasions it is right for us to press our interests against those of others—namely, when we can do so with impunity. Can we really accept this implication? If not, the reconciliation argument fails.

OURSELVES, OTHERS, AND THE PARADOX OF ALTRUISM

We have examined the arguments for ethical egoism and found them worrisome, which casts doubt on the idea that we ought to care about ourselves exclusively. Perhaps we now know what not to believe about the importance of our interests. But what should we believe?

What if we embrace the opposite of egoism—on the rebound, so to speak? If it is unreasonable to care only about ourselves, is it reasonable to care only about others? No; it would be a mistake to take this attitude too. It generates the paradox of altruism: Suppose I say that my only good is serving others, and everyone else takes a similar view about the good of others. Then there is nothing I can do to help you! I cannot even help you by letting you help me, for there is nothing you can do to help me! Unless some of us have interests apart from the good of assisting people, helping others is impossible. The fact is that unless people have interests of their own, it is hard to see how to be concerned about them. Indeed, morality itself would have no role to play, to the extent that morality is a matter of responding to the interests of others in a reasonable way. But if we do have these independent interests, it is absurd to take the attitude that the only thing that is important to us is serving others.

(But isn't it better to serve than to be served? Suppose that a woman named Ayn is the only person capable of independent interests, and everyone else is interested only in serving, not in being served. All the rest of us would fall over ourselves trying to help Ayn—without her, our lives would be senseless. And imagine our distress if Ayn announced one day that she was going to serve-and-not-be-served, like the rest of us—say, because she felt ashamed at having her own projects. Wouldn't we tell her that the most important thing she could do would be to continue her projects—and allow the rest of us to help?)

Both our own good as well as the good of others should matter to us. We should adopt neither a narrow and exclusive focus on the self nor an extreme form of altruism. But exactly how should we respond to the interests of others? Is it acceptable to help others only when they are in grave need and our help is not an undue burden for us, thus leaving ourselves free to pursue our own interests in ways that do not harm others? With this suggestion an individual is considered responsible for his or her own life, and others must assist only when the individual cannot meet that responsibility. Or should we pursue everyone's interests alike, contributing in a positive way to the welfare of each person no less than we contribute to our own welfare? With this suggestion we are as responsible for others as we are for ourselves.

To say that we are as responsible for others as we are for ourselves is to say that we should treat the interests of people in a strictly impartial way, ignoring completely the fact that some of the interests are ours and some are not. The suggestion is that morality requires us to further all concerns and all interests on a wholly impartial basis, putting aside loyalty to specific people with whom we have special ties. Consider an example devised by William Godwin (1756–1836), a political theorist.[7] Suppose that I can save only one of two persons from a burning building, one of whom is a chambermaid and the other a philanthropic archbishop. If I must make my selection on an impartial basis, then I might, as Godwin suggested, decide to save the archbishop on the grounds that he does more good for the world than does the chambermaid. But in any case I must ignore the fact that the chambermaid turns out to be . . . my mother! If I save her on the grounds that she is my mother, I am being partial, which is unacceptable, supposing that we must further all interests on an impartial basis.

Bernard Williams, a contemporary philosopher, raises a forceful objection to this demand: If the suggestion were correct, then morality could require that we detach ourselves from the self in a way that undermines our very grounds for thinking that life is worth living.[8] Surely, Williams urges, it is absurd to say that morality requires anything of the sort. The suggestion that we must pursue everyone's interests impartially is mistaken.

Williams's argument rests on a point borrowed from the Danish philosopher Søren Kierkegaard (1813–1855), considered—with Friedrich Nietzsche—to be among the earliest existentialists. In a significant sense we define who we are in terms of our most fundamental commitments and projects. For example, our relationships to loved ones and our devotion to creative projects are central to who we are. Our continuity with them enables us to see ourselves as individuals whose existence reaches forward into the future and back into the past. If our commitments and projects were somehow destroyed, we would feel that we might as well have ceased to exist. If we suffered their loss, we would be unable to judge our lives as worthwhile.

If fundamental projects and commitments give us our very reason to live, it would be unreasonable to expect us to ignore their compelling urgency and pursue them alongside the projects of other people. As well, it would be absurd to expect us to remain impartial when selecting which of two people to save when one is someone we know and love. So Williams provides grounds for saying that each of us is responsible for his or her own life.

THE MALLEABILITY OF IDENTITY

The Kierkegaardian view of the self does something else for us. It calls into question the ethical egoist's assumption that we have a clear idea of self-interest and the altruist's notion that we have a clear idea of what "selfishness" is. In defining their doctrines, egoists (and altruists) take for granted the concept of the self and define self-interest as the enhancement of the self. By doing so, they think they are getting down to brass tacks and defining self-interest in terms of such concrete concerns as existence, safety, and pleasure. But now we see that the concept of *self-interest* is malleable, because the concept of the *self* is malleable. In particular, our identities can overlap with the identities of other individuals or groups; we can take others into our identities, so that their interests are ours, and our lives are the richer for it. For example, my relationship with my wife is part of who I am; our identities overlap to a large extent. Without her, I would feel incomplete. If we bring loved ones into our identities, we profoundly alter what acting in self-interest means. It simply cannot involve harming the people with whom we align. When they flourish, so do we; enhancing their lives is as much in our interest as anything else we can do.

We can also define the self, at least in part, in terms of "altruistic" projects by which we help strangers or animals or all sentient beings. These can be so important to us that we take them into our identities; and when we do, acting in self-interest loses its narrow thrust. But are persons who see themselves this way "egoistic"? Isn't this like calling ancient perfectionists egoists because they emphasized that improving our interpersonal relationships betters us as persons and hence makes us better *off*? However unusual it might be, there is nothing to stop ethical egoists from regarding self-improvement as a form of self-enhancement. They may also identify with loved ones and define self-interest accordingly. The reason it is odd for such persons to call themselves "egoists" is that this label typically is reserved for people who consider only a very narrow set of interests as valuable in themselves—interests such as their own pleasure, safety, and power. Such egoists regard all other people as tools in the service of these narrow ends. But egoists need not take this attitude.

Once we take these points about the malleability of identity into account, we see that ethical egoism has a valuable contribution to make. Ethical egoists get into trouble when they claim that the self is the only thing with value in its own right, but their approach is helpful insofar as it suggests that developing ourselves is one morally important concern, especially when we take an expansive view of the self and construct identities that overlap with others' in generous ways. Ethical egoism is strongest when understood to be a theory of the good that equates the good with self-development. Seen this way, it can be linked to a central strand of existentialist thought, for both tend to suggest that people are self-creating beings who are at their best when they accept their creative freedom and invent an individual identity for themselves. It can also be linked to the contemporary virtue ethics approach, for both tend to view the good life as a kind of self-development, and both are suspicious of the idea that duty is prior to self-development.

QUESTIONS FOR REFLECTION

1. Some people associate the term *ethical egoism* with the view that it is right to be selfish. Is this fair to egoists? Or is selfish behavior wrong by definition? Compare murder, which is by definition wrong, since no killing qualifies as a murder unless it is impermissible. Is selfishness by definition a kind of morally objectionable behavior? Are we selfish when we neglect or harm the interests of others in impermissible ways? Or should we define selfishness in one of the two following ways:

   • An act is selfish when we do it because we want to.

   • An act is selfish when we do it because it is in our interest.

   (Consider that if either definition were correct, then eating my breakfast would be selfish, and so would nearly everything Daniel Defoe's character Robinson Crusoe did while marooned.)

2. Critically assess the following argument given by J. S. Mill in *Utilitarianism:*

   The only proof capable of being given that an object is visible is that people actually see it. The only proof that a sound is audible is that people hear it; and so of the other sources of our experience. In like manner, I apprehend, the sole evidence it is possible to produce that anything is desirable is that people do actually desire it. No reason can be given why the general happiness is desirable, except that each person, so far as he believes it to be attainable, desires his own happiness. This, however, being a fact, we have not only all the proof which the case admits of, but all which it is possible to require, that happiness is a good: that each person's happiness is a good to that person, and the general happiness, therefore, a good to the aggregate of all persons.

3. Is the ethical egoist account of the good correct? Consider just one of the goods recognized by commonsense: friendship. When are two people genuinely friends? Doesn't each of them have to consider the welfare of the other to be intrinsically valuable? And can the ethical egoist endorse this kind of regard for others? Epicurus attempts to persuade us that egoism recognizes the good of friendship, for friendship enhances our security. But does this show that friendship is good for its own sake?

4. If you had the ring of Gyges, would you refrain from stealing and from other forms of harm to others? If so, would your motive for refraining be fear of the consequences of being caught? What would your motive be?

5. Do you agree with the claim (made in the last section of the chapter) that in Godwin's case (where we can save only one of two persons in a burning building) we are not required to choose on an impartial basis? If impartiality is required, would it be all right to make our selection by tossing a coin?

6. Which describes the situation in Godwin's case more accurately: (a) You may not save your mother rather than the archbishop, (b) it is morally permissible to save your mother rather than the archbishop, or (c) you are morally required to save your mother rather than the archbishop?

7. Suppose we alter Godwin's case slightly: Now you are a professional firefighter, paid by the city. Does this affect whether or not you must be impartial when selecting whom to save? (Would the fact that you are a government official affect whether you may offer a job to your daughter rather than to an equally qualified applicant?)

8. Some acts are in our interest but do not affect the interests of others at all. For example, my decision to eat vanilla rather than chocolate cake will not affect others one way or another. Does this show that the enlightened pursuit of self-interest is one thing, while conforming to collectively advantageous social conventions is another? (Do these actions violate an applicable social convention?)

9. In his *Notes from Underground,* Part I, Section VII, Fyodor Dostoevsky's character claims that "a man, always and everywhere, prefers to act in the way he feels like acting and not in the way his reason and interest tell him, for it is very possible for a man to feel like acting against his interests and, in some instances, I say that he positively wants to act that way."[9] Is this correct? How might the psychological egoist respond?

10. What is the self? What are the interests of the self? Are these interests limited to such things as safety and pleasure? Why or why not?

11. Point out the flaws in the following argument:
    a. Acting voluntarily is doing what we want.
    b. Doing what we want is pursuing our interests.
    c. Pursuing our interests is pursuing interests of the self.
    d. Pursuing interests of the self is pursuing interest in the self.
    e. Pursuing interests in the self is acting in self-interest.
    f. So acting voluntarily is acting in self-interest.
    g. So psychological egoism is true.

12. Should we understand ethical egoism to be the view that each of us should act solely to enhance our self *however we have constructed it?* (Given the malleability of identity, it seems unlikely that egoists will want to prescribe one view of the self for everyone.) If so, then is ethical egoism correct? (Consider that some people will define the self narrowly, in terms of such things as their own pleasure and aggrandizement and little more.)

13. Try playing the following game. Divide a group into three teams, A, B, and C, and ask each to appoint a leader, who makes the final choice on behalf of the team. Each team can vote X or Y. If all three teams vote Y, each makes 2 points. If all three vote X, each loses 5 points. If team A votes X and the others vote Y, A wins 4 points, while B and C lose 2 points. If teams A and B vote X and C votes Y, A and B each lose 2 points, while Y loses 5 points. After 12 rounds, the team with the most points "wins."

FURTHER READINGS

Baier, Kurt. *The Moral Point of View.* Ithaca: Cornell University Press, 1958.

Caporael, Linnda R, et al. "Selfishness Examined: Cooperation in the Absence of Egoistic Incentives." *Behavioral and Brain Sciences* 12 (1989): 683–739.

Cottingham, William. "Partiality, Favouritism, and Morality." *The Philosophical Quarterly* 36, no. 144 (1986): 357–373.

Epicurus. *Letter to Menoeceus* and *Principal Doctrines.* In *Greek and Roman Philosophy after Aristotle,* edited by Jason Saunders. New York: Free Press, 1966.

Fletcher, George. *Loyalty: An Essay on the Morality of Relationships.* New York: Oxford University Press, 1993.

Gauthier, David. *Moral Dealing: Contract, Ethics, and Reason.* Ithaca: Cornell University Press, 1990.

——, editor. *Morality and Rational Self-Interest.* Englewood Cliffs, N.J.: Prentice-Hall, 1970.

——. *Morals by Agreement.* Oxford: Clarendon Press, 1986.

Hobbes, Thomas. *Leviathan.* In *Social Ideals and Policies: Readings in Social and Political Philosophy,* edited by Steven Luper. Mountain View, Calif.: Mayfield, 1999. First published 1651.

Kavka, Gregory. "The Reconciliation Project." In *Morality, Reason and Truth,* edited by David Copp and David Zimmerman. Totowa, N.J.: Rowman & Allanheld, 1985. Reprinted in *Social Ideals and Policies: Readings in Social and Political Philosophy,* edited by Steven Luper. Mountain View, Calif.: Mayfield, 1999.

LaFollette, Hugh. "The Truth in Psychological Egoism." In *Reason and Responsibility,* 7th ed., edited by Joel Feinberg. 500–507. Belmont, Calif.: Wadsworth, 1988.

Nagel, Thomas. *The Possibility of Altruism.* Oxford: Oxford University Press, 1970.

Nietzsche, Friedrich. *Beyond Good and Evil,* translated by Walter Kaufmann. New York: Vintage Books, 1966.

Mandeville, Bernard. *The Fable of the Bees,* edited by F. B. Kaye. Indianapolis: Liberty Classics, 1988. First published 1714.

MacIntyre, Alasdair. "Egoism and Altruism." In *The Encyclopedia of Philosophy,* edited by Paul Edwards. New York: Macmillan, 1967.

Rand, Ayn. *For the New Intellectual: The Philosophy of Ayn Rand.* New York: Random House, 1961.

——. *Fountainhead.* Indianapolis: Bobbs-Merrill, 1943.

——. *Virtues of Selfishness.* New York: Signet, 1970.

Sober, Elliott. "Did Evolution Make Us Psychological Egoists?" In *From a Biological Point of View.* 8–27. New York: Cambridge University Press, 1994.

——. "Psychological Egoism." In *The Blackwell Guide to Ethical Theory,* edited by Hugh LaFollette. 129–149. Oxford: Blackwell, 2000.

Slote, Michael. "An Empirical Basis for Psychological Egoism." *Journal of Philosophy* 61 (1964): 530–537.

Smart, J. J. C. "An Outline of a System of Utilitarian Ethics," in *Utilitarianism: For and Against,* by J. J. C. Smart and Bernard Williams. Cambridge: Cambridge University Press, 1973.

Stewart, R. M. "Butler's Argument against Psychological Hedonism." *Canadian Journal of Philosophy* 22 (1992): 211–221.

Williams, Bernard. "Persons, Character, and Morality." In *Moral Luck,* by Bernard Williams. 1–20. Cambridge: Cambridge University Press, 1981.

Wolf, Susan. "Moral Saints." *Journal of Philosophy* (1982): 419–439.

NOTES

1. These incidents are related on the World Wide Web: http://www.datvis.net/fi/columbine

2. Taking our lead from the hedonist's argument from psychological necessity offered in Chapter 5, we might defend the egoist's account of the good using the following argument:

    1. By nature each individual cares about one and only one thing for its own sake: the self.
    2. What we naturally care about is (more or less) what is good.
    3. So for each individual one and only one thing is intrinsically valuable: the self.

    But at step 1 this argument assumes the truth of psychological egoism; as we indicate in the next section, psychological egoism is questionable.

3. Epicurus, *Principal Doctrines,* in *Greek and Roman Philosophy after Aristotle,* ed. Jason Saunders (New York: Free Press, 1966), p. 56 (doctrines 31 and 33).

4. Epicurus, *Principal Doctrines,* p. 56 (doctrine 35).

5. Thomas Hobbes, *Leviathan,* in *Social Ideals and Policies: Readings in Social and Political Philosophy,* ed. Steven Luper (Mountain View, Calif.: Mayfield, 1999), p. 51.

6. Nor is it any use to argue that the theft is irrational on the grounds that your conscience will eat away at you if you steal the money. Suppose that, like about 1 percent of the general population, you are a psychopath and hence completely lacking in empathy for others. Or suppose you had a pill that prevented your feeling guilty just this once. (Actually, the billion dollars itself might be a pretty effective balm!) Clearly, then, selective cheating could be rational.

7. William Godwin, *An Enquiry Concerning Political Justice* (Harmondsworth, England: Penguin, 1985), book II, chapter 2. First published 1793.

8. Bernard Williams, "Persons, Character, and Morality," in *Moral Luck,* by Bernard Williams (Cambridge: Cambridge University Press, 1981), pp. 1–20.

9. Fyodor Dostoevsky, *Notes from Underground,* in *Existing: An Introduction to Existential Thought,* ed. Steven Luper (Mountain View, Calif.: Mayfield, 2000), p. 419.

8

Utilitarianism

Does Duty Consist in Maximizing the Collective Good?

In the late 1970s, Robert McFall's physicians discovered that he had cancer. They knew that he would die unless he had a bone marrow transplant. They told him that compatible donors would be difficult to locate and that the only likely prospects would be close relatives. The search was on. Family members were tested, and to everyone's vast relief a suitable match was found: McFall's cousin had compatible marrow. Although the likelihood of life-threatening complications was small, donation would be a painful procedure. After thinking it over, McFall's cousin chose not to cooperate. Desperate, McFall went to court to force his cousin, listed in the court record by his last name Shimp, to provide the marrow. The judge was sympathetic and went out of his way to condemn Shimp's refusal as "morally indefensible." But ultimately the court refused to force Shimp to give up his bone marrow. It noted the long-standing rule of common law that by-standers (as opposed to people involved in accidents) are not legally required to aid or rescue others. The only exceptions are cases involving special relationships, as between innkeepers and their guests, carriers and their passengers, and parents and their children (and even in these cases people may not be compelled to take actions that are risky to themselves). To require aid is incompatible with respect for the individual, the court said. "For a society which respects the rights of [the] individual, to sink its teeth into the jugular vein or neck of one of its members and suck from it sustenance for another member, is revolting."[1]

Many of us would agree with the court's objections to Shimp's behavior. Most of us think we should make certain sacrifices for others, especially family members. But we can also respect the court's view that society should not force anyone to undergo medical procedures for the benefit of others. In almost all cases we think that undergoing medical procedures, such as donating kidneys and other organs, to help others is above and beyond the call of duty and not the sort of thing people may be compelled to do.

However, in recent years proponents of a moral theory called *utilitarianism* have been challenging traditional ideas about the limits of our obligations. Utilitarianism comes in various forms, but in its classical form it combines two claims. The first is that the good is pleasure or satisfaction of desire or happiness as experienced by any sentient being. The second claim is the *consequentialist thesis* that the right choice is the option that maximizes the good. Utilitarianism (and consequentialism generally) challenges traditional ideas because it says we must do as much good as we possibly can—a heavy demand indeed.

In this chapter we will explore some of the attractions and failings of utilitarianism and examine the case some of its proponents make for saying that our altruistic responsibilities are surprisingly demanding.

CLASSICAL UTILITARIANISM AND EXTREME ALTRUISM

Like Aristotle's virtue ethics, and ethical egoism, utilitarianism is a *teleological theory*, which means that it defines proper behavior in terms of the good. Although utilitarianism had its roots in the work of Epicurus (341–270 B.C.), Francis Hutcheson (1694–1746), and David Hume (1711–1776), it was first clearly stated in its classical form by the British philosopher Jeremy Bentham (1748–1832). Bentham suggested that happiness is both the good and the only thing we seek for its own sake, where happiness is understood in the hedonist way as pleasure and the absence of pain. Bentham then claimed that the right action is the one that maximizes the aggregate good of all sentient beings. Why is this the right way to behave? Bentham seemed to think the point obvious: Once we have identified what is good, the right response is whatever brings about the greatest good.

Bentham's hedonistic version of utilitarianism worried critics from the start. Consider, for example, how difficult it is to measure levels of pleasure or to determine whether the pleasure you are experiencing is equivalent to the pleasure I am experiencing. Unfortunately, we cannot build hedonometers, or devices that would detect and measure pleasure. Also, the hedonist version of utilitarianism is vulnerable to the charge that pleasure and pain are not the only things intrinsically worthy of concern. For example, being hated by people whom we love is a very bad thing, even if they hide their betrayal from us so successfully that we never find out and hence never suffer.

For these and other reasons, contemporary utilitarians have tended to reject the hedonistic approach in favor of a view called *preferential utilitarianism,* according to which the good consists in the satisfaction of desires. If we understand the good this way, we can handle some of the concerns about hedonism, such as the example of betrayal: Assuming that we want to be loved by the people we love, their hatred thwarts our desire and hence is a bad thing, even if we never undergo the painful experience of discovering our misfortune.

Characteristic of Bentham's philosophy was his hostility toward the idea of natural rights, or freedoms that may not be limited even in the interest of pressing social concerns:

> Natural rights is simple nonsense: natural and imprescriptible rights [is] nonsense upon stilts.

However, Bentham did think that protecting certain freedoms could be expedient, and in such cases he called the protected freedoms "rights":

> As there is no right, which ought not to be maintained so long as it is upon the whole advantageous to the society that it should be maintained, so there is no right which, when the abolition of it is advantageous to society, should not be abolished.[2]

Later utilitarians adopted Bentham's roundabout way of defining rights. According to John Stuart Mill (1806–1873), conformity to a rule of conduct is our duty only if enforcing the rule will result in the greatest good. Rights Mill defined in terms of duties: An individual has the right to do something when and only when others are duty-bound not to interfere. For example, I have the right to adopt any philosophical position I choose, for it is expedient for society to prevent others from stopping me.

Also characteristic of Bentham's approach was his commitment to strict impartiality concerning those whom we are to please. What is important is how much pleasure there is, not who has it or how it is distributed over time.[3] Moreover, what makes a creature an object of moral concern is its capacity to experience pleasure and pain. This means that animals as well as human beings are owed moral consideration, and Bentham was one of the first philosophers in the West to criticize the mistreatment of animals. Responding to the rather dismissive views of Immanuel Kant concerning animals, Bentham wrote

> A full-grown horse or dog is beyond comparison a more rational, as well as a more conversable animal, than an infant of a day, or a week, or even a month, old. But suppose the case were otherwise, what would it avail? The question is not, Can they *reason?* Nor, Can they *talk?* But, Can they *suffer?*

It counts to their credit that utilitarians have always criticized animal abuse. In recent years, a growing number of people have pressed for improvements in the treatment of animals, and utilitarianism provides them with a theoretical backing; no doubt, this helps account for the popularity of utilitarianism. Peter Singer, a consequentialist philosopher, has been especially visible in this regard. Expanding upon Bentham's attack on animal abuse, Singer has suggested that utilitarianism's implications concerning the moral status of animals are quite radical. According to Singer, since animals can suffer, Bentham's slogan "everybody to count for one, nobody for more than one" commits the utilitarian to treating individual animals as the moral equals of individual human beings. According to Singer, to take an animal's suffering less seriously than a person's—simply because the animal is not a person—is arbitrary. Singer calls this practice *speciesism,* and suggests that it is on a par with racism.[4]

Utilitarianism has another, related feature that attracts people: It seems to set a high standard, by comparison to which theories that emphasize individual rights and duties can seem mean and grudging. To emphasize the point that utilitarianism sets a high standard, Bentham and Mill attempt to equate the disinterested pursuit of utility (where utility is the good we are to maximize) with the golden rule. Mill puts the claim this way: "'To do as you would be done by,' and 'to love your neighbor as yourself,' constitute the ideal perfection of utilitarian morality."[5] Most of us admire people who help others, and utilitarianism seems more demanding in this regard than does any other moral perspective. We must sacrifice to help provide others with the things they need. We may also have to sacrifice to provide others with things they *want.* In fact, it is easy to get the impression that anyone who criticizes utilitarianism must be indifferent to others and to the suffering of others. James Rachels, himself a utilitarian, seems to hold this view, judging from the words with which he ends the chapter on utilitarianism in one of his books:

> Could it be . . . that future generations will look back in disgust at the way affluent people in the 20th century enjoyed their comfortable lives while third-world children died of easily preventable diseases? Or at the way we slaughtered and ate helpless animals? If so, they might note that utilitarian philosophers of the day were criticized as simple-minded for advancing a moral theory that straightforwardly condemned such things.[6]

To see why classical utilitarianism is so demanding, consider that we can relieve much suffering in the world by helping the needy (and animals)–by working to improve their situations and by giving them goods. How much is enough? Well, according to the utilitarian, we must continue our effort until further sacrifices would reduce our ability to help. We need not compromise our productivity, because that would make us less able to help in the future. In fact, if we can increase our productivity, we must. If such high levels of altruism are required, there is really no room for optional altruism. Any good we can do, we must. For the classical utilitarian, the case for extreme altruism is overwhelming:

Argument for Extreme Altruism

1. We are morally required to boost the overall good as high as we can. (This is the classical utilitarian view.)

2. Given the present state of suffering in the world, it is necessary to make extreme sacrifices on behalf of the needy in order to maximize the overall good, giving up everything we have except what we need to work as productively as possible.

3. So we must make these extreme sacrifices. (Call this view *extreme altruism.*)

If this argument is sound, you and I are worse people than we might have thought. It is true that a median two-income American family will spend about 40 percent of its income on taxes (the figure was 41.5 percent in 1996, 40.9 in 1997, and 39 in 1998), which is a substantial contribution to the community.[7] These funds help meet the needs of those who are relatively poor in the United States. According to the Census Bureau, about 13 percent of the money spent by states in 1996 went to public welfare ($193 billion), a little less than half of what states spent on education ($399 billion).[8] On average, Americans also contribute about 3 percent of their annual income to nonprofit organizations, some of which aid poor Americans.[9] In 1995, a bit over 80 percent of the $144 billion in contributions made to nonprofit organizations in the United States came from individuals. However, Americans do little for the poor in other countries, even though the needy there are far worse off than the poor here. In the United States, about 13 percent of us (34.5 million Americans, including 14 million children under the age of six) live below the officially designated poverty level, but the average poverty threshold for a family of four in 1998 was $16,660, and $13,003 for a family of three. Elsewhere, there are 1.2 billion people living on less than a dollar a day, and 2.8 billion living on less than two dollars a day.[10] Admittedly, many of them live in rural settings, where earning money is less important, since they are able to grow food–an option available to relatively few Americans. Nonetheless, according to the Food and Agricultural Organization, in the world as a whole, over 800 million people are malnourished.

Utilitarianism makes still more demands of us. It is one thing to meet people's needs and another to enable them to have what they want (but do not need). Admittedly, the line between needs and wants is not clear, but surely it exists. And even if no one in the world were in need, there would be the issue of what we must do to help others acquire what they want. In answer to this question, utilitarianism demands, as a general rule, redistributing goods equally across the world, taking from those who have more and giving to those who have less, since doing so tends to make it more likely that desire satisfaction will be maximized.[11]

RESERVATIONS ABOUT CLASSICAL UTILITARIANISM

Does classical utilitarianism really require better behavior than the moral tradition? And is the utilitarian account of the right correct? To help us decide, let's consider three of its consequences.

Forcibly Harming People to Benefit Others

One concern about classical utilitarianism is that in some circumstances it permits or requires us to harm some people in order to benefit others. Two examples illustrate the point.

The Case of the Ruthless Mayor   Imagine a city in turmoil over an unsolved hate crime that is causing escalating rioting and bloodshed. Suppose you are the mayor of this city; you soon come to realize that the perpetrator has probably fled and is not going to be caught. You also realize that if an innocent person confessed to the crime, people would be satisfied that the criminal had been apprehended, and city life would return to normal. However, no volunteers have come forward. But then you realize that you can force someone to take the blame, and if that person doesn't cooperate you can frame him or her. In doing so, you will end the turmoil and maximize the aggregate good. Now, it might well be admirable (albeit misguided) for some innocent person to confess, but is it admirable for you to force one to? Not at all. It benefits many people, but it is a despicable act of naked aggression that harms someone terribly.[12]

The Organ "Donor" Case   On any given day, people die because suitable donor organs are unavailable. Suppose that scientists solve compatibility problems, so that anyone's healthy organs can be successfully transplanted. Suppose you are a physician, and you realize that all of the organs of one healthy individual can be distributed among several needy people, thus saving their lives. You also notice that no one is volunteering. However, you are in a position to kill a healthy person who refuses to donate and save several people using the organs, thus increasing the total good as much as possible. Perhaps it is admirable for people to give up life for others. But is it admirable for you—or a state official or anyone else—to kill an unwilling victim to accomplish the same end? Is it what is best for all concerned? Or is it plain murder?

These two examples, which are standard fare in the critical literature, show that classical utilitarians are committed to the objectionable general principle that harming people, even in grievous and fatal ways, is justified as long as it is offset by the good we do others. But can't we say at least this much on behalf of utilitarians: When they demand sacrifices by individuals, the harm done is always offset by good others accrue? If so, then utilitarians can try to convince us that the people who refuse to make the sacrifices are displaying a petty disregard for others. However, it is not true that harm sanctioned by utilitarianism is always offset by the good enjoyed by others. And this brings us to another troublesome consequence of utilitarianism.

Forcibly Harming People to End Their Suffering

A second worry about utilitarianism is that in some circumstances it permits or requires us to kill people against their wills in order to minimize their suffering. Let's spell this out with another example.

The Case of the Chronic Sufferer   Consider that there are people who suffer from mental or physical pain who cannot make themselves happy and whom others cannot make happy. Many of them can function and still want to live, perhaps out of a sense of duty. Our hearts go out to such persons, and we are frustrated that we cannot solve their problem. But the utilitarian formula suggests that we treat them as wrongdoers, even if unintentional ones, since their unhappiness brings down the aggregate good. Worse, utilitarianism supports a grisly and abhorrent general policy for handling such persons: Kill them, for when their unhappiness is ended, it is no longer added into the computation of the total happiness, and so the sum rises. (Why not just drug them into a stupor rather than killing them? Well, the utilitarian formula suggests that killing them is better since preserving the lives of drugged people is a drain on medical resources and hence a source of substantial disutility.) Of course, there will be exceptions, for we must weigh into our calculations the utility of family members—which might count in favor of the killing or against it.

Notice, however, that the utilitarian formula favors killing these suffering people even if their deaths do not help others. We needn't suppose that others will be made happier by their deaths (although that will be one more nail in the coffin, as far as the utilitarian calculus is concerned). When others do not benefit, the utilitarian cannot say that good enjoyed by others offsets the horror of the killings, nor portray those who refuse to die as petty and selfish. By continuing their existence, all the unhappy are doing is lowering the sum. Does that really matter? Can it possibly justify the general policy of eliminating the chronically unhappy against their wills? Why is this abstract quantity called *total good* so important?

Requiring Strict Impartiality

There is a third reason to resist the classical utilitarian view: It forces us to be strictly impartial as concerns those whose good we are to maximize. Strict impartiality has two especially worrisome consequences.

First, requiring strict impartiality implies that it is wrong to give special consideration to our interests and those of our friends and loved ones. As we noted when we discussed ethical egoism, this demand seems unacceptable, since it can require us to give up pursuits that, in our view, make our lives worth living. Suppose, for example, that although I am not especially good at it and will never make a contribution, I am driven to make paintings; yet I have a clear talent as a biologist and am already on the verge of seeing ways to boost crop productivity. I can do far more good as a biologist, and so choosing my career on impartial grounds requires that I pursue biology, even though my life will feel empty unless I am an artist. Godwin's example (see Chapter 7) provides another illustration: Suppose you must choose between saving your mother (or someone else who plays a central role in your life) or a stranger. The latter happens to be an archbishop who contributes more to the greater good than your mother does. According to the utilitarian, you must ignore your family ties and save the archbishop. Yet no one except a doctrinaire utilitarian (and perhaps the archbishop!) would agree.

A second consequence of the strict impartiality required by utilitarianism concerns animals. As we suggested in Chapter 2, the fact that animals have interests is grounds to acknowledge that we owe them consideration. We do not have to accept utilitarianism to object to animal abuse. But few of us will accept the utilitarian view that it is wrong to treat human beings better than animals, as we do, for example, when we save a person rather than several mice. Bentham was correct when he rejected the notion that rationality is the only feature relevant to whether a creature is an object of moral concern. But he was wrong in assuming that the capacity to suffer is the only relevant feature. Also significant are the following: being a moral agent, being self-aware, and having interests.

Over the years, utilitarians have offered a wide range of responses to their critics. Let us consider the most important of these.

TWO-TIERED UTILITARIANISM

Many utilitarians abandoned the classical view in favor of substantially different versions of utilitarianism; let's see if the newer approaches avoid our criticisms. Bentham's view was that, on each occasion, we are to choose the action that has the best overall consequences. This doctrine is now called *act utilitarianism*. A newer version is called *rule utilitarianism*. Instead of focusing on individual acts, as Bentham's version does, the new version learns from Kant (whom we discuss in the next chapter), and defines itself in terms of policies or types of acts. It identifies general rules that maximize the good if everyone accepts them and says we are obligated to conform to these rules in all cases. Mill himself flirted with rule utilitarianism; however, he never backed away from the view that, strictly speaking, act utilitarianism determines the right thing to do, not rule utilitarianism. Act utilitarianism is the final arbiter of morality, Mill thought, but he hinted that people normally will serve the collective good best by adopting a two-tiered system: applying expedient and familiar rules or principles in normal situations and submitting these to the test of utility-maximization only when new considerations arise or the principles clash or need justification.[13] To determine whether to add or subtract a rule of conduct we ask whether it increases utility. When choosing how to act, however, we put aside the question of utility and steer by the rules that maximize utility.[14] Rules are chosen on one level, where utility is the deciding consideration, while actions are chosen on a separate level, where the rules are the deciding consideration.

Considerations in Favor of Two-Tiered Utilitarianism

Abandoning the original form of utilitarianism in favor of the two-tiered system seems to help us deal with some standard counterexamples, such as the overzealous mayor. On particular occasions framing an innocent person might maximize the good. However, a policy of framing innocent people would not, if for no other reason than that the policy will be public knowledge, and framing people is impossible if everyone is aware of what is going on, as Kant might have noted.

Some say two-tiered utilitarianism also helps with our concerns about impartiality. Perhaps it is expedient to encourage people to adopt policies by which they give special attention to their families and friends, as well as policies by which they are partial toward their own projects and interests. If so, the two-tiered system can deal with our cases requiring objectionable impartiality: You may become an unproductive but happy artist rather than a productive yet despondent biologist, and you may save your mother rather than the good archbishop.

Let us note, however, that if they deal with our counterexamples by dropping the requirement of impartiality, rule utilitarians will undermine the case for extreme altruism. If we may pursue our own interests and those of our loved ones and neglect the interests of strangers, then we need not be extreme altruists. Apparently, utilitarians must choose between offering a plausible version of their view or defending extreme altruism. They cannot do both.

Objections to Two-Tiered Utilitarianism

Even if the new utilitarians can handle the Case of the Ruthless Mayor and cases involving objectionable impartiality, their worries are not at an end. There are many more criticisms to be made.

The Exceptions Objection   One problem is that two-tiered utilitarianism seems ad hoc as compared to act utilitarianism: What is distinctive about the utilitarian view is the idea that (boosting) the total good is what matters; but if utility maximization is so important, why shouldn't we make exceptions to expedient rules when we can bring about even more utility? For example, even if it is true that, generally, utility is maximized when people put their families ahead of strangers, we can do still better by putting the occasional (especially needy) stranger ahead of our family. So why isn't it right to do so?

Utilitarians usually respond to the Exceptions Objection by saying that people are too biased and ignorant to work out expedient exceptions to rules, especially when pressed for time. If they try, the effort will backfire, and over-all utility will decrease. This response places the utilitarian in danger of defending absolutism—the view that the moral principles we must conform to lay down unqualified and narrow demands—thus undermining one of the chief attractions of the view. But whether we accept the (rather demeaning) response or not, the fact remains that utilitarians cannot solve all their problems by forbidding us to make exceptions to expedient rules, which brings us to a second concern about the two-tiered system.

The Bad Rules Objection   The problem is that objectionable rules sometime maximize utility and hence receive the endorsement of the two-tiered system. In fact, we have already mentioned two cases in point. Like the old, the new form of utilitarianism supports the general policy of killing chronic sufferers who want to live, since this policy boosts the aggregate utility. The new form also endorses the actions of the overly ambitious physician in our Organ "Donor" Case. To argue to the contrary, the rule utilitarian would have to argue that (1) killing healthy individuals and giving their organs to people who cannot otherwise be saved is objectionable because it produces less overall good than a policy of (2) letting the potential donors live and the potential organ recipients die. However, isn't it far more plausible to say that policy 1 produces the most good overall? It is true that many healthy people will be upset at the prospect of being the next "donor," and some will die. Fear is bad and must be considered in the utility calculus; but does fear offset the deaths of the potential recipients and their consequent loss of happiness? Aren't fewer deaths better than more deaths? And wouldn't many unhealthy people be enormously relieved to know that if they need organs they will get them? Is the objection to killing healthy people for the sake of the dying really that it would not promote the overall good? Or is it that individuals are forcibly sacrificed – used – for the sake of others, as Kant might say?

Responses by Two-Tiered Utilitarians

Can utilitarians respond to the Bad Rules Objection? Let us test the strength of the most common rejoinders.

First, they might say that only real cases should be used to assess utilitarianism, not fanciful examples involving far-fetched situations. This gambit might allow them to postpone facing the objectionable policy of killing for "donor" organs, but the solution to organ compatibility is not far in the future. In any case, our other objection stands: Chronic sufferers are not creatures in the pages of science fiction; they are real people, and utilitarianism sanctions the policy of killing them against their will.

Second, utilitarians might argue as follows: "The Bad Rules Objection is viable only if the policies mentioned – killing the chronic sufferers and organ "donors" – really are bad rules. Why say they are? Isn't it because they are contrary to common sense? But why not say that the fault lies in common sense rather than in the policies? Common sense isn't infallible, and even if a policy is contrary to common sense it does not follow that the policy is bad."

As this response illustrates, utilitarians may raise suspicions about the probative power of common sense. However, their critics will ask how we are supposed to test theories unless we rely on commonsense examples. Realizing they need to respond to this reasonable question, some utilitarians seem to offer the following answer: If accepting a theory maximizes the good, it is the best theory! Of course, this answer simply begs the question: Unless we are already card-carrying utilitarians or attempting to show that utilitarianism is self-refuting, we will not test the truth of utilitarianism by asking whether its acceptance maximizes the good.

Other utilitarians appear to think that their ideal – maximizing the good – is compelling enough that it needs no (or little) defense, so compelling, in fact, that none of its implications could possibly serve as counterexamples, no matter how contrary to common sense, and that it is common sense we must adjust instead. And indeed, we have seen that maximizing the good would relieve a great deal of suffering, which is an attractive goal. But we have also seen that utilitarianism has unattractive implications. Is the utilitarian ideal so forceful it should override our commonsense intuitions? Or is its force the result of misunderstanding its nature? The second option is worth considering; let's see if we can locate a misleading interpretation of utilitarianism that might be responsible for its appeal to many people.

OPTIMIZING VERSUS AGGREGATING

Utilitarianism can appear to call on us to do the best for all concerned, which is an attractive, if demanding, ideal. Some people might even resist commonsense objections to this ideal. But here is the point: "Do the best for all concerned" is not the utilitarian's ideal! (Nor is it the consequentialist's.) To be sure, "Do what is best for all concerned" is not a completely straightforward policy; however, the main idea seems plain enough. To do the best for *one* person is to benefit him or her as much as possible. To do the best for all of us is to benefit each of us as much as possible. More precisely, it is to apply the following policy:

- When you can improve someone's situation without worsening someone else's, do so, and keep doing so until no one can be made any better off without making someone else worse off.[15] (Call this policy *optimizing.*)

It is easy to confuse this with the principle of utility, which is

- Maximize the good. (Call this policy *aggregating.*)

But utilitarian aggregating is very different from optimizing. To optimize, we must limit ourselves to benefiting people. By contrast, nothing in the utilitarian policy rules out harming people in terrible ways (recall the organ donation case). It says the only thing that matters is making the aggregate good as great as possible; if we can increase this total by grievously harming individuals, too bad for them. A policy that makes you worse (even worst) off is not what is best for you. Hence maximizing the aggregate good is one thing, and doing what is best for all concerned is clearly quite another.

All right, perhaps some are drawn to utilitarianism because they think it requires optimizing. But does this mean we have to give it up? Why not just reinvent utilitarianism yet again, understanding it now as the view that we are morally required to optimize?

Doing so certainly seems to constitute progress, but problems remain. One difficulty is that the policy of optimizing still seems to favor killing chronic sufferers who prefer to live. From the standpoint of utility, aren't the chronic sufferers better off dead, so that killing them is a way to optimize? Yet sufferers have the right to remain alive if they want to, and it would be wrong for us to override their decision.

A second difficulty arises once we remind ourselves about what we are trying to accomplish in devising an ethical theory. Traditional moral philosophers were trying to work out principles that specify minimally acceptable conduct. They sought principles that lay out duties we must meet in order to protect the interests of others (including principles that require aiding others in certain circumstances) and rights others must respect in order to protect our interests. Devising these principles was the central task of ethics as they understood it. Obviously, these principles would not tell us what conduct is best, either for the individual or for everyone. Answering the question, What makes our lives go best? is another, separate task for the ethicist. People will no doubt try to live the best lives they can, and many will try to help others do the same. But it is not wrong to aim for less, either for ourselves or others, and there is such a thing as going above and beyond the call of duty. When we do more good for others than we must, we perform praiseworthy deeds called *supererogatory acts.*

Utilitarians give the impression that they, too, want to identify what sort of conduct is minimally acceptable, for they claim to tell us what is "right" and "wrong." But if we understand the utilitarian answer in terms of optimizing, something seems seriously askew. "Do the best for all concerned" seems bizarre as an answer to the question, What is the least it is permissible to do? Can the least we may do for ourselves or for everyone be the very best we can do? Anyone who answers the traditional question by saying "Do the best for all" seems to misunderstand the question. Nonetheless, it is always possible to revise the tradition or to begin a new one. We can abandon the traditional task of specifying minimally acceptable conduct. Perhaps that is the way to understand utilitarianism.

ACTS AND OMISSIONS: KILLING AND LETTING DIE

Whether we accept utilitarianism or not, utilitarians may still be correct when they say that we must do everything we can to relieve suffering in the world. The thesis we have called extreme altruism can be defended on other grounds, as James Rachels has made clear.

Rachels offers a way to defend extreme altruism without appealing directly to utilitarianism. He says that when people stand by as others die, they assume that a particular sort of omission—namely, not doing something that would prevent a death—is, in itself, not as morally objectionable as a particular kind of act—namely, killing someone. In fact, however, the assumption is false. In both cases the result is a death, so surely whatever reasons we might have for not killing bar us from omitting to save. In itself, letting people die is as wrong as killing, Rachels says, and this *equivalence thesis,* as he calls it, taken together with the fact that we must not kill innocent people, implies that we must save everyone we can. Indeed, because killing the innocent is terrible, so is not rescuing the starving; as a result, we must contribute to famine relief all the money we do not devote to our minimal needs.[16] Thus it is gravely wrong for parents to buy their son a pricey pair of shoes that catches his eye or to send their daughter to an expensive private college or even to send in a pledge to National Public Radio.

Rachels is aware that sometimes it is difficult to distinguish between cases involving killing and cases involving letting die. There are cases in which the distinction is clear enough—shooting someone fatally is a killing, and removing a respirator at a patient's request is letting the patient die—but sometimes a killing in one context is a letting-die in another. For example, if Mary the physician puts Fred on a respirator, then later takes him off at his request, Mary lets Fred die. But things are quite different if Fred's greedy niece Betty sneaks in, turns off the respirator, and watches her Uncle Fred die: Betty has killed Fred. In both cases a respirator is turned off, but we are killers when we thwart the efforts of someone saving a life (assuming that those efforts would have succeeded).

Is Rachels correct when he says that people who refrain from giving all they can to famine relief think that killing is, in itself, worse than letting die? Perhaps some of us do, but upon reflection most of us acknowledge that sometimes an omission that permits a death is as serious as an act of killing. Imagine, for example, that our physician Mary is in charge of treating her rich Uncle Fred and really wants him to die so that (like her sister Betty) she can inherit his estate; suppose she omits to provide some treatment knowing that without it he will die. Her omission is as morally objectionable as killing would be. Or suppose a physician were late for a golf game and simply abandoned a patient, who them died from a treatable complication. The physician's omission would be comparable to a decision to drive drunk, knowing that someone could be killed.

So most of us would not accept the unqualified view that "killing is worse than letting die." In some circumstances, such as when we are involved in certain relationships, we have a special obligation to preserve others' welfare, and our neglect can be so seriously wrong as to invite comparison to a killing. The relationships are ones in which the lives of some people are entrusted to others; examples include the physician-patient relationship and the parent-child relationship. This is not to say that a physician cannot, under any circumstances, allow patients to die, for a patient might wish to refuse treatment, releasing the physician from any obligation to provide care that otherwise would have been provided.

A more accurate statement of our position, then, is that *unless* I have a special obligation to preserve your welfare, omitting to help you is not to be compared with killing you. Where such an obligation does not exist, my neglect is, at worst, an ordinary violation of my general duty to provide emergency assistance, which is a much less serious moral failing than a killing. In order to defend his equivalence thesis, Rachels must convince us that we have an obligation to everyone that is as demanding as parents' responsibility for their children. But this claim presupposes that morality requires us to treat others in a strictly impartial way, which is a thesis we have questioned. Rachels's defense of extreme altruism is therefore unconvincing.

QUESTIONS FOR REFLECTION

1. According to J. S. Mill, sometimes enforcing an otherwise useful rule of conduct will backfire or have no useful effects. In such cases we should not speak of a duty to abide by the rule. Instead, conformity to a rule of conduct is our duty only if enforcing the rule will result in the greatest good—that is, only if enforcing the rule is right.[17] (Mill's terminology is misleading and confusing, since it implies that we are not always duty-bound to perform actions that are morally required. Only some beneficial acts are "duties," yet failing to do as much good as possible is always morally wrong.)[18] But can't we be accountable for tasks even when it is onerous to force us to avoid doing them? Imagine supercriminals, who cannot be stopped without killing thousands of innocent people: Apprehending such villains may well entail more harm than good, but does this support the idea that the criminals have done nothing wrong? (And can Mill get away with saying that the criminals are not duty-bound to cease their wrongful behavior?)

2. Peter Singer defends a strong obligation to assist others on the basis of the following principle: "If we can prevent something bad without sacrificing anything of comparable significance, we ought to do it."[19] Critically assess this principle. Can it support a plausible argument for extreme altruism? Why or why not?

3. What does Singer's principle suggest when applied to people in Shimp's situation—that is, to people who are suitable donors of bone marrow? Does it require that they make the donation? Does it require that all of us donate one of our kidneys if by doing so we can save a life? Does it permit a physician to kill a healthy but unwilling "donor" to save several people who need organs?

4. Are there circumstances in which rule and/or act utilitarianism requires healthy people to give up their lives to provide tissues needed to save several others? If no one is willing to volunteer, will it sanction killing unwilling donors? *Should* people be compelled to do such things?

5. Is it possible for a consequentialist to reject Rachels's equivalence thesis? What should a consequentialist say about the significance of the acts versus omissions distinction? Explain.

6. Rachels says that "there are the same reasons for and against letting die as for and against killing"; therefore, "killing and letting die are morally equivalent—neither is preferable to the other." Critically assess his position.

7. Critically assess the following argument: It is far easier to control how we act than it is to control the things we omit to do. So we are always responsible for how we act, but only sometimes responsible for how we omit to act.

8. Should society punish failures of generosity? If so, which kinds? Explain.

9. Critically assess the following argument: Even if people are obligated to help the needy in reasonable ways, they have the right to choose whom to help. Hence they should be allowed to designate how the money taken from them in taxes is to be spent.

10. Respond to the following argument: Shimp did not act immorally, because undergoing a painful surgical procedure to save a life is an act of considerable self-sacrifice. Had he helped his cousin, we would have praised his generosity and expected his cousin to be grateful. This suggests we think that Shimp was being asked to do more than his duty, for it is inappropriate to praise people merely for doing their duty and inappropriate to condemn people for not doing more than they must.

11. Suppose Schmitt the Nazi holds a gun to your head and tells you that unless you push Lucy in front of an oncoming train he will shoot you. May you kill Lucy? (Is killing an innocent bystander who is not threatening you self-defense? May you do anything whatever to save your own life?) Now suppose Schmitt tells you that unless you kill Lucy, he will kill twenty innocent bystanders and that he will spare them if you do kill Lucy. May you kill Lucy? Is it your duty? What would the utilitarian say?

12. In *Justice as Fairness,* John Rawls offers the following charge against utilitarianism:

The most natural way . . . of arriving at utilitarianism . . . is to adopt for society as a whole the principle of rational choice for one man. . . . The correct decision is essentially a question of extending to society the principle of choice for one man, and then, to make this extension work, conflating all persons into one. . . . Utilitarianism does not take seriously the distinction between persons.[20]

Does utilitarianism ignore the distinction between persons, as Rawls charges? Are these grounds for rejecting utilitarianism? *Ought* we to take the distinction between persons seriously? (For a response to Rawls, see Derek Parfit, "Later Selves and Moral Principles.")[21]

13. Consider the following series of questions: (1) Suppose you have acquired your money legitimately, and that although I am living comfortably, I can make myself happier by taking 10 percent of your money—so much happier that our combined utility is greatest if I take your money. Must you turn over your cash when I demand it? (2) Now suppose two of us want to split 20 percent of your money, and the combined utility of all three of us is greatest if we take it. Is it morally permissible for us to take your money? (3) Now suppose that utility is maximized if several of us take 40 percent of your money. Are you obligated to turn it over? If the answer to the first question is no, why isn't the answer to the last question no? Or is the answer to all three questions yes? What would utilitarians say? Are they correct?

FURTHER READINGS

On Utilitarianism

Bentham, Jeremy. *Anarchical Fallacies,* Article II. *Social Ideals and Policies,* edited by Steven Luper. Mountain View, Calif.: Mayfield, 1999.

——. *An Introduction to the Principles of Morals and Legislation,* edited by J. Burns and H. L. A. Hart. London: Athlone Press, 1970. First published 1823.

Frey, R. G. *Utility and Rights.* Oxford: Blackwell, 1984.

Goodin, Robert. "Utility and the Good." In *A Companion to Ethics,* edited by Peter Singer. Cambridge: Blackwell, 1991.

Hare, R. M. *Moral Thinking: Its Levels, Method, and Point.* Oxford: Clarendon Press, 1981.

Jamieson, Dale, editor. *Singer and His Critics.* Oxford: Blackwell, 1999.

Lyons, David. *Forms and Limits of Utilitarianism.* Oxford: Clarendon Press, 1965.

Mill, J. S. *Utilitarianism.* In *Social Ideals and Policies,* edited by Steven Luper. Mountain View, Calif.: Mayfield, 1999. First published 1863.

Parfit, Derek. *Reasons and Persons.* Oxford: Oxford University Press, 1984.

Rachels, James. "The Debate over Utilitarianism." In *The Elements of Moral Philosophy,* 3rd ed., by James Rachels. Boston: McGraw-Hill, 1999.

Sen, Amartya, and Williams, Bernard. *Utilitarianism: For and Against.* Cambridge: Cambridge University Press, 1973.

Sidgwick, Henry. *The Methods of Ethics.* London: Macmillan, 1907. First published 1874.

Smart, J. J., and Williams, Bernard. *Utilitarianism and Beyond.* Cambridge: Cambridge University Press, 1982.

On the Obligation to Provide Emergency Relief

Aiken, William, and LaFollette, Hugh. *World Hunger and Moral Obligation.* Englewood Cliffs, N.J.: Prentice-Hall, 1977.

Dower, Nigel. "World Poverty." In *A Companion to Ethics,* edited by Peter Singer. Cambridge: Blackwell, 1991.

Dreze, Jean, and Sen, Amartya. *Hunger and Public Action.* Oxford: Oxford University Press, 1989.

Fishkin, James. *The Limits of Obligation.* New Haven: Yale University Press, 1982.

Goodin, Robert. *Protecting the Vulnerable.* Chicago: University of Chicago Press, 1996.

Lappe, Frances Moore, and Collins, Joseph. *World Hunger: Twelve Myths.* San Francisco: Institute for Food and Development Policy, 1982.

O'Neill, Onora. *Faces of Hunger.* London: Allen & Unwin, 1986.

——. "Hunger, Needs, and Rights," in *Problems of International Justice,* edited by Steven Luper, Boulder: Westview Press, 1988.

Rachels, James. "Killing and Starving to Death," *Philosophy* 54 (1979): 159–171.

Shue, Henry. *Basic Rights: Subsistence, Affluence, and U.S. Foreign Policy.* Princeton: Princeton University Press, 1980.

Singer, Peter. "Rich and Poor." In *Practical Ethics,* 2nd ed., by Peter Singer. Cambridge: Cambridge University Press, 1993.

Unger, Peter. *Living High and Letting Die: Our Illusion of Innocence.* Oxford: Oxford University Press, 1996.

NOTES

1. *McFall v. Shimp,* 10 Pa.D. & C. 3d 90 (1978).

2. Jeremy Bentham, *Anarchical Fallacies,* Article II, in *Social Ideals and Policies,* ed. Steven Luper (Mountain View, Calif.: Mayfield, 1999), p. 243.

3. The point is emphasized by Mill, too, in chapter II of *Utilitarianism,* ed. Oskar Piest (Indianapolis: Bobbs-Merrill, 1957), p. 22: "As between his own happiness and that of others, utilitarianism requires him to be as strictly impartial as a disinterested and benevolent spectator."

4. Peter Singer, "Animal Liberation," in *Moral Problems,* ed. James Rachels (New York: Harper & Row, 1975).

5. Mill, *Utilitarianism,* chapter II.

6. James Rachels, *The Elements of Moral Philosophy,* 3rd ed. (New York: McGraw-Hill, 1999), pp. 121–122.

7. Claire Hentz, "The Tax Burden of the Median American Family," Tax Foundation Publications (March 2000), No. 96.

8. From the World Wide Web: http://www.census.gov

9. Najeeb Halaby, "It's Time for Charities to Get More Benefit from the Donation Buck," *Christian Science Monitor* 22 December 1995, p. 19.

10. From the World Wide Web: http://www.worldbank.org

11. For elaboration of this point, see Richard B. Brandt's *A Theory of the Good and the Right* (Oxford: Clarendon Press, 1979), in which he argues that a welfare-maximizing moral system will select the following principle for allocating income and goods:

    > The real income (monetary income adjusted for differing price-levels) after any taxes should be equal, except (a) for supplements to meet special needs, (b) supplements recompensing services to the extent needed to provide desirable incentive and allocate resources efficiently, and (c) variations to achieve other socially desirable ends such as population control. (p. 310)

    Brandt expresses the principle in terms of money, since "money is something we can easily hand out in equal amounts," and it is efficient to leave to individuals the decision about how to use allocated money to maximize individual happiness. The main reason for distributing equally is that utility declines at the margin. Here's an example to illustrate the point: A car will have some specific utility for an individual, but a second car will have far less utility for that individual (basically, it will serve only as a backup mode of transportation). The value of a third car is even less. In general, the utility to an individual of additional goods of the same sort falls precipitously, and economists refer to this fact by speaking of the phenomenon of declining marginal utility. From the standpoint of maximizing utility, it is best to give the second car to someone who has no car. Because of declining marginal utility, the way to maximize utility, as a general rule, is to distribute goods equally and to allocate money for purchasing goods equally.

12. Unlike the remaining cases, the Case of the Ruthless Mayor works only against the hedonist version of classical utilitarianism, not the preferential version. The preferential utilitarian says desire satisfaction is what counts, but most people in a town outraged by a crime want the real criminal punished, which is not accomplished by framing an innocent person.

13. See, for example, the end of chapter II of *Utilitarianism* and Mill's treatment of principles in chapter V. It is later utilitarians who develop the two-tiered system fully. See, for example, R. M. Hare, *Moral Thinking* (Oxford: Oxford University Press, 1981).

14. Mill, for one, did not advocate putting considerations of utility completely aside when deciding how to act. He thought it best that we cultivate in people

"a direct impulse to promote the general good," making it "one of the habitual motives of action" (chapter II, p. 23).

15. Economists use the term *Pareto optimal* to refer to situations in which no one can be made any better off without making someone else worse off, after the Italian economist Vilfredo Pareto (1848–1923).

16. James Rachels, "Killing and Starving to Death," *Philosophy* 54 (1979): 159.

17. Mill, *Utilitarianism,* chapter V, reprinted in *Social Ideals and Policies,* p. 148.

18. Mill, *Utilitarianism,* chapter II, reprinted in *Social Ideals and Policies,* p. 140.

19. Peter Singer, "Rich and Poor," in *Practical Ethics,* 2nd ed., by Peter Singer (Cambridge: Cambridge University Press, 1993).

20. John Rawls, *A Theory of Justice* (Cambridge, Mass.: Harvard University Press, 1971), p. 27.

21. Derek Parfit, "Later Selves and Moral Principles," in *Philosophy and Personal Relations,* ed. A. Montefiore (London: Routledge & Kegan Paul, 1973).

9

Kantianism
Is Duty Respect for Humanity?

In a March 1991 issue of the *New England Journal of Medicine,* physician Timothy Quill stunned his colleagues by admitting that he had given the necessary drugs to a patient who wanted to commit suicide and then told less than the truth to cover it up.[1] Years later Quill was in the public eye again when he, along with others, sued the New York State Attorney General, urging that New York retract its ban on assisted suicide; in 1997 the matter came before the U.S. Supreme Court (*Dennis C. Vacco, Attorney General of New York, et al., Petitioners v. Timothy E. Quill et al.*), which left New York's ban in place.

In his article, Quill said that his patient, whom he called Diane, had leukemia, a disease that was curable only 25 percent of the time—and then only after chemotherapy and a bone marrow transplantation process involving whole body irradiation to kill all existing marrow. Rather than submit to these horribly unpleasant procedures for the sake of a 25 percent chance of recovery, Diane decided to refuse treatment, knowing that death within months was certain.

After making her decision, she met with Quill repeatedly; eventually he came to see her point of view clearly and concluded that "it was the right decision for her." But Diane also told Quill that she wanted to "maintain control of herself and her own dignity during the time remaining to her," and after that she wanted to take her life as painlessly as possible. Quill told her that the Hemlock Society provided information about suicide, and shortly thereafter she asked Quill for barbiturates for sleep. Quill described his reaction:

> Since I knew that this was an essential ingredient in a Hemlock Society suicide, I asked her to come to the office to talk things over. She was more than willing to protect me by participating in a superficial conversation about her insomnia, but it was important to me to know how she planned to use the drugs and to be sure that she was not in despair. . . . I made sure

that she knew how to use the barbiturates for sleep, and also that she knew the amount needed to commit suicide. We agreed to meet regularly, and she promised to meet with me before taking her life. . . . I wrote the prescription with an uneasy feeling about the boundaries I was exploring— spiritual, legal, professional, and personal. Yet I also felt strongly that I was setting her free to get the most out of the time she had left, and to maintain dignity and control on her own terms until her death.

As her end approached, Diane talked with Quill one last time. She invited her friends over to say goodbye and said her final words to her husband and son. After she died, her husband called Quill for advice about what to do, and he came over. Quill described what happened when he called the medical examiner:

> When asked about the cause of death, I said, "acute leukemia." . . . Although acute leukemia was the truth, it was not the whole story. Yet any mention of suicide would have given rise to a police investigation and . . . the decision to perform an autopsy would have been made at the discretion of the medical examiner. The family or I could have been subject to criminal prosecution, and I to professional review. . . . I said "acute leukemia" to protect all of us, to protect Diane from an invasion into her past and her body, and to continue to shield society from the knowledge of the degree of suffering that people often undergo in the process of dying.

Seeing that Quill made it possible for Diane to die with dignity and with minimal loss of control, many of us will support Quill's decision to assist her. Some of us will also excuse his decision to mislead the authorities, on the grounds that it played an essential role in skirting objectionable laws that make it impossible for people to die well. Still others, however, are likely to condemn Quill on both counts. Chief among Quill's detractors would be the eighteenth-century German philosopher Immanuel Kant, who argued that neither lying nor suicide is ever permissible.[2] Both are wrong precisely because they are incompatible with our dignity and with the respect we owe ourselves as persons. Lying, in Kant's view, is "the obliteration of one's dignity as a human being"[3] and to commit suicide is "to degrade the humanity in one's person."[4] In spite of Kant's harsh indictments, his claims are controversial, and we will need to examine them carefully. But before we do, a review of Kant's approach to ethics is in order.

MORALITY VERSUS PRUDENCE

Suppose that you need new pants, yet your funds are limited. You mention your situation to a friend, and he says "if you want the best deal on jeans, go to the Acme Jeans Outlet." Your friend's advice takes the form of a directive or *imperative:* It contains the clause, "go to the Acme Jeans Outlet," which tells you what to do. However, it is also conditional: The clause "if you want the best deal on jeans" makes it clear that the directive applies to you only if you seek inexpensive jeans.

Now suppose that your friend responds in a slightly different way. After thinking about your situation, he realizes that you are looking for cheap jeans, so he says, "Go to the Acme Jeans Outlet." Your friend's counsel is offered in the form of a directive; however, it is still conditional, because the "if" clause is intended, even though it is not explicitly stated. He said "Go to the Acme Jeans Outlet," but he certainly would not expect you to comply if you no longer wanted to buy jeans.

Kant called such directives *hypothetical imperatives,* to signal that they apply to us only when we have certain desires, whether these are mentioned explicitly or not. Principles issuing hypothetical imperatives are important to rational agents, because these principles can help us satisfy our desires and ultimately make ourselves happy. To mark off principles that help us if we want to achieve happiness (or desire satisfaction) efficiently, as any prudent person does, Kant used the term *principles of empirical practical reason.*

Insofar as we are purely prudent (and in this sense rational) beings, desire satisfaction is our concern; but if we are also reasonable, or moral, beings, our highest priority is meeting our obligations. In fact, the principles that set out our obligations bind us unconditionally, so they cannot be hypothetical imperatives. The duty expressed by the principle "Do not kill innocent people" is not contingent upon our having this desire or that, whether explicitly or not. The requirement cannot be restated as "If you want to avoid risking jail time or pangs of conscience, do not kill innocent people," which would not apply to risk takers or the remorseless. The directive issued is *categorical,* not hypothetical, according to Kant: It applies to us no matter what our desires are. This is true of all moral principles. To distinguish them from the counsels of prudence, Kant called them *principles of pure practical reason.*

While all moral principles bind categorically, some are more fundamental or basic than others are. In his *Groundwork of the Metaphysic of Morals,* Kant attempted to identify the most fundamental principle of all. His aim was to "seek out and establish *the supreme principle of morality.*"[5] This basic categorical imperative would express the core idea of morality, the heart of the moral law.[6]

But what would it say? Kant thought that the answer is implicit in the very idea of a categorical imperative: It suggests that we are bound by a law that applies to all agents no matter what their desires are. In other words, it suggests that we are required to conform to "the universality of a law as such"– and "it is this conformity alone that the imperative properly asserts to be necessary." [7] Hence the supreme moral principle can be put as follows: If you intend to act in a certain way or according to a certain policy, be sure that your intention is *universalizable;* that is, make sure you can also intend for everyone to act in the same way. Otherwise, your way of acting is not permissible. Using the term *maxim* for the rule or policy that expresses the intention behind your action, Kant stated the supreme moral principle this way:

> Act only on that maxim through which you can at the same time will that it should become a universal law. [8]

This way of stating the categorical imperative is known as the *universal law formulation.* Later, Kant supplied two other formulations and said that the three amounted to the same thing. However, the three formulations seem quite different; here are the other two:

> Act in such a way that you always treat humanity, whether in your own person or in the person of any other, never simply as a means, but always at the same time as an end. [This is the *end-in-itself formulation.*] [9]
> Act always on the maxim of such a will in us as can at the same time look upon itself as making universal law. [This is the *formulation of autonomy.*] [10]

Of the three, the clearest version is the first. It is also the most authoritative, according to Kant. Let's examine it further and attempt to come to terms with Kant's difficult notion of universalizability.

APPLYING THE CATEGORICAL IMPERATIVE

Kant's requirement that a maxim be universalizable is supposed to rule out "making an exception to it for ourselves." [11] It precludes treating ourselves as enjoying special privileges. Kant wants us to resist exempting ourselves from requirements we impose on others. To see how Kant's approach works, consider one of his own illustrations: The case of the deceitful promise. Suppose that I need money and realize that if I promise to pay it back, then the bank will loan me the money. I also realize, however, that I will not be able to keep my promise. May I make a promise I do not intend to keep? To answer this question, I must work through a series of steps. [12]

First, I must express the intention behind my action in the form of a rule that Kant calls a "maxim." Schematically, it might look like this:

> When I am in circumstances C, I will do A.

Kant himself expresses the maxim behind my action as follows:

> Whenever I believe myself short of money, I will borrow money and promise to pay it back, though I know that this will never be done. [13]

While Kant's way of expressing my intention is sufficiently detailed for Kant's purposes, the exact form of a maxim is not fixed; maxims may be more or less complicated depending on the complexity of the considerations involved in one's policy. It is conceivable that I am the sort of person who would borrow under false pretenses only when my life or my family's survival depended on it, whereas Kant has me borrowing every time I am short of money. It is also conceivable that I would not make a deceitful promise if I could find a job quickly or if I believed that my action would cause bank loan officers to lose their jobs. What is important is that one's maxim be sincere: It must express one's intentions accurately.

My next step is to use my maxim as the basis of a thought experiment that helps me detect whether acting from my maxim is in some sense irrational, incoherent. Basically, I must figure out what the world would be like if everyone adopted my maxim. I have to imagine what we might call *the world my maxim yields.* I start with the world as it is and imagine changing it just enough for two conditions to be met. First, everyone adopts my policy as it is spelled out in my maxim. As Kant says, they do so as if compelled by a law of nature or by psychological necessity. Second, it is public knowledge that everyone acts from this maxim. Thus the world yielded by the deceitful promise maxim would be one in which people always attempt to secure loans under false pretenses whenever they find themselves short of cash, and this proclivity is common knowledge.

Finally, I ask whether the world my maxim yields involves one or the other of two contradictions:

- A *contradiction in conception* would occur if the world my maxim yields is impossible.

- A *contradiction in will* would occur if I could not "will" the world my maxim yields.[14]

If neither contradiction arises, then my maxim is universalizable and acting on it is morally permissible. Otherwise, I may not proceed; doing so is unreasonable and forbidden by the categorical imperative, which we can now state as follows:

Act only on the basis of maxims that yield worlds that involve neither contradiction.

This means that I may not make my deceitful promise after all, for the world it yields involves a contradiction in conception. If everyone had a policy of making deceitful promises to get loans whenever they were short of money, and this were common knowledge, no one would take the promises seriously. There is an inconsistency in imagining that (1) everyone gets a loan using deceptive promises, yet (2) no one gets a loan using deceptive promises since no one accepts anyone's word.

As our example illustrates, some maxims are flawed because the attempt to universalize them generates a contradiction in conception. However, other maxims are flawed for a different reason: Attempting to universalize them generates a contradiction in will. To illustrate this point, let us ask whether it would be permissible to act from the *maxim of indifference,* namely:

> When I can worsen someone's situation, I will not, but when others are in distress, and I can help, I will not.

According to Kant, the world generated by this maxim does not involve a contradiction in conception; in fact, "if such an attitude were a universal law of nature, mankind could get on perfectly well." [15] However, it is not possible to will a world of indifference,

> for a will which decided in this way would be in conflict with itself, since many a situation might arise in which the man needed love and sympathy from others, and in which, by such a law of nature sprung from his own will, he would rob himself of all hope of the help he wants for himself. [16]

What exactly does Kant mean here? It is tempting to read him as follows: To will a world is to want to take part in it. This reading seems plausible since it gets Kant to the conclusion he wants to reach about his example. We can will the world of indifference only if we welcome the prospect of entering it, knowing that we must forgo all assistance from others. But we would not be willing to enter such a world, since we want to receive help when we really need it.

Unfortunately, this straightforward way of spelling out the idea of universalizability creates difficulties. The main problem is that people differ in what they want, so when they ask whether they can will a world yielded by a given maxim, they reach different results. Suppose, for example, that I am a rugged individualist; I want to make it solely on my own—or die trying. In that case, I have no trouble "willing" the world of indifference, since it is the sort of world I want to be part of, the sort of world in which I can satisfy my desires, including my desire neither to help others nor to receive help. Yet people who are less independent cannot "will" the world of indifference. They want to receive help, but they won't if they are in the world of indifference. Hence we seem forced to reach an embarrassing conclusion: I may act from the maxim of indifference, but others may not act from this maxim. Instead of providing us with a way to identify universally applicable moral principles, Kant will have ended up defending a version of moral relativism!

To will a world does not mean that we can satisfy all of our desires in that world—Kant cannot have that in mind. Instead, Kant must mean that we can accommodate a particular set of interests in the world yielded by our maxim. Which interests? Presumably these will be interests all rational beings share, so that the requirements of morality will be the same for everyone and not vary depending on people's specific desires. But which will these interests be?

We can be a bit more specific about them if we take into account a passage in which Kant notes that all rational beings have their rationality itself as a goal:

> *Rational nature exists as an end in itself.* This is the way in which [every rational being] necessarily conceives his own existence.[17]

Kant's thought is this: Part of being rational (where rationality is understood to encompass reasonableness as well) is taking on the task of developing our rational abilities as thoroughly as possible. Suppose, for example, that we would lose our ability to resolve moral issues if we spent all of our time in a drunken stupor: In that case it would be irrational to become a lush. We need something as rational beings if it is a necessary condition for us to become or remain as rational as possible, and Kant thinks that neglecting these needs is always irrational.

Apparently, it is these needs that Kant has in mind when he proposes his contradiction in the will test. Therefore, we might interpret his test as follows:

> We are able to will a world when and only when bringing about (and taking part in) that world is not an impediment to our meeting our needs as rational beings.

Consider, once again, the maxim of indifference. Now, one thing we need if we are to become and remain rational is life. But in the world yielded by the maxim of indifference, no compassionate people will save us if our lives are threatened. A "contradiction," or tension, arises when we try to will this world: As rational beings we necessarily want to remain rational, and hence we want our lives secured (at least while rationality is possible); and given this goal, it makes no sense to place ourselves in a world where others who can easily save us will always refuse to do so. In this interpretation, Kant would say that the rugged individualists we imagined earlier (who would rather die than receive aid) betray an irrational neglect for their continued existence as rational beings. The world yielded by the maxim of indifference cannot be willed–by anyone.

In this way we are led to Kant's view that helping people to become and remain rational is a duty, albeit an *imperfect* one, meaning that we have a great deal of discretion in choosing how we help, whom we help, and when we help. By contrast, some duties, such as the obligation not to lie or commit suicide, are *perfect* and admit of no discretion at all.

Before we leave Kant's test for universalizable maxims, let us consider a criticism that is frequently made and yet easily answered. John Stuart Mill put the objection this way:

> [Kant] lay down a universal first principle as the origin and ground of moral obligation; it is this: "So act that the rule on which thou actest would admit of being adopted as a law by all rational beings." But when he begins to deduce from this precept any of the actual duties of morality, he fails, almost grotesquely, to show that there would be any contradiction, any logical (not to say physical) impossibility, in the adoption by all rational beings of the most outrageously immoral rules of conduct. All he shows is that the consequences of their universal adoption would be such as no one would choose to incur.[18]

In Mill's reading, Kant's categorical imperative says we may perform an action as long as it is endorsed by a set of principles or rules that meets one simple test: It is not incoherent to imagine everyone adopting those rules.

Admittedly, Kant said things that facilitate Mill's reading; the following passage is not atypical: "Nothing but the idea of the law in itself . . . —so far as it, and not an expected result, is the ground determining the will—can constitute that pre-eminent good which we call moral."[19] And Mill certainly was right when he suggested that in his interpretation Kant would have to accept outrageously immoral rules of conduct. It is entirely possible to imagine everyone adopting the following rules, for example: Put your cigarette out using the skin of the nearest child; torture your parents when they are elderly; break people's noses whenever you feel like it. However, Mill's version of the categorical imperative is much weaker than Kant's; in effect, in Mill's version, we may act on a maxim as long as the world yielded does not involve a contradiction in conception. This overlooks the fact that Kant explicitly insisted on a second condition; he required that the world yielded does not involve a contradiction in will.

CONSEQUENCES AND INTENTIONS

For Kant, as we have seen, the moral assessment of conduct is fundamentally the assessment of an agent's intentions rather than the consequences of what an agent does. In fact, Kant is probably a bit too emphatic about this point, for he suggests to some readers—including Mill—that the consequences of our actions are entirely irrelevant from the moral point of view, a suggestion that seems implausible. Let's take a moment to dispel this impression.

Kant's first sentence in his *Groundwork* is that "it is impossible to conceive anything at all in the world, or even out of it, which can be taken as good without qualification, except a good will." [20] A bit later he adds that "a good will is not good because of what it effects or accomplishes—because of its fitness for attaining some proposed end: It is good through its willing alone—that is, good in itself." [21] In these passages Kant is contrasting (1) grasping duty and forming the intention to act from it, with (2) affecting the world one way or another. He says that whether we are moral persons (or people whose wills are good) is not determined by the ways we change the world. Instead, our response to and grasp of duty determine whether we are moral. To be moral, we must take duty seriously for its own sake, but this is not enough, for we might want to do our duty, yet have a wholly skewed idea of what is involved. In addition, we must have an accurate grasp of our duty. But as long as we are aware of our duty and are fully committed to acting as duty dictates, we are morally worthy in the fullest sense, no matter how ineptly we might perform and no matter how badly things turn out. Imagine that some powerful and malicious demon or alien decides to follow you around, and every time you attempt to act properly, the demon thwarts your plans. When you try to throw a life preserver to a child to save her from drowning, the demon takes over and causes the preserver to knock her unconscious, and she drowns. When you try to tell someone the truth, the demon seizes control, and you come out with a falsehood. Nonetheless, you have done everything required of you, and your good will "would still shine like a jewel for its own sake as something which has its full value in itself." [22]

While underlining the point that moral merit attaches only to getting our duties and intentions right, Kant sometimes overstated himself, saying implausible things unnecessarily. In particular, he denied that helping others because we feel sympathy for them (and hence want to help) has any moral worth—only actions done from duty have moral worth, since duty is a more reliable and accurate basis for action than is sympathy. Kant is not suggesting that acting from sympathy is reprehensible, but what he is saying here is still too harsh, since people who act from sympathy might still be du*tiful.* They might be prepared to forgo an action prompted by sympathy if it conflicted with duty. If I am limping to my car, you might be inclined to carry my bags—but not if you discover that I am a criminal injured in a bank robbery. Here you act from sympathy, but duty would override in case of conflict. In such circumstances it seems overly rigid to deny that your action has moral worth.

It seems plausible enough to say, with Kant, that people are only required to grasp their duties and form the right intentions; they are not morally responsible when things go wrong. However, it would be a mistake to conclude that, for Kant, the consequences of our actions do not matter at all. They can be morally important in two ways.

First, persons, or "rational beings," have "absolute" value: They are ends in themselves.[23] Hence it is unfortunate when a moral agent is harmed or killed—for example, when my brakes (which I just had serviced) fail, and I kill someone accidentally. To harm an innocent human being is a misfortune for the victim as well as myself, even if my intentions are unimpeachable, and I am in no way blameworthy for what occurred. Nor does Kant deny this. He says that having a good will is the only "unqualified" good, and the "highest" good, but he does not say that it is the "sole and complete good."[24] Even happiness is good, but only if it is the result of morally permissible activities. A fundamental feature of Kantian ethics is that the concept of the right precedes the concept of the good: To know whether something is valuable, we first must know what is right. This feature is typical of *deontological* theories, which explain proper conduct in terms of duty.

There is a second way the consequences of our actions matter: Consequences help determine what our duties are. When we ask whether a maxim is universalizable, we are assessing (hypothetical) consequences: We work out the consequences of everyone's adopting our policy, and we determine whether we can "will" such a world. Acknowledging that consequences matter in this way is entirely consistent with Kant's claim that "a good will is not good because of what it effects or accomplishes," by which Kant meant only to say that dutiful conduct is praiseworthy even if the results are a complete disaster.[25] It is also consistent with Kant's repeated claim that principles of morality "must have an origin entirely and completely a priori."[26] Kant's view is that the supreme principle of morality—the categorical imperative—can be established without appealing to experience. The fundamental moral principle is like a mathematical proposition in that its truth can be established without consulting experience. Be that as it may, it does not follow that particular moral injunctions must also be established using unaided reason, as Kant realized.[27]

ABSOLUTISM AND CONFLICTS OF DUTIES

Kant left his readers with another false impression that needs dispelling—namely, that Kantian ethics forces us to conform to rigid and narrow moral principles (at least when these define perfect duties). Unfortunately, Kant wanted to be read this way: He made it absolutely clear that he was an *absolutist,* or someone who holds that moral principles lay out unqualified and narrow requirements. "Reason," he wrote, "enjoins its commands relentlessly," and he complained that people tend to "quibble with these strict laws of duty, . . . and to make them, where possible, more adapted to our wishes and inclinations."[28] In applying his theory to concrete issues, such as lying or suicide, he invariably set out the narrowest moral principle possible and stridently rejected reasonable qualifications. When a philosopher named Benjamin Constant (1767–1830) pointed out circumstances in which telling the truth would be monstrous, Kant insisted that we may not lie–period. Suppose, Constant said, that your friend Sue, whom you know to be a good person, rushes to your door and asks you to hide her from an ax-wielding maniac, who, moments later, bursts in, and says, "Where is Sue? I'm going to hack her to bits!" Surely it would be permissible to say that Sue is elsewhere or that you do not know where she is. "No one," Constant said, "has a right to a truth which injures others."[29] Kant would not hear of it: "Truthfulness in statements which cannot be avoided is the formal duty of an individual to everyone, however great may be the disadvantage accruing to himself or to another." This is because "by telling an untruth . . . , I cause that declarations should in general find no credence, and hence that all rights based on contracts should be void . . . , and this is a wrong done to mankind generally."[30] Kant did not tell us exactly what to say to the murderous maniac, but he really did seem to expect something like, "I cannot tell a lie, Mr. Maniac; she's in the closet."

Upon reading Kant's response to Constant, one has to ask how the duty to tell the truth squares with our duty to respect the rational agency of others.[31] As a rational being, Sue is an end in herself, and she will remain a rational being as long as she is alive. But to save her life, all you have to do is tell a lie that steers the maniac away from your door, and then phone 911 so that the police can pick him up. Your duty to respect Sue's rational agency seems to conflict with your duty not to lie. What are we supposed to do when our duties clash? Does Kant have an answer?

The best way to help Kant out here is to say that he has created difficulties where none need arise. Kant's absolutism is especially troublesome; not only should we reject it on the grounds that it leads to inflexible moral demands, but Kant himself should also have rejected it, because it is in tension with his own procedure for identifying our duties. Suppose, for example, that I were considering whether to act from the maxim, Never lie. The world yielded by this maxim is one in which no one will be helped by a lie no matter what is at stake, and we could not will such a world. Since we might find ourselves in Sue's circumstances, we need people to feel free to lie on occasion. And knowing that police officers sometimes cannot deal with murderers without deception, such as when they are working in undercover operations, we would not want to tie their hands. Considerations like these suggest that a far better moral principle is this:

Don't lie unless it is necessary to prevent the killing of innocent people.

If everyone acted from this principle, rare lies would be permitted, but otherwise lies would be forbidden, and so the practice of truth telling would not melt down, as Kant feared.

Thus one way to handle conflicts of duty within the general framework Kant laid out is to reject absolutism and qualify each moral principle so that the duty it lays out does not compete with the duties enjoined by other principles, at least in circumstances people are likely to face. This is essentially what we have attempted in designing our qualified principle concerning lying, and it is Kant's best bet.[32]

There are two other ways to handle conflicting duties. First, we might try to explain away conflicting duties using W. D. Ross's distinction between *prima facie duties* and *proper duties*.[33] We have a prima facie duty to do something when our obligation can be overridden, and a proper duty to do something when, all things considered, our obligation is not overridden. Ross treats familiar duties such as "Do not lie," and "Help others in need" as prima facie duties. He says there are situations where they clash (like Constant's case), but no situations in which our proper duties clash. In a case like Constant's we must weigh competing prima facie duties and see which wins out, thereby determining what our proper duty is. Unfortunately, however, Ross does not tell us how to decide when one prima facie duty outweighs another.

A second strategy for handling conflicts of duty might also help fill in the details of Ross's strategy: Instead of testing the universalizability of maxims one at a time, we might test pairs of maxims, or a complete moral framework, including rules for assigning some duties priority over others, all at once.[34] If we want to retain Ross's idea of a prima facie duty, we could do so by treating maxims tested one at a time as defining prima facie duties and the complete moral framework as defining proper duties.

RESPECT FOR PERSONS

So far our discussion has centered on Kant's first formulation of his categorical imperative. However, of the three versions he provided, it is the second that has had the greatest popular influence:

> Act in such a way that you always treat humanity, whether in your own
> person or in the person of any other, never simply as a means, but always
> at the same time as an end.

Exactly what this injunction meant is the subject of extensive controversy. But the thrust seems clear enough.

The gist of Kant's requirement is that we *respect moral agency*, our own as well as others'. Moral agency involves three things: first, *moral competence,* or the ability to work out our duties and to act accordingly; second, *moral responsibility,* which is the willingness to act on our duties; and, third, *self-determination,* which embraces choosing values, setting ends for ourselves, and shaping our lives accordingly. To respect moral agency, we must never impair any of these three, and we should help create conditions that foster their development. Let's look at some of the most important implications Kant drew from his requirement of respect for moral agency.

1.   We have the (imperfect) duty to perfect ourselves as moral agents. This means that we must develop our moral capacities as well as we can. But Kant did not think our duty ends there. He added that we may not eat and drink to excess: "When a man is gorged with food, he is temporarily incapacitated for activities which require adroitness and deliberation in the use of his powers." [35] He also claimed that the duty to perfect ourselves rules out suicide; a man who commits suicide destroys "the subject of morality in his own person." [36]

2.   Given the importance of self-determination, we may not interfere with people's freedom to choose their ends and values and to design their own lives in responsible ways. It is always acceptable to argue with them, in the hope of influencing their decisions, for this acknowledges that they are reasonable beings. But ultimately we must give way to their decisions concerning their lives, unless these are irresponsible.

3.   Nor may we treat people as if they were not self-determining. It is never acceptable to act as if someone were a mere tool or mindless object or a resource to exhaust. For this reason, we may not manipulate people or involve them in our plans against their wills. We may ask or hire people to perform services, such as cutting our hair or teaching us philosophy. In these cases we are not using others as mere means, because we engage with them as fellow moral beings: We let them consider their own priorities and freely accept—or reject—our plans. By contrast, in conning them into going along with plans they would otherwise reject, we bypass the apparatus of rationality. However, even mutually consensual activities can involve treating others as mere means, according to Kant, although his grounds are considerably more obscure. Here he cited prostitution, as well as consensual sex motivated solely by sexual pleasure. Kant considered plain sexual gratification degrading, whether consensual or not, on the grounds that any person involved is "used as a thing"—because "the desire is . . . directed only toward sex and not towards the person as a human being." [37]

4.   The importance Kant placed on self-determination was also the driving force behind his view of justice. In *Metaphysical Elements of Justice,*

Kant claimed that the laws of a just state (which Kant called "external," in contrast to the moral law, which he called "internal") should limit our freedom to pursue our life plans only for one reason: To permit others to exercise the same freedom. And in *On the Old Saw, That May Be Right in Theory but It Won't Work in Practice* (1793), Kant said that the proper goal of legislation is to create an order in which (1) people's freedom is as extensive as possible and (2) the freedoms granted are compatible with everyone's having the same freedoms. Among other things, this means that legislators should not be in the business of making people happy. Instead, their task is to maintain a system of rules by which people may pursue happiness as they wish, as long as they do not infringe on "another's right to do whatever can coexist with every man's freedom under a possible universal law."

AUTONOMY

Recall that the third (and final) formulation of Kant's categorical imperative, the *formulation of autonomy,* reads as follows:

> Act always on the maxim of such a will in us as can at the same time look upon itself as making universal law.

This formulation emphasizes that moral agents are autonomous beings: They impose moral rules upon *themselves* and have the capacities and motivation necessary to do so. More important, however, Kant meant to suggest that only a moral law that people in some sense *construct* binds them. By this Kant meant at least two things.

First, our moral obligations are based ultimately on our deliberations as reasonable beings, not on anything outside of these. In particular, Kant rejected the idea that morality can be grounded in God's will, the dictates of a political regime, facts about human nature, or the teleological structure of the world. Moral principles are not preexisting facts we discover. To conceive of morality as given by preexisting facts is not consistent with our autonomy; it is to fall into "heteronomy"—the absence of autonomy.

Second, the deliberative process by which we decide whether it is permissible to act in a certain way is simultaneously a process by which moral principles are devised. In considering whether we may not lie, for example, we begin with the maxim behind our proposed action, which might be, I may not lie in any circumstances. We generalize this maxim into a principle applying to everyone: No one may lie in any circumstances. If our maxim leads us to a world that generates neither a contradiction in conception nor a contradiction in will, the generalized maxim will be a binding moral principle.

Thus, moral beings are autonomous in the sense that through their moral deliberations they construct a law that they apply to themselves, and they are bound only by this self-given law.

DIANE'S SUICIDE

We have seen that Kant vehemently rejected suicide and lying. However, we have also seen that the Kantian approach to ethics is far more flexible than its inventor made it out to be and allows us to defend some actions Kant rejected. In light of these competing considerations, how should we assess Diane's decision to commit suicide and Timothy Quill's role in her suicide?

Recall that Kant was wrong when he declared the principle "Never lie" to be universalizable; from the standpoint of universalizability, we need a more sophisticated principle, such as, "Don't lie unless it is necessary to prevent the killing of innocent people." Now let us add that the principles "Do not commit suicide" and "Do not help anyone commit suicide" can be criticized on similar grounds. For a world in which no one ever commits suicide is one in which people with untreatable illnesses spend their twilight days in unbearable pain or in drug-induced unconsciousness—unable to control their lives, unable to appreciate the relationships and activities that gave their lives meaning, and yearning only for release. Such persons must endure the slow degradation of their humanity and the gradual loss of their self-determination. Is this tragic world really one we could will? Isn't suicide sometimes a way to forestall the indignity of lingering after we have ceased to be self-determining?

Kant's most convincing reason for criticizing suicide was that it "degrades the humanity in one's person" and hence violates the injunction that we never use anyone, including ourselves, as a mere means. But did Diane really degrade her own humanity, or was her leukemia doing that? Wasn't it respect for her own humanity that led her to draw a line and refuse to endure the breakdown of her body and faculties indefinitely?

On the other hand, it is troubling to adopt a principle that is too permissive concerning suicide, assuming we cannot will a world in which people commit suicide in moments of heightened but temporary emotionality, as far too many young people have done. What we seem to need is a principle that avoids the extremes, such as the qualified principle, "Morally competent people may commit suicide when they face an irreversible illness that is so debilitating or painful it undermines the incentive for living."

These remarks go a long way toward exonerating Quill, for Diane's suicide was permitted by our qualified principle. Hence the following argument seems correct:

1. It is all right to help morally competent people act in permissible ways when they ask us to.

2. Diane's decision to commit suicide was competent and permissible, as was her choice of means—namely, barbiturates—and she asked Quill to help her obtain the drugs.

3. So assisting Diane by prescribing barbiturates was acceptable.

Assuming it is all right to help people act in permissible ways when they ask us to do so and that Diane's suicide was acceptable, then the assistance Quill provided was above reproach.

QUESTIONS FOR REFLECTION

1. According to Kant, having sex for the sake of pleasure "is a degradation of human nature."[38] What exactly does he mean? Is he correct?

2. According to Kant, one person can "use another human being as an instrument for his service; he can use his hands, his feet, and even all his powers; he can use him for his own purposes with the other's consent."[39] Yet consensual sex among two people motivated solely by sexual desire is wrong. Is Kant's position consistent? Is it plausible?

3. Kant says, "There are many spirits of so sympathetic a temper that, without any further motive of vanity or self-interest, they find an inner pleasure in spreading happiness around them and can take delight in the contentment of others as their own work. Yet I maintain that in such a case an action of this kind . . . has . . . no genuinely moral worth." This is because the action is not performed "from duty"—only when we act "for the sake of duty alone" does our action have "genuine moral worth."[40] Why does Kant say this? Is his claim justified in the context of his moral theory? Or might he say something more like this: Actions have moral worth even if motivated by delight in others so long as duty is also a sufficient motive?

4. According to Kant, when, if ever, is it permissible for a physician to lie to a patient? Is Kant correct? Explain.

5. Why does Kant hold that moral laws hold "with absolute necessity?"[41] Is he correct?

6. Why did Kant treat the duty not to lie as a perfect duty? Would it have been better to treat it as an imperfect duty, thus giving us leeway in deciding when to tell the truth?

7. In a footnote, Kant says that "Don't do unto others what you don't want done to yourself" is "trivial" and cannot serve as standard, "for it

is merely derivative from our principle [namely, the categorical imperative], although subject to various qualifications: It cannot be a universal law since it contains the ground neither of duties to oneself nor of duties of kindness to others . . . , nor finally of strict duties towards others; for on this basis the criminal would be able to dispute with the judges who punish him, and so on." Why does Kant think the "trivial" principle cannot ground the duties he mentions? Is he correct?

8. Quill deceived authorities to cover up Diane's suicide and his part in it. But die he lie? Was his deception permissible? What would Kant say about the following argument:

    a. Lying is permissible as a way to prevent wrongs.
    b. It is wrong for the state to bar people from helping others do morally appropriate things.
    c. Quill lied to prevent the state from punishing people (namely, Quill and Diane's husband) for helping others (Diane) act in a morally acceptable way.
    d. So Quill's lie was permissible.

9. Suppose Schmitt the Nazi holds a gun to your head and tells you that unless you push Lucy in front of an oncoming train he will shoot you. May you kill Lucy? (Is killing an innocent bystander who is not threatening you self-defense? May you do anything whatever to save your own life?) Now suppose Schmitt tells you that unless you kill Lucy, he will kill twenty innocent bystanders, and that he will spare them if you do kill Lucy. May you kill Lucy? Is it your duty? What would the Kantian say? What would the utilitarian say? Whose view is more plausible?

10. May healthy people voluntarily give one of their kidneys to someone who needs one in order to live? May people sell their organs? May someone who will die without a kidney transplant demand that a healthy person provide that kidney? May force be used to procure the organ from an unwilling "donor"? (If so, may the healthy "donor" insist on compensation?) Is it permissible to kill healthy people when it is possible to use their organs to save many lives? What would Kant say? What would utilitarians say? Which position is more plausible?

FURTHER READINGS

Works by Kant

Anthropology Considered from a Pragmatic Viewpoint. Translated by Mary J. Gregor. The Hague: Martinus Nijhoff, 1974. First published 1798.

Critique of Judgment. Translated by James Meredith. Oxford: Clarendon Press, 1964. First published 1790.

Critique of Practical Reason. Translated by L. W. Beck. Indianapolis: Bobbs-Merrill, 1956. First published 1788.

Critique of Pure Reason. Translated by Norman Kemp Smith. New York: St. Martin's Press, 1963. First published 1781.

Groundwork of the Metaphysics of Morals. Translated by H. J. Paton. New York: Harper Torchbooks, 1964. First published 1785.

Metaphysics of Morals. Metaphysical Elements of Justice (Part I, *Metaphysics of Morals*). Translated by John Ladd. Indianapolis: Bobbs-Merrill, 1965; *Immanuel Kant, The Doctrine of Virtue, Part II of the Metaphysic of Morals.* Translated by Mary J. Gregor. Philadelphia: University of Pennsylvania Press, 1964. First published 1797.

On the Old Saw, That May Be Right in Theory but It Won't Work in Practice. In *Perpetual Peace and Other Essays,* translated by Ted Humphrey. Indianapolis: Hackett, 1983. First published 1793.

Perpetual Peace. In *Perpetual Peace and Other Essays.* Translated by Ted Humphrey. Indianapolis: Hackett, 1983. First published 1795.

Prolegomena to Any Future Metaphysics. Translated by James Ellington. Indianapolis: Bobbs-Merrill, 1970. First published 1783.

Religion within the Limits of Reason Alone. Translated by Theodore Greene and Hoyt Hudson. New York: Harper & Row, 1960. First published 1793.

Works on Kant

Beck, L. W. *A Commentary on Kant's Critique of Practical Reason.* Chicago: University of Chicago Press, 1961.

Gewirth, Alan. *Reason and Morality.* Chicago: University of Chicago Press, 1978.

Herman, Barbara. *The Practice of Moral Judgment.* Cambridge: Mass.: Harvard University Press, 1993.

Hill, Thomas, Jr. *Autonomy and Self-Respect.* Cambridge: Cambridge University Press, 1991.

——. *Dignity and Practical Reason in Kant's Moral Theory.* Ithaca: Cornell University Press, 1992.

Körner, Stephen. *Kant.* New Haven: Yale University Press, 1982.

Korsgaard, Christine. *Creating the Kingdom of Ends.* Cambridge: Cambridge University Press, 1996.

Mulholland, Leslie. *Kant's System of Rights.* New York: Columbia University Press, 1990.

O'Neill, Onora. *Constructions of Reason.* Cambridge: Cambridge University Press, 1989.

Paton, H. J. *The Categorical Imperative.* Chicago: University of Chicago Press, 1948.

Ross, W. D. *Kant's Ethical Theory.* Oxford: Oxford University Press, 1954.

Van der Linden, Harry. *Kantian Ethics and Socialism.* Indianapolis: Hackett, 1988.

Williams, Bernard. *Ethics and the Limits of Philosophy.* Cambridge, Mass.: Harvard University Press, 1985.

Wood, Allen. *Kant's Moral Religion.* Ithaca: Cornell University Press, 1970.

NOTES

1. Timothy Quill, "Death and Dignity: A Case of Individualized Decision Making," *New England Journal of Medicine* 324, no. 10 (March 7, 1991): 691–694.

2. For example, in *Lectures on Ethics* (given 1775–1780), trans. Louis Infield (Indianapolis: Hackett, 1924), Kant said "suicide is in no circumstances permissible" (p. 151).

3. Immanuel Kant, *The Metaphysical Principles of Virtue,* trans. James Ellington (Indianapolis: Bobbs-Merrill, 1964), 429 (p. 91). [The first number (429) corresponds to the pagination in the standard edition of Kant's works, called *Kants Gesammelte Schriften* (Berlin: Preussische Akademie der Wissenschaften, 1900–1942). These numbers appear in the margins of most translations of Kant's writings. The second number refers to the page number in the Ellington translation.]

4. Kant, *The Metaphysical Principles,* 423 (p. 84).

5. Kant, *Groundwork of the Metaphysic of Morals,* trans. H. J. Paton (New York: Harper Torchbooks, 1964), preface, p. 60.

6. Kant, *Groundwork,* 420 (p. 87).

7. Kant. *Groundwork,* 421 (p. 88).

8. Kant, *Groundwork,* 421 (p. 88).

9. Kant, *Groundwork,* 429 (p. 96).

10. Kant, *Groundwork,* 432 (p. 100).

11. Kant, *Groundwork,* 424 (p. 91).

12. In interpreting Kant's first formulation, I follow John Rawls, "Themes in Kant's Moral Philosophy," in *Kant's Transcendental Deductions: The Three Critiques and the Opus Postumum,* ed. Eckart Forster (Stanford: Stanford University Press, 1989).

13. Kant, *Groundwork,* 422 (p. 90).

14. Kant, *Groundwork,* 424 (p. 91).

15. Kant, *Groundwork,* 423 (p. 91).

16. Kant, *Groundwork,* 423 (p. 91).

17. Kant, *Groundwork,* 429 (p. 96).

18. John Stuart Mill, *Utilitarianism,* chapter 1; p. 6 in *Utilitarianism,* ed. Oskar Piest (Indianapolis: Bobbs-Merrill, 1957). Compare chapter V, p. 65.

19. Kant, *Groundwork,* 399 (p. 67)

20. Kant, *Groundwork,* 393 (p. 61).

21. Kant, *Groundwork,* 394 (p. 62). Compare 399 (p. 68), 402 (p. 69), and 435 (p. 102).

22. Kant, *Groundwork,* 394 (p. 62).

23. Kant, *Groundwork,* 428 (p. 96).

24. Kant, *Groundwork,* 396 (p. 64).

25. Compare *Groundwork,* "the moral worth of an action does not depend on the result expected from it." 401 (p. 69).

26. Kant, *Groundwork,* 426 (p. 93).

27. Their "origin" is the categorical imperative; but in Kant's view, their derivation requires working out whether our maxims are universalizable, which depends on facts about the basic nature of human beings (together with facts about whatever additional "rational beings" there might be) and the world they live in.

28. Kant, *Groundwork,* 405 (p. 73).

29. Immanuel Kant, "On a Supposed Right to Lie from Altruistic Motives," *Living Well,* ed. Steven Luper (Fort Worth: Harcourt Brace, 2000), p. 350.

30. Kant, "On a Supposed Right to Lie," p. 350. Compare *Groundwork* 403 (p. 71).

31. I am grateful to Dorothy Orzech for this way of stating the concern.

32. Certainly it is the only way he will be able to preclude conflicts of duty, as he wished to do, judging from the following passage in *The Metaphysics of Morals:*

    A conflict of duties . . . would be that relationship between them in which one would (wholly or partially) cancel the other. But since duty and obligation in general are concepts which express the objective practical necessity of certain actions, and since two opposite rules cannot be necessary at the same time, then if it is a duty to act in accordance with one of them, it is not only not a duty, but contrary to duty, to act in accordance with the other. It therefore follows that a conflict of duties and obligations is inconceivable. 224 (p. 24).

33. W. D. Ross, *The Right and the Good* (Oxford: Oxford University Press, 1930).

34. Occasionally, Kant hinted at rules giving priority to some duties over others. For instance, in *Lectures on Ethics,* he said "the duties dictated by right or by generosity are inferior to the duties we owe to ourselves" (p. 211).

35. Kant, *The Metaphysical Principles of Virtue,* 427 (p. 88).

36. Kant, *The Metaphysical Principles of Virtue,* 423 (p. 83).

37 . Kant, *Lectures on Ethics,* p. 166.

38. Kant, *Lectures on Ethics,* p. 163.

39. Kant, *Lectures on Ethics,* p. 163.

40. Kant, *Groundwork,* 398 (p. 66).

41. Kant, *Groundwork,* 408 (p. 76).

10

Contractarianism
Is Duty the Outcome of an Ideal Agreement?

On April 25, 1999, ten thousand members of a peaceful group called Falun Gong quietly formed a ring around Zhongnanhai compound, which houses China's leaders in Beijing, hoping to encourage the government to grant them official recognition. The protest worried China's leaders, because it seemed to come out of the blue and because Falun Gong is an enormous organization. Some say it numbers near 60 million in China and includes people in all walks of life. It is gaining membership in the United States as well, with centers in New York, Louisville, Cleveland, and Salt Lake City, and elsewhere.[1]

Falun Gong was started in 1992 by a former soldier named Li Hongzhi (pronounced "Lee Hungjur"), who lives in exile in New York City. Hongzhi developed Buddhist and Daoist teachings into a way of life that emphasizes truthfulness, benevolence, and forbearance. He also recommends exercise techniques called qigong, which are thought to enhance the flow of qi ("tchee"), or vital energies, improving health and self-healing. As well, Falun Gong hints that Hongzhi's techniques can give "supernormal capabilities"; Hongzhi himself is sometimes said to be able to see through objects, for example.

In spite of – or perhaps because of – the air of mystery surrounding Falun Gong, it has become the fastest growing movement in China. Its practitioners communicate using fax machines and the Internet, and it clearly is able to amass people quickly. However, the protest it staged in April 1999 alarmed the Communist leaders in China so much that on July 22 they banned Falun Gong and began a massive campaign of intimidation and propaganda against it. Thousands of members have been detained, and its leaders are being charged with undermining the "social order." The media are filled with reports about Falun Gong practices leading people to commit suicide or die

161

from treatable illnesses. One Chinese official claimed that "Falun Gong is an anti-scientific, anti-human, anti-social, anti-government and illegal organization with all the characteristics of an evil religion."[2] Another official recently pledged to "maintain with full effort social stability," to "criticize, arrest and indict key members," and to halt the "criminal activities of the devil cult."[3]

The Chinese have never accepted the contemporary Western attitude about the importance of individual liberty, and Western nations regularly condemn China for human rights violations. The crackdown on Falun Gong provoked predictable criticism by European nations and the United States. A typical reaction was that of James Foley of the U.S. State Department: "We do not believe people should be persecuted or prosecuted simply for peaceful assembly or for exercising their religious beliefs or practices, as long as they are not harming anybody."[4]

However, it is important to put the tension between China and the West into historical perspective, for our emphasis on liberty is a comparatively recent event. Not that long ago, what we now call individual rights were not recognized in Western nations. Indeed, the subjugation of the individual to the state and even slavery itself were viewed as proper by nearly everyone. The earliest clear defense of the importance of individual liberty came in the seventeenth century from the English philosopher John Locke (1632–1704). According to Locke, our right to liberty is fundamental, and it greatly restricts the power a government may legitimately exercise over us. To support his claim, Locke adopted a version of the *contractarian* idea that the rules of justice (or morality generally) are those reasonable people would (or could) adopt through a suitable agreement. According to Locke, people cannot properly agree to a form of government unless it protects individual liberty, so justice requires the protection of liberty.

While all contractarians analyze justice in terms of a suitable "contract," they split over what it takes for the agreement to be "suitable." In this chapter we will discuss alternatives proposed by two of the most influential contractarians, Thomas Hobbes and John Locke.

HOBBES AND INTEREST-BASED CONTRACTARIANISM

When Thomas Hobbes wrote his famous book *Leviathan* (1651), there was growing skepticism about the ancient view that people naturally seek goods that bring them into harmony with others in a mutually supportive way. According to the Italian diplomat Niccolò Machiavelli (1469–1527) and the Dutch Lawyer Hugo Grotius (1583–1645), by nature people pursue interests that tend to divide them, making them competitive and contentious. In *The Prince* (1513) Machiavelli suggested that people are interested in safety, in matters of relative standing, such as honor and glory, and in the means to these ends–power. But the more people emphasize the importance of power over others, the more competitive they become. As Machiavelli wrote, "whoever is responsible for another's becoming powerful ruins himself."[5] A century later, the Dutch Lawyer Hugo Grotius (1583–1645) adopted a similar view. In *The Law of War and Peace* (1625), Grotius suggested that individuals (and states) are preoccupied with their own preservation and relative standing and the things that help them advance these ends, and hence they are prone to clash with each other, even to the point of warfare. Given the hostility of our fellow human beings, Grotius thought we must look after ourselves; to do so, it is best to establish a framework of *rights,* which tell people what they may do without interference from others, and *duties,* which tell them how they must accommodate others. In particular, people have a duty to preserve themselves, and a right to acquire and keep things that are "necessary and useful to life."[6]

The State of Nature and Absolute Sovereignty

Following in the wake of Machiavelli and Grotius, Hobbes argued that we need rules and a political authority to enforce them if we are ever going to get along with one another. Without these, we would be in a "state of nature," which is Hobbes's term for a state of affairs without government or political arrangements of any sort. In the state of nature our situation is grim indeed, given several features of the human context:

- People's basic needs and desires are more or less the same. Everyone is concerned about his or her own well-being, and everyone needs food, shelter, clothing, and security.

- But the resources people need or want are scarce. There are never enough resources for all people to get what they desire.

- So people are led to compete for the things they need or want.

- This competition then leads people to distrust others and to regard them as enemies.

- Distrusting others, people often strike out at them in an effort to preempt the violence they expect from them.

- Moreover, people are evenly matched in power and intelligence. It is true that a few individuals are stronger than others, but even the strongest person can be killed by the weakest using weapons or by several people acting in concert. So people cannot overcome the tensions among themselves by having a decisive fight.

Hence, given their natural proclivities, people are likely to find themselves perpetually at war with one another, even when they are not actually at blows. "For Warre, consisteth not in Battell only, or the act of fighting; but in a tract of time, wherein the Will to contend by Battell is sufficiently known."[7] The "state of nature" is a state of war that Hobbes describes in one of the most famous passages in literature:

> In such condition, there is no place for Industry; because the fruit thereof is uncertain: and consequently no Culture of the Earth; no Navigation, nor use of the commodities that may be imported by Sea; no commodious Building; . . . no Arts; no Letters; no Society; and which is worst of all, continuall feare, and danger of violent death; And the life of man, solitary, poore, nasty, brutish, and short.[8]

As dire as the natural situation is, Hobbes thought it could be overcome. The first step is to identify a framework of rules he called "natural laws," which are "dictates of reason" that lay down "what conduces to the conservation and defense of people."[9] In other words, we need to work out rules whose acceptance by all would be *collectively advantageous*. Recall the way we defined this notion in Chapter 7: If everyone's accepting a set of rules (or conventions) makes each person better off (or at least no worse off) than he would be in the absence of those rules, then it is collectively advantageous. If we can identify collectively advantageous rules, we can go a long way toward establishing a peaceful coexistence with each other. For even if people are basically egoists, it should be possible to persuade them to agree to go along with the rules on condition that everyone else does. After all, the agreement is in each person's interest, Hobbes thought, since each of us is better off under collectively advantageous rules than she would otherwise be—especially if Hobbes is right in saying that the alternative is a state of war.

Unfortunately, however, Hobbes thought we would be unable to convince people that others would abide by the rules. The problem is that others are too likely to renege on their agreement to live by the rules and to take advantage of us. Suppose, for example, that you and I agree not to kill each other and to refrain from stealing from each other, after seeing that this arrangement is helpful to both of us. Suppose, too, that you keep your end of the bargain. What's to stop me from turning on you, seeing that I can improve my situation by killing you and taking your stuff? Our situation is much like a prisoner's dilemma (which we discussed in Chapter 7). "He which performeth first, does but betray himself to his enemy,"[10] and since we both realize this, our effort to agree to follow mutually advantageous rules breaks down.

Is there a way to solve the assurance problem—the difficulty of convincing ourselves that others will follow the rules if we do? According to Hobbes, the only way is to agree with one another to place ourselves under the authority of a sovereign who has absolute power over us. We must agree to go along with the sovereign's policy, whatever it turns out to be. The sovereign then identifies and promulgates collectively advantageous rules and has the power to force people to abide by them. In Hobbes's view, absolute sovereignty is a legitimate form of government because people in a state of nature would agree to it in order to resolve the assurance problem. The agreement that legitimates absolute sovereignty is merely hypothetical, however: Absolute sovereignty is legitimate, in Hobbes's view, whether or not people ever actually agree to it; it is justified by the fact that we would agree to it because it is in each person's interest to do so.

Has Hobbes offered a convincing defense of absolute sovereignty? Most of us would acknowledge that his argument is resourceful and suggestive. But few will accept his conclusion because we question his solution to the assurance problem. How much reassurance do we need before we will abide by mutually advantageous rules? Is it really true that only the threats of a sovereign with absolute power can convince us that others will do their part? Most of us do not take as grim a view of human nature as Hobbes does; we think that ordinary people are usually prepared to behave cooperatively. Hobbes portrays humanity as Mafia families just itching to attack one another unless restrained by the all-powerful godfather. He exaggerates, and present-day constitutional democracies attest to the fact that absolute sovereignty is not the only stable form of government.

While no one accepts Hobbes's defense of absolute sovereignty, other elements of his system continue to intrigue theorists today. Contemporary neo-Hobbesians, such as David Gauthier, think that Hobbes's idea of beneficial rules is useful even if we reject his defense of absolute sovereignty.[11] Gauthier himself thinks that the assurance problem is solved quite easily: People who violate the rules are soon known as cheaters and are avoided by others. Hence it is rational to develop a strong habit of abiding by the rules.

Interest-Based Contractarianism

Probably the most persuasive form of neo-Hobbesianism would set aside the assurance problem and limit itself to the claim that justice—perhaps even morality itself—is determined by rules we would agree to (if everyone else did) on the grounds that they are collectively advantageous. To be just, people must abide by those rules. This view of morality we might call *interest-based contractarianism*. Should we accept it?

It can be tempting to criticize interest-based contractarianism on the grounds that in some circumstances ethical egoists will violate the moral rules picked by interest-based contractarians. Equipped with the ring of Gyges, we could make ourselves invisible and steal with impunity. And even without the ring we might find ourselves in circumstances in which we stand to gain a great deal if we break the rules and our chance of being detected is very small.

However, this is not really a fair criticism. Interest-based contractarianism implies that we are better off under the moral rules it selects than we would otherwise be, but that is consistent with the possibility that in some circumstances certain people can do still better for themselves by violating the rules. In fact, interest-based contractarianism requires that we sometimes avoid individual acts that would make us best off—namely, when the acts would violate the rules. For example, it requires that we refrain from stealing, even on occasions when we stand to gain a great deal and even if the ring of Gyges or some feature of our situation ensures our anonymity. It is true that some neo-Hobbesians such as David Gauthier wish to reconcile ethical egoism with interest-based contractarianism, but the latter can be true even if the reconciliation is impossible. It might be helpful to draw an analogy. Ethical egoism is to interest-based contractarianism as act utilitarianism is to rule utilitarianism (see Chapter 8): Ethical egoism can be called *act egoism* since it holds that the correct act to perform is the one that is (maximally) in one's interest. Interest-based contractarianism is a kind of *rule egoism* since it says that rightful conduct is a matter of conforming to collectively advantageous rules. Rule egoism no more implies act egoism than rule utilitarianism implies act utilitarianism.[12]

Once it is disassociated from ethical (act) egoism, much can be said in favor of interest-based contractarianism. To its credit is the fact that it requires a powerful form of reciprocity: Rules that are in every single person's interest will not require anyone to be sacrificed for the sake of others. Acts of self-sacrifice will be entirely optional and considered supererogatory. Arguably, this feature might give it an edge over utilitarianism. Interest-based contractarianism has two other virtues as well. It provides a clear motivation for morality: It is in our interest to be moral. And it gives a clear picture of the objective basis for morality: Roughly speaking, a set of rules is correct in virtue of being collectively advantageous.

Nonetheless, substantial difficulty confronts any form of contractarianism that is treated as a theory of morality generally, rather than as a theory of justice. The problem is that mentally incompetent human beings and animals are not reasonable; hence they cannot take part in any agreement, even a hypothetical one, whereby principles of conduct are selected. And there is no guarantee that competent people who are choosing rules to govern their mutual interactions will worry about the interests of the incompetent. Yet the incompetent, too, have rights. However (as we saw in Chapter 2), it may be possible to deal with this objection by stipulating that in choosing rules of conduct, competent people deliberate on behalf of the incompetent and ensure that their interests are accommodated in reasonable ways.

LOCKE AND DEMOCRATIC CONTRACTARIANISM

According to interest-based contractarians, the only rights and duties we have are the ones selected by the social contract. But some other contractarians, notably John Locke, disagree. According to Locke, our most basic rights and duties are independent of the social contract. In fact, they help determine when a contract is appropriate, for it is improper to enter into an agreement that violates our rights or prevents us from honoring our duties. Chief among our rights are two: liberty and political equality. Let's look at the argument Locke gives for these rights in his *Second Treatise of Government* (1689), and then we can discuss the form of contractarianism Locke defends.

The Basis of Liberty and Equality

Locke's defense of the rights of liberty and political equality comprises three steps. First, he claims that virtually everyone is "furnished with like faculties, sharing all in one community of nature." [13] He is not explicit about which faculties he has in mind, but it is not difficult to supply a plausible sketch of the most important details: We have the faculties that enable us to be self-determining, morally competent, and morally responsible.

We are self-determining when we choose values and shape our lives in accordance with them. When I develop a conception of how—ideally—my life would unfold and attempt to realize my vision in fact, I am self-determining. Locke believed that all of us are able to take charge of our own lives in this way.

We are morally competent when we can perform two key tasks. First, we can identify, with adequate accuracy, which moral principles are defensible. Among other things, this means that we can see matters from the point of view of others and assess the ways our principles affect their well-being. For Locke, these justifiable principles are laws of nature. Second, we ourselves can conform to our principles, even when considerations of self-interest might tempt us to violate them.

Finally, we are morally responsible when we are willing to conform to justifiable moral principles. Unlike Hobbes, Locke believed that normally people are concerned about the impact their behavior has on others and will act in ways they can justify to them.

In saying that people are self-determining, competent, and responsible, Locke did not mean to imply that there are no differences among people in these respects. Some may be especially skilled at assessing the impact a policy will have on others, for example. Nonetheless, in ordinary circumstances, normal adults have these three features to a fully adequate extent; and, for Locke, being adequately self-determining, competent, and responsible means that people are moral equals. Thus Locke's first step was this:

1. Normal adults are self-determining, morally competent, and responsible; in this sense they are moral equals.

Locke's second step concerned the implications of moral equality. Moral equals, he said, are entitled to political equality and freedom. That is, if you and I are self-determining, as well as morally competent and responsible, the control I may exert over you should be no greater than the control you may exert over me: We are political equals, and neither is the subordinate of the other. As Locke put the point, all should be "equal one amongst another without subordination or subjection."[14] But it is not enough to say that we are political equals; a stronger claim is justified: As far as possible, each of us should be free from the control of the other. I am no more entitled to tell you what to do than you are entitled to tell me what to do, for morally competent and responsible people will shape their lives in ways that are entirely appropriate without coercion by others. Locke's second and third moves, then, were these:

2. Moral equals should be politically equal and free.

3. So normal adults are entitled to political equality and liberty.

To say that people should be free is not, however, to say that they may engage in immoral behavior. The "state of liberty" is not a "state of license" in which people may act on their whims.[15] For in all matters, we must live up to our moral responsibilities. But normal people are willing and able to do so, which makes them moral equals and hence entitled to "perfect freedom to order their actions and dispose of their possessions and persons as they think fit, within the bounds of the law of nature, without asking leave or depending upon the will of any other man."[16]

Locke thought that competent, responsible adults have a natural right to be in charge of their own lives. By contrast, incompetent people should be cared for, and their liberty must be qualified to accommodate their caregivers.[17] Children are morally incompetent, and in many areas they must obey their parents, but that does not mean that parents may kill their child or take its property.[18] On the contrary, parents are responsible for raising their children in a way that will enable them to attain the capacities requisite for moral equality, and children must cooperate in this endeavor. Likewise, mentally deficient adults must be cared for. We also have an important duty to ourselves: We must preserve our own lives.

In order to meet our responsibilities to live and to help the innocent, we must have the right to keep property we have acquired legitimately. We must also have the right to judge whether someone has acted in a morally improper way; and when, in our judgment, someone is guilty of impropriety, we may "retribute to him, so far as calm reason and conscience dictate, what is proportionate to his transgression, which is so much as may serve for reparation and restraint."[19] These rights allow us to protect responsible people, who act morally, from irresponsible people, who will do so only if forced to.

Locke's defense of freedom and political equality was profoundly influential and contributed to the English Revolution of 1688, which substantially limited the king's powers; the American Revolution of 1776; and the French Revolution of 1789. It is echoed by Thomas Jefferson's words, "all men are created equal," which appear in the Declaration of Independence, and in the words, "men are born and remain free and equal in rights," from the French Declaration of the Rights of Man and Citizen.[20] However, the battle for emancipation had many fronts, and the freedom people have won came at a great price. As Martin Luther King, Jr., said in his *Letter from Birmingham Jail* (1963), "freedom is never voluntarily given by the oppressor; it must be demanded by the oppressed."[21] The struggle by which power was transferred from the king to the people, ruling collectively, had to be followed by the struggle to overthrow colonial rule. Then slaves had to fight for emancipation. As if that were not enough, women had to mount a separate fight to end patriarchal rule, and liberal feminists such as Mary Wollstonecraft, Harriet Taylor, and John Stuart Mill hammered home the fact that women are morally competent and responsible, so they too are entitled to freedom and political equality.[22] Finally, there is the ongoing battle between individuals and "the people." In his masterful defense of freedom, *On Liberty* (1859), Mill warned us that we must constantly be on guard against the tyranny of the majority:

> The "people" who exercise the power are not always the same people with those over whom it is exercised; and . . . "self-government" . . . is not the government of each by himself, but of each by all the rest. The will of the people, moreover, practically means the will of the most numerous or the most active *part* of the people; the majority . . . ; the people, consequently, may desire to oppress a part of their number; and precautions are as much needed against this as against any other abuse of power.[23]

Locke's Account of the Social Contract

If we are morally competent people with a natural right to self-determination
and even a right to enforce morality, it is difficult to imagine a legitimate way
we can become subject to the power of any kind of political authority. How
can this come about? Locke's answer has two parts. First he tells us what it
takes for an individual to become subject to a political authority. Then he
tells us what it takes for political arrangements to be just.

As for the individual: In view of the natural right to liberty and equality,
Locke thinks that there is one—and only one—way in which we as individuals can become subject to a particular government: We must agree to accept
its authority; we must give our actual consent. Our consent need not be explicit; we need not say, "I hereby agree to submit to the rule of such and such
a government." Locke thought that we sometimes give our consent tacitly, by
doing certain things that imply our acceptance of the government's authority.
But our consent must at least be tacit. It is as simple as that. Without your consent, no government has authority over you.

As for justice, Locke reasoned as follows: Since a government may rule
over an individual if and only if the individual consents, then the only just
forms of government are ones people could consent to. To be just is to be the
sort of government that free and politically equal people could adopt through
a proper, but merely hypothetical, agreement.

But not just any agreement can legitimate a form of government. The
agreement must meet two conditions. First, it must be prudent for people to
make the agreement. That is, it must be clear that by agreeing they will advance their interests. Otherwise there is no reason to think people would consent to that form of government. Second, the agreement must not violate
anyone's rights nor cause people to neglect their duties to themselves or to
others. Otherwise it would be impermissible for people to consent. In sum,
then, a form of government is just if and only if free and politically equal
people could agree to submit to it without making themselves worse off and
without neglecting their moral responsibilities to themselves and others.
Locke's view might be called *democratic contractarianism* since freedom and political equality are democratic ideals and Locke thinks that these ideals help
determine which political arrangements are just.

Absolute sovereignty is an example of a political arrangement whose un-
justness is shown by the fact that we cannot give proper consent to it. To see
why, imagine offering a government complete control over our property or
unlimited power over our lives (as Hobbes proposed that we do). Giving others this unlimited power is tantamount to enslaving ourselves, which is both
imprudent and morally improper, Locke thought. We may not enslave our-

selves or give up all rights to property without violating our duties to ourselves and others. Rather than accepting a form of government that exercises absolute sovereignty over us, we would be better off in the state of nature.[24] Unless a regime leaves us self-determining, submitting to it is neither prudent nor permissible. Hence only forms of government with sharply limited power over their citizens are legitimate.

Locke's Successors: Rousseau, Kant, Rawls, Scanlon

Theorists influenced by Locke's democratic contractarianism include the French philosopher Jean-Jacques Rousseau (1712–1778), the German philosopher Immanuel Kant (whom we discussed in the previous chapter), and, recently, John Rawls and T. M. Scanlon.

In *On the Social Contract* (1762), Rousseau defends a version of the social contract; according to this view, the compact welds individuals into a community with something Rousseau calls a "general will" that everyone takes as his or her own will; as a result, people are transformed into free moral beings. In forming the social contract, people are trying "to find a form of association which will . . . protect . . . the person and goods of each associate, and in which each . . . may still obey himself alone, and remain as free as before."[25] The solution, according to Rousseau, is a compact in which "each of us puts his person and all his power in common under the supreme direction of the general will, and, in our corporate capacity, we receive each member as an indivisible part of the whole."[26] This maneuver allows us to remain as free as before, but not free in the same sense as before. Freedom in the state of nature is the liberty to act as we please—with this kind of freedom, we are not yet moral beings. Leaving the state of nature, we give up our natural liberty; and what we gain, as both Kant and Rousseau emphasize, is "moral liberty"— that is, autonomy, which "makes [a man] truly master of himself; for the mere impulse of appetite is slavery, while obedience to a law which we prescribe to ourselves is liberty." We undergo another transformation in leaving the state of nature: When we unite (contract, undergo an "act of association") with others, we cease to be individual personalities and instead become "a moral and collective body" with a "common self" and a common "life" and "will." The sovereign power "is only a collective being." The only form of association that is consistent with our moral freedom is one that consists in our transforming ourselves into a collective person with a collective, or general, will. Once we become such a person, we give *ourselves* a law and act accordingly. The object of the general will is the common good and is expressed in the form of generalizations that apply to everyone, thus excluding from its scope the good of particular individuals insofar as these are not captured by such general policies.

In recent years Locke's approach has been revived and revised by John Rawls and T. M. Scanlon, who use the idea of a reasonable agreement to clarify morality and justice. By *reasonableness* they mean, basically, the willingness to handle interpersonal conflicts in a way that others can endorse. According to Rawls, society is bound by principles of justice that reasonable and rational people would agree to starting from a position of equality.[27] Scanlon expresses his own view this way: "When we address our minds to a question of right and wrong, what we are trying to decide is, first and foremost, whether certain principles are ones that no one, if suitably motivated, could reasonably reject."[28]

FREEDOM OF RELIGION

The treatment of Falun Gong, mentioned at the beginning of this chapter, prompted the question, How important is freedom of religion? Let us return to this issue, and discuss Locke's view on the matter.

In *A Letter Concerning Toleration* (1689) Locke argued in favor of tolerating religious diversity on several grounds.[29] First, belief cannot be coerced, so it is improper to enforce religious conformity.[30] Second, given human fallibility, you and I are more likely to discover the truth if we are free to explore alternatives instead of professing one doctrine forced on us by a state official, who "certainly is less concerned for my salvation than I myself am."[31] Finally, he thought, political instability results from religious persecution, not from diversity in religious beliefs.

Nonetheless, Locke defended only a very restricted freedom of religion. It is enough, he thought, to separate church and state; that is, the state should limit its attention to the "worldly" concern of protecting people's rights and leave "the salvation of souls" to religious organizations.[32] However, this means the exercise of religion may be limited in any way that helps promote "legitimate" state interests, such as maintaining order. Unfortunately, this view led him to advocate the suppression of atheism and Catholicism — atheism because he feared it weakens people's commitment to morality by undermining belief in eternal damnation and Catholicism because it encourages loyalty to the pope.[33] On "worldly" grounds such as these, a state may justify all sorts of policies that inadvertently restrict religious practice.

In his day, Locke was a remarkably forward thinker and a pioneer in defending religious toleration. Three hundred years later, however, his vision of religious toleration might strike us as narrow, since it sweeps aside perspectives such as atheism and Catholicism. Consider China's campaign to eliminate Falung Gong. Because China's leadership saw Falung Gong as a threat to the national order, its crackdown seems entirely consistent with the right to religious liberty as Locke understood it. But even if Falung Gong's ways might lead to changes – even substantial changes – in China's existing social order, isn't it still wrong to suppress this peaceful organization?

Given the narrow scope of the form of religious toleration Locke advocated, it might come as some surprise to find that in recent decisions the U.S. Supreme Court's views closely resemble Locke's. The key case was *Employment Division v. Smith*, decided in 1990. It focused on Alfred Smith and Galen Black, who were denied unemployment compensation benefits by the State of Oregon after they were dismissed from their jobs as drug counselors at a private drug rehabilitation organization. Smith and Black were denied compensation because their use of peyote at a Native American church violated Oregon's law concerning controlled substances. The Court had to decide whether prohibiting the sacramental use of peyote violated Smith's and Black's constitutional rights; specifically, whether it violated the First Amendment of the Constitution, which says that "Congress shall make no law respecting an establishment of religion, or prohibiting the free exercise thereof."

In earlier decisions, the Court had made it clear that the right to exercise one's religion is not absolute; that is, there can be legitimate grounds for restricting religious freedom in some cases. But it had also set two precedents. First, it decided that the government could not restrict religious practice without providing a "compelling" reason for doing so. And second, even if it met this burden, it had to design legislation so as to restrict religious practice as little as possible.

These precedents are easily defended. Proper respect for (morally competent and responsible) persons, one might argue, requires that the freedom to shape one's own life in accordance with one's values and beliefs not be restricted unless there are extremely weighty and uncontroversial reasons for doing so. This means that one should be free to live in accordance with one's religious convictions, too; these play an especially central role in the lives of most people. However, self-determination does not mean other-determination; while we should be free to shape our own lives, it does not follow that we should be free to shape others' lives. Nor should freedom of religion be construed as the freedom to do whatever one's religious beliefs dictate. The right to exercise one's religion is not like freedom of thought. One may believe or value anything one likes and embrace any doctrine of faith without having any direct impact on anyone else. Freedom of thought is a necessary component of self-determination and should be absolute. But acting on our religious beliefs might harm others, and therefore the freedom to exercise one's religion cannot be absolute. Restrictions on religious liberty are legitimate when they can be justified on compelling grounds, such as when the lives of others are at stake.

But in *Smith* the Court put its two precedents aside. It held that as long as legislators do not pursue antireligious motives when they target a practice, they are free to promulgate (generally applicable) laws that interfere with the exercise of religion.[34] The government may not set out to eliminate a Native American religion by preventing its members from gathering in a place they have considered sacred for hundreds of years or by forbidding the use of peyote. But it may pass laws that block these practices as an incidental effect.

Some would question the wisdom of the Court's decision in *Smith,* on the grounds that the right to develop and act upon one's own religious and philosophical views creates a very powerful presumption against interference by others. Arguably, this presumption supports the older precedent. In fact, many legislators across the country came to this conclusion, and *Smith* has been widely criticized. Nearly half of the states' legislatures, including Oregon's, have passed laws permitting the sacramental use of peyote, thus restoring the religious rights of Native Americans, at least in certain jurisdictions. More significantly, Congress attempted to reinstate the presumption in favor of religious freedom by passing the Religious Freedom Restoration Act of 1993. This act required that the government not "substantially burden" the exercise of religion unless it showed that the burden "(1) is in furtherance of a compelling governmental interest; and (2) is the least restrictive means of furthering that compelling governmental interest."[35]

However, at the moment the Court has had the last word. In *City of Boerne v. Archbishop of San Antonio* (1997), which considered a local zoning authority's decision to deny a church a building permit, the Court declared the Religious Freedom Restoration Act to be unconstitutional. The problem, according to the Court, was that instead of enforcing the First Amendment's free exercise clause, the act changed the meaning of the clause. And while Congress has enforcement power, it does not have the power to determine when the Constitution has been violated. That is the prerogative of the Court. Ironically, then—for the time being, at least—the government (in the form of the Court) has decided that it (or Congress) does not have the power to bar itself from restricting religious freedom.

QUESTIONS FOR REFLECTION

1. According to Grotius, people may legitimate any form of government at all, including an absolute sovereignty, by consenting to its rule. People may "entirely relinquish their rights, and surrender them to

another."[36] Was he correct? Why did Locke disagree with Grotius on this matter? Was Locke correct?

2. According to Grotius, "the silence of the law . . . prohibits any one from impeding another in doing what the law permits."[37] Is this claim correct? How would Locke have reacted to it?

3. Hobbes says in chapter 16 of *Leviathan* that "a multitude of men, are made One Person, when they are by one man, or one Person, Represented," suggesting that everyone in the "leviathan" takes on a group identity whose policy is determined by the sovereign. Insofar as the subject is the leviathan, its policies are the subject's. Is Hobbes's view plausible? If so, what follows concerning the importance of individuals and their rights?

4. According to Hobbes, it is in our rational self-interest to support or, along with others, to set up a sovereign who has absolute power over us. For the absolute sovereign enforces arrangements that are in the collective interest. Was Hobbes correct? What would Locke say? Which theorist's view is more accurate?

5. While Locke defended the claim that people should be free, he, like Grotius, said that we have a duty to preserve ourselves. Are these two claims consistent? If we have the right to self-determination, isn't it permissible to let ourselves die?

6. Do people have the right to self-determination? May our liberty to shape our own lives (insofar as doing so has no significant impact on others) be restricted? If so, when? What if people harm themselves— say, by taking debilitating drugs or smoking or committing suicide?

7. Suppose that Fred is the most informed expert about what makes life go best, and Fred wants to improve everyone's lives by telling everyone what to do. Must people obey Fred? Why or why not?

8. According to Locke, ordinary people are morally competent and responsible. Is he correct? If not, is he wrong when he says that ordinarily people should be free?

9. Substantial inequalities in possessions may occur in the state of nature consistently with the law of nature. Such inequalities are therefore legitimate in Locke's view. Moreover, a just government will not attempt to transfer the property of one person to another—for example, to make holdings more equal. Indeed, "the preservation of property [is] the end of government and that for which men enter into society."[38] Are these implications of Locke's view plausible? If not, how should Locke's view be altered?

10. What does Locke mean when he says that people are free and equal? What is his justification? Is he right? How would he respond to the following possible reasons for arguing that some people are superior: (a) Some people are stronger than others; (b) some are smarter; (c) some act better, morally speaking; (d) some work harder and contribute more; (e) women are superior because they are capable of giving birth; (f) children and people who are severely mentally handicapped need supervision.

11. Hobbes thinks that the state of nature (the situation we would be in if we were not subject to coercive political authority) is extremely unpleasant. Locke does not; his view is much more like that of the early American patriot Tom Paine, who suggested that the community manages well through voluntary choices made by individuals and is rarely helped by the coercive intervention of authorities. Who is more accurate?

12. Have you consented to the authority of the U.S. government? (Remember, Locke claimed that forced "consent" is not binding.) If so, how and when did you do so? (Note that the consent of minors is not binding.) If not, what are your responsibilities to the United States, and its to you? (Are they the same as your responsibilities to France and its to you?)

13. Locke says that we have a natural duty to help others. Does it follow that we have a duty to participate in a society that renders such aid to others and to help set one up if it does not already exist? Or should individuals be free to act on their humanitarian duties as they understand them?

FURTHER READINGS

Dunn, John. *The Political Thought of John Locke.* Cambridge: Cambridge University Press, 1969.

Finnis, John. *Natural Law and Natural Rights.* Oxford: Clarendon Press, 1980.

Freeman, Samuel. "Reason and Agreement in Social Contract Views." In *Philosophy and Public Affairs* 19 (1990): 122–157.

Gauthier, David. *Morals by Agreement.* Oxford: Clarendon Press, 1986.

Grotius, Hugo. *The Law of War and Peace.* Translated by A. C. Campbell as *The Rights of War and Peace.* New York: M. Walter Dunne, no date.

Hobbes, Thomas. *Leviathan,* edited by Michael Oakeshott. New York: Collier Books, 1962. First published 1651.

King, Martin Luther, Jr. *Letter from Birmingham Jail.* In *Civil Disobedience: Theory and Practice,* edited by Hugo Bedau. Indianapolis: Pegasus, 1969. First published 1963.

Locke, John. *Letter Concerning Toleration,* edited by P. Romanell. Indianapolis: Bobbs-Merrill, 1955. First published 1689.

——. *The Second Treatise of Government,* edited by Thomas Peardon. Indianapolis: Bobbs-Merrill, 1952. First published 1689.

Machiavelli, Niccolò. *The Prince,* translated by George Bull. Harmondsworth, England: Penguin, 1961. First published 1513.

Mill, John Stuart. *On Liberty.* In *Three Essays.* Oxford: Oxford University Press, 1975. First published 1859.

——. *The Subjection of Women.* In *Three Essays.* Oxford: Oxford University Press, 1975. First published 1869.

Rawls, John. *A Theory of Justice.* Cambridge, Mass.: Harvard University Press, 1971.

Rousseau, Jean-Jacques. *On the Social Contract.* In *On the Social Contract, Discourse on the Origin of Inequality, and Discourse on Political Economy,* translated by Donald Cress. Indianapolis: Hackett, 1983. First published 1762.

Scanlon, T. M. *What We Owe to Each Other.* Cambridge, Mass.: Harvard University Press, 1998.

Simmons, A. John. *On the Edge of Anarchy.* Princeton: Princeton University Press, 1994.

Wollstonecraft, Mary. *A Vindication of the Rights of Women.* New York: Prometheus Books, 1989. First published 1792.

NOTES

1. Nanaho Sawano, "Tracing Falun Gong's Roots in the US," *Christian Science Monitor,* 6 January 2000, p. 18.
2. Marcia Kunstel and Joseph Albright, "Chinese Act Decisively to Stifle Popular Meditation Cult," *Atlanta Journal and Constitution,* 29 August 1999, p. A15.
3. Pamela Pun, "Sect Man Dies in Custody," *Hong Kong Standard,* 26 January 2000, carried by Worldsources Online.
4. Marcia Kunstel and Joseph Albright, "Chinese Act Decisively to Stifle Popular Meditation Cult," *Atlanta Journal and Constitution,* 29 August 1999, p. A15.
5. Niccolò Machiavelli, *The Prince,* trans. George Bull (Harmondsworth, England: Penguin, 1961), chapter I, section III.
6. Hugo Grotius, *The Law of War and Peace,* trans. A. C. Campbell as *The Rights of War and Peace* (New York: M. Walter Dunne, no date), chapter II, section I.
7. Thomas Hobbes, *Leviathan,* ed. Michael Oakeshot (New York: Collier Books, 1962), part I, chapter 13.
8. Hobbes, *Leviathan,* part I, chapter 13.
9. Hobbes, *Leviathan,* part I, chapter 15.

10. Hobbes, *Leviathan*, part I, chapter 14.

11. See David Gauthier, *Morals by Agreement* (Oxford: Clarendon Press, 1986).

12. In effect, premise 1 of the reconciliation argument that we discussed in Chapter 7 is the thesis that rule egoism is correct.

13. John Locke, *Second Treatise of Government*, edited by Thomas Peardon (Indianapolis: Bobbs-Merrill, 1952), section 4.

14. Locke, *Second Treatise*, section 4.

15. Locke, *Second Treatise*, sections 6 and 63.

16. Locke, *Second Treatise*, section 4.

17. Locke, *Second Treatise*, section 60.

18. Locke, *Second Treatise*, section 65.

19. Locke, *Second Treatise*, section 7.

20. Referred to in Georges Lefebvre's *The Coming of the French Revolution*, trans. R. R. Palmer (Princeton: Princeton University Press, 1947).

21. Martin Luther King, Jr., *Letter from Birmingham Jail*, in *Civil Disobedience: Theory and Practice*, ed. Hugo Bedau (Indianapolis: Pegasus, 1969).

22. Mary Wollstonecraft, *A Vindication of the Rights of Women* (New York: Prometheus Books, 1989). First published 1792; John Stuart Mill, *The Subjection of Women*, in *Three Essays* (Oxford: Oxford University Press, 1975). First published 1869.

23. Mill, *On Liberty*, in *Three Essays* (Oxford: Oxford University Press, 1975), p. 8. First published 1859.

24. Locke, *Second Treatise*, section 13.

25. Jean-Jacques Rousseau, *On the Social Contract*, in *On the Social Contract, Discourse on the Origin of Inequality, and Discourse on Political Economy*, trans. Donald Cress (Indianapolis: Hackett, 1983), book I, chapter VI.

26. Rousseau, *Social Contract*, book I, chapter VI.

27. See John Rawls, *A Theory of Justice* (Cambridge, Mass.: Harvard University Press, 1971).

28. T. M. Scanlon, *What We Owe to Each Other* (Cambridge, Mass.: Harvard University Press, 1998), p. 191.

29. John Locke, *A Letter Concerning Toleration*, edited by P. Romanell. (Indianapolis: Bobbs-Merrill, 1955). First published 1689.

30. Locke, *Letter*, pp. 18 and 45.

31. Locke, *Letter*, pp. 19 and 32.

32. *Letter*, p. 17.

33. *Letter*, pp. 51–52.

34. "The Clause does not relieve an individual of the obligation to comply with a law that incidentally forbids . . . the performance of an act that his religious belief requires . . . if the law is not specifically directed to religious practice and

is otherwise constitutional as applied to those who engage in the specified act for nonreligious reasons" (494 U.S. 872, *873, 110 S.Ct. 1595, **1597).

35. S. Rep. No. 103–111.
36. Grotius, book I, chapter III, section VIII.
37. Grotius, book I, chapter I, section IX.
38. Locke, *Second Treatise,* section 138.

11

The Contemporary Debate

What Are Some Contemporary
Approaches to Ethics?

Contemporary theorists are still struggling to decide which normative theory is correct. There is much agreement in broad outlines about what an ethical theory should do for us: Utilitarians, Kantians, and contractarians all try to provide a scheme of rights and duties—*rights* so that it is clear what individuals may do without interference from others, and *duties* so that it is clear what each of us must do regardless of our other plans. But even this broad outline has received significant criticism.

In this final chapter we will briefly sketch the moral framework that many contemporary ethicists seem to favor and then lay out and evaluate objections by three groups of critics. These critics include (1) communitarians, who say that emphasizing individual rights is a mistake since the community is the proper object of moral concern; (2) contemporary virtue ethicists, who argue that moral behavior is the product of a virtuous character, not the product of dutiful conformity to moral principles, and (3) feminist advocates of the ethics of care, who join other virtue ethicists in rejecting a vision of morality centered on following rules and suggest that proper moral behavior is the outcome of a caring outlook. Perhaps it is possible to take these criticisms into account and shape elements from different moral traditions into a plausible and useful moral view.

A MORAL FRAMEWORK

In the ethical literature, four moral principles are widely discussed, and many theorists seem to think that these principles constitute the backbone of an acceptable normative theory, even while disagreeing about their precise formulation and about their relative importance. These principles are as follows:

- The principle of respect for self-determination
- The principle of beneficence
- The principle of nonmaleficence
- The principle of justice

Let's consider each of these principles.

The principle of respect for self-determination says that competent, responsible people should be free to be self-determining: They ought to be free to choose values and ends for themselves and to shape their own lives accordingly, insofar as these choices do not affect others. And everyone must behave in ways that allow people to be self-determining. Let us make a few observations about this fundamental principle.

First, it does not apply to everyone. It concerns responsible, morally competent people. To be morally competent is to have an adequate idea about which moral principles are justifiable and to be capable of acting in accordance with them. Competent people may be called responsible when they are willing to conform to justifiable principles. Thus the principle of respect for self-determination is consistent with the view that incompetent or morally irresponsible people should not be completely in charge of their lives. Children, for example, do not know right from wrong; and to the extent that they cannot take responsibility for their actions, others must supervise them.

Second, the principle of respect for self-determination is largely neutral concerning competing conceptions of what makes life go best. Arguably, this is a virtue, for reasonable people disagree about the best life's ingredients. Of course, some points are clear enough. Almost everyone, upon reflection, will grant that pleasure, knowledge, interpersonal relationships of various sorts, and self-realization are all intrinsically good and that the best life will involve all of these elements. However, many further issues may be irresolvable. For example: Precisely what mix of these goods makes for the best life? Are there other goods? If there is no clear-cut basis for forcing people to conform to a particular conception of the good, isn't it best if our moral principles are as neutral as possible among views of the good? This neutrality is achieved by the principle of respect for self-determination, which leaves to individuals the task of constructing visions of the best life.

A third point about our right to be self-determining is that it helps explain why, as a general policy, we ought to be honest in our interactions with others. Typically, when we deceive others, or manipulate them, we are attempting to direct their actions, rather than letting them determine their own affairs. As deceivers, we believe that they will reject our wishes if they have full knowledge of what we are up to; we aim to control them by misleading them. Hence deceivers usually do not respect the self-determination of their victims.

Finally, by appealing to the principle of respect for self-determination, we may justify several familiar rights, in that they help create the conditions under which we may forge our lives:

1. Freedom of tastes and pursuits, which is the right to adopt our own preferences and any pursuits that do not affect others

2. Freedom of association and movement, or the right to move about freely in public areas and to unite with others to pursue mutually agreeable ends

3. Freedom of thought and conscience, or the right to believe anything we choose and to adopt any religious or philosophical position

4. Freedom of expression, or the right to share one's views with others

5. Bodily integrity, or the right to choose what happens to one's own body

6. The right to private property, which is basically the right to possess and exploit items we have acquired legitimately, together with the right to transfer this right to others

So much for the principle of respect for self-determination. Now let's discuss a second moral principle.

The principle of beneficence says that when doing so is not an unreasonable burden, we ought to assist others who cannot meet their needs through their own efforts. The duty this injunction expresses typically is considered "imperfect" in Kant's sense, which means that we may exercise our own discretion in deciding what we will do to help and who will receive our assistance. However, those with utilitarian leanings might defend a stronger duty of beneficence than do those who favor Kantianism.

There are two distinct ways to help people and hence two forms of beneficence. We may speak of a *humanitarian* obligation when we are duty-bound to help others in ways they welcome. By contrast, our "assistance" is *parentalistic* (or paternalistic) when we ignore or override people's preferences and force people to do things or submit to things on the grounds that it is in their interest.

When we treat mentally incompetent people in parentalistic ways, our behavior is fully consistent with the principle of respect for self-determination. However, imposing parentalistic requirements on competent and responsible adults is problematic. Some theorists argue that such intrusions can be justified in certain limited contexts.[1] We may ban harmful recreational drugs, for example, on the grounds that rational people would not take them if they were fully aware of all of the consequences of doing so. Out of respect for self-determination, other theorists reject all parentalistic intrusions in the lives of competent, responsible adults.[2]

The principle of nonmaleficence says we ought not harm people; and, except when doing so is reasonable given critical human interests, we ought not harm animals. This principle overlaps with the principle of beneficence, since not harming people can be viewed as a mode of helping them. However, the principle of nonmaleficence is usually said to take priority over the principle of beneficence, in the sense that it is more important not to harm others than it is to help them. A clearer way to state what is essentially the same point is this: We may help others only in ways that are consistent with respect for their rights, as required by the principle of respect for self-determination. For we saw in Chapter 8 that an unqualified injunction to benefit others can lead to objectionable conduct, as illustrated by the Case of the Chronic Sufferer. But while the duty to respect people's rights trumps our parentalistic duties, our (imperfect) humanitarian duties may restrict our individual freedom.

The principle of justice is something ethicists often refer to, but in fact there is considerable disagreement about what justice entails. Two views command a great deal of support: one defended by *libertarians,* such as John Hospers and Robert Nozick, and the other defended by *egalitarian (or welfare) liberals,* such as John Rawls.[3]

Some libertarians argue on broadly Kantian grounds, suggesting that individual rights express the inviolability of, and respect for, persons. Rights protect us from being used as mere means. Hence rights are themselves inviolable, and the central function of a just government is to protect our rights.

Prominent among our prerogatives is our right to property, which libertarians understand as follows: First, we may always claim ownership of our selves (our persons) and our labor. For all other items, the right of acquisition depends on whether the item is a natural material or a humanmade thing. Natural materials are items that we do not produce, such as soil, water, and wild animals and plants. Humanmade items are things (cars and crops, for example) that people produce by applying their labor to natural materials. According to libertarians, I may acquire a natural item when my doing so does not make anyone else significantly worse off or when others (who have already acquired it without harming anyone) freely transfer it to me, perhaps in exchange for something else. Of course, I may also acquire money and other items that people are willing to give me in exchange for my labor or possessions. Property rights entitle people to possess and use their property as long as they wish and to transfer these rights to others. To seize people's property and give it to others, as the state might do in order to bring about a more equitable distribution of wealth or income, violates people's rights and is therefore unjust.

Unlike libertarians, some theorists maintain that justice requires that goods be redistributed to achieve a substantial degree of material equality. Rawls is the most influential of these theorists. His view, called "justice as fairness," is complex. However, he expresses his main idea as follows:

> All social values—liberty and opportunity, income and wealth . . . —are to
> be distributed equally unless an unequal distribution of any, or all, of these
> values is to everyone's advantage.
>   Injustice, then, is simply inequalities that are not to the benefit of all.[4]

Generally speaking, Rawls's view is that departures from equality need special justification. Inequalities must be shown to benefit members of the least-well-off social group in society. Libertarians counter by insisting that justice has nothing to do with distributing goods equitably, but it does forbid violating people's rights, which is what happens when others seize property acquired legitimately.

As the dispute over the principle of justice illustrates, there is plenty of disagreement among theorists concerning the interpretation of the principles that would constitute the backbone of normative ethics. Nor is controversy limited to the interpretation of principles. Several theorists reject the very idea of morality as dutiful conformity to moral principles. Let's turn to some of their criticisms of the dominant view.

COMMUNITARIANISM

Writers grouped under the label *communitarians,* such as Michael Sandel, Roberto Unger, and Charles Taylor, charge that the dominant view undermines community ties and thereby distances people from one of the most important sources of fulfillment, which is participation in the community. Communitarians hope to revive an approach that was widespread in the ancient world. The idea is to *prevent genuine clashes of interests from occurring from the outset* by encouraging people to identify with the community: To the extent that members of a group share an identity, they share interests and will pursue their common good as enthusiastically as they might have pursued individual well-being.[5] According to this ideal, ethics is about creating the conditions under which everyone identifies with the group, rather than thinking of themselves as separate persons with their own lives to live. The main thrust of morality is to draw people to the perspective suggested by the terms "we" or "us," rather than that suggested by the terms "I" or "me."

Much in the communitarian vision is appealing, for close ties with others are genuinely good. If you and I are bound together by true community ties, we are brought into a reciprocal relationship of a special sort: In large measure I take the values adopted by you (and the others) seriously *because* these are *your* values, and I want to share them with you. The fact that others in my community care about something is itself a reason for me to care about it. What matters to them matters to me, and vice versa. It also matters to me that what matters to me matters to them—and vice versa! We want to share certain core commitments and relationships for the sake of sharing, and out of these shared goods is built a public life in which each participates in a harmonious, self-reinforcing way.

Moreover, when the common goals are attained, it is perceived as our accomplishment, not that of one or more separate individuals. When we identify with the ends and values of the group, we expand the boundaries of the self. We may join with others on a small scale, as when we form friendships or marriages; on a medium scale, as when we join sororities, fraternities, or other closely knit organizations; or on a large scale, as when we join churches or form civic associations. When our identities are bound up with others, furthering our common life can be a rich and rewarding experience. We do not value friendships, for example, simply because they help us to advance our more narrow ends. And many of the things we do would not be rewarding if done in solitude. When we do things in concert with friends or with members of certain groups, we are rewarded with a sense of belonging and participation, for our comrades want us to take part in their lives, and we return their good will in kind.

These points about community are important, and it is not unreasonable to expect an adequate moral view to take them into consideration. However, nothing in our list of four principles prevents us from acknowledging the good of community. We can concede that human beings are social beings whose shared ends give them an identity that overlaps with others and who want to participate in community life for its own sake. Our first principle emphasizes the importance of self-determination, but self-determination is consistent with forming any sort of voluntary association that respects the rights of others. Given that sharing our lives with others is a great good, the vast majority of people will choose to participate in communities of various sorts, and will want to remain part of communities that helped shape them during their formative years. Of course, we will want to insist that participation in each community be voluntary, but surely this caveat is reasonable.

Even if we acknowledge the rich social dimensions of humanity, we will want to resist the communitarian idea that ethics is fundamentally a matter of creating harmony by encouraging people to identify with their community. For this idea faces at least two objections.

First, the communitarian formula for harmony is both impractical and undesirable in the contemporary setting. Not even the communities in the ancient world were able to maintain their integrity solely by dint of a shared identity; they were hierarchical societies that maintained order by using force to subordinate masses of people. Furthermore, ancient communities such as Athens were far smaller and much more homogeneous than societies such as the United States, where extremely diverse groups are scattered over thousands of miles. There are too many people pursuing too many visions of happiness for us ever to reduce morality to a matter of fostering and maintaining national ties. To deepen these ties sufficiently, we would have to compel everyone in the country to embrace only one among many possible ways of life, and doing that is neither possible nor desirable. Genuine ties cannot be created by force.

Second, while it is fulfilling for people to shape themselves into groups with shared identities, it is also rewarding to develop as separate individuals. People value close interpersonal relationships, but they also want to be autonomous and independent. Many of the most impressive figures in the world have been relatively self-contained people who made great contributions while living largely in solitude.[6]

So we will remain different selves with different interests, even while joining communities when we choose. Given this diversity, we must recognize the inevitability of clashes among individual and group interests—hence the appeal of conducting ourselves on the basis of a framework of duties and rights that remains as neutral as possible among competing conceptions of the good.

VIRTUE ETHICS

The dominant moral view has also drawn criticism from theorists such as G. E. M. Anscombe and Alasdair McIntyre who are sympathetic to aspects of the ancient idea that good behavior is the outcome of possessing the virtues responsible for good character, and these critics have been influential.[7] Modern virtue ethicists reject the idea that morality is entirely a matter of acting from obligatory moral principles, and they make a good case. Three charges are especially noteworthy:

1. According to Anscombe, the modern notion of a duty is based on the outmoded view that moral principles are binding because they express the commandments of a divine being. Because modern theorists no

longer take this view seriously, they can no longer explain the binding force of moral principles. They cannot tell us why moral injunctions must be obeyed. Hence moral philosophy cannot be built around a framework of obligatory principles.

2.   Virtue ethicists have also expanded upon Bernard Williams's argument (touched on in Chapter 3) that advocates of the standard rule-based approach tend to formulate overly demanding rules that endanger the projects and relationships that partly constitute our identities and characters. Suppose, to use William Godwin's example once more, that I can save just one person, my mother or someone else, from a burning building. Suppose also that I have a duty to provide emergency assistance on an impartial basis, as Godwin suggested. Then in selecting whom to help I must ignore my ties to my mother. Yet allowing her to burn to death would be unspeakably horrible. A virtue ethicist would say that Godwin's view is wrongheaded; it is only fitting that I respond to the special bond I have to my mother and rescue her.

3.   A third charge is that some moral behavior is not prompted by duty at all. As Michael Stocker has pointed out, for example, friends do not help each other because they think it is their duty.[8] Consider how you would react if you asked your friend for advice, and the response was, "I don't really want to help, but I suppose it is my duty." Insofar as they are friends, people do not act from duty, and we don't want them to. Nonetheless, it is morally repugnant when a friend gives us a cold shoulder in times of need. These points suggest that the objectionable nature of neglecting friends cannot be explained as a violation of duty and must be accounted for on some other basis. A virtue ethics approach supplies what we need: We examine the specific nature of the intrinsically good relationship called friendship and show that callous disregard is inconsistent with it. Two people are friends only if each considers the well-being of the other to be important for its own sake. Hence only when we are moved to assist others out of genuine concern for them are we truly friends.

Before we attempt to respond to these three charges, let's lay out a further complaint, this one offered by some contemporary feminist writers.

FEMINISM AND THE ETHICS OF CARE

Whereas the theorists who began the feminist movement were figures like Mary Wollstonecraft (1759–1797), John Stuart Mill (1806–1873), and Harriet Taylor (1807–1858), who relied on traditional democratic values to defend equal rights for women, many contemporary feminists charge that aspects of the dominant moral view reflect a male bias. Some of these theorists have been influenced by the work of a psychologist named Carol Gilligan.

According to Gilligan, mainstream theorists such as Sigmund Freud, Erik Erikson, and Lawrence Kohlberg define healthy moral development in terms of masculine values, basing their studies primarily on young men. In view of the values women come to hold, these theorists concluded that females are less morally developed than males, but their conclusion is erroneous, according to Gilligan: We cannot identify the values held by morally mature human beings by ignoring half of the world. Males tend to be competitive and individualistic; they understand morality in terms of rules of fair play and look to these rules to adjudicate disputes. By contrast, females tend to value cooperation and caring relationships and attachments. But this does not mean females are morally defective. Moral development tends to be different for women, not inferior. It is centered on "the understanding of responsibility and relationships, just as the conception of morality as fairness ties moral development to the understanding of rights and rules."[9]

Gilligan does not say that moral development is always one thing for men and another for women or that the difference is rooted in human nature. Her claim is only that there is a tendency for contemporary Western women and men to end up with different values. Her claims about this tendency are modest:

> [It] is not absolute, and the contrasts between male and female voices are presented . . . to highlight a distinction between two modes of thought and to focus a problem of interpretation rather than to represent a generalization about either sex. . . . No claims are made about the origins of the differences described or their distribution in a wider population, across cultures, or through time.[10]

The modesty of her claim seems well advised given the fact that men, too, value close relationships. As we have seen, systems of virtue ethics built around developing relationships (rather than meeting obligations specified by rules) were espoused by several figures in the ancient world, including Confucius, Plato, and Aristotle. These figures underlined the importance of love and friendship, for example. And many female theorists have elaborated ethical doctrines that emphasize fairness, equality, rights, and duties. For example, in the eighteenth century, Mary Wollstonecraft argued that women were rational beings who deserved the same rights as men.[11] She also warned against classifying virtues along gender lines, for it can steer women away from traditionally male pursuits. Singling out certain attributes, such as submissiveness, as "feminine," can also serve as an instrument for gender-based subordination.

But suppose that Gilligan is correct when she speculates that contemporary Western males tend to gravitate toward value schemes centered on rights and rules, while contemporary Western females tend to gravitate toward value schemes that emphasize relationships. What should we conclude about the adequacy of these values? Here is one way to represent the possibilities:

1. Feminine values are (or can be developed into) a moral vision that is complete and fully adequate in its own right, and the same is true of masculine values.

2. Feminine values constitute a completely adequate moral view, while masculine values are defective and incomplete.

3. Feminine values are defective and incomplete, while masculine values constitute a completely adequate moral view.

4. Feminine as well as masculine values are incomplete on their own, but they can be combined into a completely adequate view.

Roughly speaking, Gilligan criticizes psychologists for defending possibility 3; her own thesis that values are gendered and that moral development is different for women but not inferior is consistent with all of the other three possibilities. However, possibility 1 seems to commit us to a kind of relativism: The moral truth is relative to one's gender. If we are not prepared to accept relativism or the idea that the moral development of women is somehow defective, which option would Gilligan's thesis suggest, 2 or 4?

One line of thought that may seem to support possibility 2 is this: If values are gendered, it is tempting to suspect that values linked to males are male-furthering; that is, they enhance the dominance of males over females. And if this is so, then "masculine" values are defective, and anyone who is concerned about the dominance of males over females will then move up a level in the hierarchy of abstraction, and work to prevent the dominance of male values over female values. All this prompts suspicion about the dominant moral view precisely because many males helped create it. Perhaps women ought to put these "masculine" values aside and center their ethics on "feminine" values.

However, there is a problem with this line of thought. It said that if values are gendered, then "masculine" values are probably male-furthering. But isn't it just as likely that "feminine" values are female-furthering? And if that is true, mustn't we conclude that both "masculine" and "feminine" values are defective and incomplete? If so, possibility 4 seems to be the best conclusion, not 2.

There is another problem: By itself, the fact that males tend to hold certain values or the fact that given values are associated with males is not convincing grounds for saying that these values are male-furthering, especially when the values labeled "masculine" are the values embodied in our four moral principles, which are fully consistent with Western democratic ideals. The vast majority of people living in the modern Western world – including males – reject the idea that members of one sex should be granted privileges and rights denied to members of the other sex. According to Western democratic ideals, both sexes should be treated as moral equals, and the autonomy of both sexes ought to be respected. We can apply the label "masculine" to the values expressed in this claim, and to our four principles, because they involve rights and autonomy, but these values do not further the domination of men over women. Indeed, since calling these values "masculine" may create the impression that they are covertly male-furthering, it is a good idea to avoid such misleading labeling.

There is another way to support possibility 2. We might get to work developing "feminine" values into a moral system that is fully adequate to life and show that it has features that make it superior to the values embodied in the principle-based moral view. We have already questioned the claim that these values are male-furthering, so the superiority of "feminine" values would have to consist in something else. Nonetheless, it is conceivable that the strategy would succeed.

Many feminists – including some inspired by Gilligan's portrayal of the feminine orientation – have developed sophisticated ethical perspectives in which close relationships take center stage. One such writer is Nel Noddings, a professor of child education at Stanford University. Noddings's contribution is a system of virtue ethics called the "ethics of care."[12] According to her, morality can be understood in terms of two human interests, or "sentiments." The first is "natural caring," or the concern each of us naturally and spontaneously feels for certain people (or animals) whom we know. "In situations where we act on behalf of the other because we want to do so, we are acting in accord with natural caring."[13] The second interest is prompted by a personal ideal Noddings calls a "vision of best self," which specifies our vision of who, ideally, we should be, as well as how, ideally, we should behave. Applying it helps us to evaluate the concern we feel for others; it leads us to "accept and sustain the initial feeling rather than reject it" and guides us in developing it. Under the influence of our ideal, we come to regard caring for specific individuals as necessary, since it is the way the person we strive to be would respond. But this obligation "is limited and delimited by relation."[14]

Because of my existing ties, I bear all sorts of responsibilities to certain people; meeting these might preclude my forming new ties, thereby incurring new responsibilities. Moreover, "we are not obligated to summon the 'I must' if there is no possibility of completion in the other." [15] For example, "I am not obliged to care for starving children in Africa, because there is no way for this caring to be completed in the other unless I abandon the caring to which I am obligated." Also, "in connection with animals, . . . we may find it possible to refuse relation itself on the grounds of a species-specific impossibility of any form of reciprocity in caring." [16]

Will its proponents develop the ethics of care into a complete and adequate moral vision and show that it should displace the rule-based moral framework? Time will tell. But there is another distinct possibility. Suppose that a close examination of the rule-based framework shows that it cannot adequately deal with certain aspects of life, such as caring relationships. Instead of abandoning it in favor of an approach such as Noddings's in which caring relationships take pride of place, why not combine insights we learn from both? This option will be especially attractive if each moral vision has strengths the other lacks. And feminists, together with communitarians and virtue ethicists, are surely correct when they claim that the existing principle-based moral framework is not fully adequate. In light of the concerns raised by feminists, communitarians, and virtue ethicists, we should discuss whether it is better to abandon the dominant moral framework or strengthen it using insights offered by its critics.

PRIVATE AND PUBLIC SPHERES OF LIFE

Clearly, communitarians, care ethicists, and virtue ethicists have made important contributions. Communitarians have developed insights concerning the value of community and what is required for communities to flourish, while care and other virtue ethicists have made important points about the emotions and virtues that help us to achieve worthwhile lives. These theorists have made it abundantly clear that morality is not simply a matter of conforming to principles that set out minimally acceptable conduct. To respond to the needs of friends and loved ones with minimally acceptable conduct is both inappropriate and offensive. Yet identifying such conduct has been the central task of the dominant moral tradition. So shouldn't we conclude that the tradition is developing a misleading vision of morality?

No, that conclusion would be inaccurate. The theorists who have attempted to develop a framework of duties do not claim that morality is entirely a matter of conforming to minimalist principles or that these principles are recipes for a worthwhile life or flourishing relationships. It is true that they have said relatively little about what it takes to make life worthwhile. But they do not deny that this is an important area of moral inquiry. They simply focus primarily on a different area of ethics. They have made little effort to account for the moral scheme by which we shape our lives in the private sphere; that is, they say little about how we should behave toward those with whom we have special ties of affection, kinship, or identity. And this is a significant omission. For most people, both male and female, by far the most enriching, meaningful, and important aspects of life are part of the private sphere. But it does not follow that their contribution is worthless.

Communitarianism and care and virtue ethics are better suited than the rule-based approach to guide us in designing our relationships and communities. However, these approaches cannot completely displace the rule-based tradition, for we cannot get along without a framework of moral principles. It is needed to help us solve a thorny problem, which is this: Even if we are good people, our interests sometimes conflict with the interests of others in ways that cannot be overcome by appeals to shared identity or close interpersonal relationships. When these clashes occur, we need to decide what to do, and it is hard to see how we can without formulating and evaluating moral principles that would constitute the framework of morality operative in the public sphere.

Critics might respond that a good character ensures appropriate conduct even toward those with whom we have no special ties. Perhaps they would add that it is appropriate to show only a moderate degree of concern for strangers since we do not share with them the ties that in large part both produce and define good behavior. But even if our good characters and feelings of concern lead us to act well in the public sphere, we still must explain and justify our actions to others and ourselves when challenged. In order to resolve these moral disputes, a public dialogue is indispensable, and people cannot expect to win their case by pointing out that they are, after all, good. They must do the best they can to spell out the truth as they see it and explain why they see it as they do. In practice this means formulating explicit principles for conduct and arguing that reasonable people would accept them.[17]

If it is true that our approach in the private sphere will differ significantly from our approach in the public sphere, how will the two fit together? The two systems must cohere with each other so that there is a smooth transition between our public lives and our private lives. Moreover, it seems likely that as our thoughts about the two mature, our ideas about the one system will influence our views about the other. Meanwhile, one general point about the relationship between the two spheres of life seems defensible: Decisions about private matters should fall within the scope of the principle of respect for self-determination. In this way, we leave it to individuals to work out the details of the moral view governing the close relationships they form with others, insisting only that they respect others' rights.

QUESTIONS FOR REFLECTION

1. In "Virtue Theory," Greg Pence writes, "the reason it is wrong to steal property or force hysterectomies on unsuspecting women cannot be totally explained by discussing the vices of criminals."[18] In order to express the objection, we need to appeal to moral principles. Is he correct?

2. What should we do when virtues clash with each other? For example, the virtue of friendliness might prompt us to do something the virtue of truthfulness opposes—such as telling a lie—and in certain circumstances, it can be difficult to know which virtue to side with. A case in point: You overhear your friend Mary being insulted by a very dangerous man, but she does not understand him and asks you what he said about her. You know that the truth would be a devastating blow to her pride. Do you tell the truth and allow your friend to be distressed? In deciding what to do, would it be useful to formulate and consider alternative principles of conduct? (One policy: Always tell the truth. Another: Never cause your friends distress.)

3. Do all moral principles express obligations? Or might some supply guidance for achieving goods such as friendship? How would moral principles that express obligations relate to moral principles that do not?

4. In "Public and Private Morality," Stuart Hampshire expresses sympathy for a view he attributes to the Italian political writer Niccolò Machiavelli (1469–1527), that "it was irresponsible and morally wrong to apply to political action the moral standards that are appropriate to private life and to personal relations: standards of friendship and of justice."[19] Is it true that what we are required to do in the public sphere might seem objectionable if assessed by standards appropriate in the private sphere?

5. Do males and females have different values? If so, is this due to human nature or to contingent features of society? Should everyone be encouraged to develop the same values?

6. Is the good life for women different from the good life for men? Are the obligations women bear different from those binding men? If so, how?

FURTHER READINGS

Justice

Nozick, Robert. *Anarchy, State and Utopia.* New York: Basic Books, 1974.

Rawls, John. *A Theory of Justice.* Cambridge, Mass.: Harvard University Press, 1971.

Communitarianism

Buchanan, Alan. "Assessing the Communitarian Critique of Liberalism." *Ethics* 99 (1988): 852–882.

Kymlicka, Will. *Liberalism, Community, and Culture.* Oxford: Oxford University Press, 1989.

Mulhall, Stephen, and Swift, Adam. *Liberals and Communitarians.* Oxford: Oxford University Press, 1992.

Pence, Greg. "Virtue Theory." In *A Companion to Ethics,* edited by Peter Singer. Oxford: Blackwell, 1991.

Sandel, Michael. *Liberalism and the Limits of Justice.* Cambridge: Cambridge University Press, 1982.

Taylor, Charles. "Atomism." In *Philosophy and the Human Sciences,* edited by Charles Taylor. Cambridge: Cambridge University Press, 1985.

Unger, Roberto Mangabeira. *Knowledge and Politics.* New York: Free Press, 1975.

The Ethics of Care

Gilligan, Carol. *In a Different Voice.* Cambridge, Mass.: Harvard University Press, 1982.

Jaggar, Alison. "Feminist Ethics." In *Encyclopedia of Ethics,* edited by Lawrence Becker and Charlotte Becker. New York: Garland Press, 1992.

Jaggar, Alison, and Young, Iris, editors. *A Companion to Feminist Philosophy.* Oxford: Blackwell, 1998.

Larrabee, Mary Jeanne, editor. *An Ethic of Care: Feminist and Interdisciplinary Perspectives.* New York: Routledge, 1993.

Noddings, Nel. *Caring: A Feminine Approach to Ethics and Moral Education.* Berkeley: University of California Press, 1984.

Okin, Susan Moller. "Thinking like a Woman." In *Theoretical Perspectives on Sexual Difference,* edited by Deborah Rhode. New Haven: Yale University Press, 1990.

Contemporary Virtue Ethics

Anscombe, G. E. M. "Modern Moral Philosophy." *Philosophy* 33 (1958): 1–19.

Bennett, Jonathan. "The Conscience of Huckleberry Finn." *Philosophy* 49 (1974): 123–134.

Crisp, Roger, editor. *How Should One Live? Essays on the Virtues.* Oxford: Oxford University Press, 1996.

Foot, Philippa. *Virtues and Vices.* Berkeley: University of California Press, 1978.

MacIntyre, Alasdair. *After Virtue,* 2nd ed. Notre Dame, Ind.: University of Notre Dame Press, 1981.

——. "Virtue Ethics." In *Encyclopedia of Ethics,* edited by Lawrence Becker and Charlotte Becker. New York: Garland Press, 1992.

Pence, Greg. "Virtue Theory." In *A Companion to Ethics,* edited by Peter Singer. 249–258. Oxford: Blackwell, 1993.

Schneewind, J. B. "The Misfortunes of Virtue." *Ethics* 101 (October 1990).

Slote, Michael, and Crisp, Roger, editors. *Virtue Ethics.* Oxford: Oxford University Press, 1997.

Stocker, Michael. "The Schizophrenia of Modern Ethical Theory." *Journal of Philosophy* 73 (1976): 453–466.

Wallace, James. *Virtues and Vices.* Ithaca: Cornell University Press, 1978.

Williams, Bernard. "A Critique of Utilitarianism." In *Utilitarianism: For and Against,* edited by J. J. Smart and Bernard Williams. Cambridge: Cambridge University Press, 1973.

Wolf, Susan. "Moral Saints." *Journal of Philosophy* 79 (1982): 419–439.

NOTES

1. One such theorist is Gerald Dworkin; see "Paternalism," *Monist* 56 (January 1972), and *The Theory and Practice of Autonomy* (Cambridge: Cambridge University Press, 1988).

2. For example, John Hospers, "What Libertarianism Is," in *Libertarian Alternative,* ed. Tibor Machan (Chicago: Nelson-Hall, 1974).

3. See John Hospers, "What Libertarianism Is," in *Libertarian Alternative,* ed. Tibor Machan (Chicago: Nelson-Hall 1974), and Robert Nozick, *Anarchy, State and Utopia* (New York: Basic Books, 1974).

4. John Rawls, *A Theory of Justice,* rev. ed. (Cambridge, Mass.: Belknap Press, 1999), p. 54. First published 1971. This general conception of justice Rawls then refines by replacing it with the following two principles (where the first takes priority over the second):

   First: Each person is to have an equal right to the most extensive scheme of equal basic liberties compatible with a similar scheme of liberties for others.

   Second: Social and economic inequalities are to be arranged so that they are both (a) reasonably expected to be to everyone's advantage, and (b) attached to positions and offices open to all.

   However, Rawls abandons the first principle in later writings, such as his *Political Liberalism* (New York: Columbia University Press, 1993), replacing it with the following principle:

   Each person has an equal claim to a fully adequate scheme of equal basic rights and liberties, which scheme is compatible with the same scheme for all. (p. 5)

   He adds that "the first principle . . . may easily be preceded by a lexically prior principle requiring that citizens' basic needs be met" (p. 7).

5. Although Mill attacked parentalistic intrusions into the lives of individuals, he also recommended – in chapter II of *Utilitarianism,* ed. Oskar Piest (Indianapolis: Bobbs-Merrill, 1957), p. 22 – the strategy of convincing people to identify with the group: "Utility would enjoin, first, that laws and social arrangements should place the happiness or . . . the interest of every individual as nearly as possible in harmony with the interest of the whole; and secondly, that education and opinion . . . should . . . establish in the mind of every individual an indissoluble association between his own happiness and the good of the whole."

6. For accounts of some of these people, see Anthony Storr, *Solitude: A Return to the Self* (New York: Free Press, 1988).

7. G. E. M. Anscombe, "Modern Moral Philosophy," *Philosophy* 33 (1958): 1–19; Alasdair McIntyre, *After Virtue* 2nd ed. (Notre Dame, Ind.: University of Notre Dame Press, 1981).

8. Michael Stocker, "The Schizophrenia of Modern Ethical Theory," *Journal of Philosophy* 73 (1976): 453–466.

9. Carol Gilligan, *In a Different Voice* (Cambridge, Mass.: Harvard University Press, 1982), in *The Moral Life,* 2nd ed., ed. Steven Luper and C. Brown (Fort Worth: Harcourt Brace, 1992), p. 109.

10. Gilligan, *In a Different Voice,* p. 2.

11. Mary Wollstonecraft, *A Vindication of the Rights of Women* (Buffalo: Prometheus Books, 1989). First published 1792.

12. Nel Noddings, *Caring: A Feminine Approach to Ethics and Moral Education* (Berkeley: University of California Press, 1984), partially reprinted in *Living Well,* ed. Steven Luper (Fort Worth: Harcourt Brace, 2000).

13. Noddings, *Caring,* p. 452.

14. Noddings, *Caring,* p. 456.

15. Noddings, *Caring,* p. 456.

16. Noddings, *Caring,* p. 456.

17. Stuart Hampshire noted that "there is a greater requirement of explicitness of reasoning in public morality than in private"; see "Public and Private Morality," in *Public and Private Morality,* ed. Stuart Hampshire (Cambridge: Cambridge University Press, 1978), p. 50.

18. Greg Pence, "Virtue Theory," in *A Companion to Ethics,* ed. Peter Singer (Oxford: Blackwell, 1993), pp. 249–258.

19. Hampshire, "Public and Private Morality," p. 49.

Index

197

Equality
  moral, 167
  political, 167
Equivalence thesis, 133
Erikson, Erik, 188
Ethics, defined, 15
Ethics, normative, defined, 15
Ethics of care, 180, 187–191
Eudaimonia, 90. *See also* Happiness
Evaluative (normative) considerations, 5
Exceptions objection, 130
Existentialism, 87, 114
  and ethical egoism, 116
Exxon Valdez, 25

Factual considerations, 5
Falun Gong, 161, 172
Feminism, 20, 180, 187–191
Filial piety, 85
Fingarette, Herbert, 87, 98, 100, 100nn2, 3, 101n8
Finnis, John, 66, 176
Firth, Roderick, 33, 34, 36n15
Fishkin, James, 138
Fletcher, George, 119
Flourishing. *See* Happiness
Foley, James, 162
Foot, Philippa, 194
Forster, Eckart, 159n12
Freedom, 154, 162, 167, 182
  of association and movement, 182
  of expression, 182
  of religion, 172–174, 182. *See also* Freedom of thought and conscience
  of tastes and pursuits, 182
  of thought and conscience, 172–174, 182
Freeman, Samuel, 176
Freud, Sigmund, 188
Frey, R. G., 35, 137
Friendship, 91, 94, 96–98, 101n16, 117, 128, 185, 187

Gautama, 69, 75, 79, 82n9
Gauthier, David, 119, 165, 166, 176, 178n11
Gewirth, Alan, 158

Gilligan, Carol, 188, 194, 196nn9, 10
Godwin, William, 114, 117, 120n7, 128, 187
Golden rule, 84, 156
Good
  agent-neutral account of, 16, 104
  agent-relative account of, 16, 104
  concept of, 2–3, 19, 22n9, 91, 122
  instrumental versus noninstrumental, 16. *See also* Value, instrumental
  nature-based account of, 87–93
  good will, 149
  unqualified, 150
Good, I. J., 80, 82n7
Good, Robert, 4
Goodin, Robert, 137, 138
Graham, Angus, 100
Green, Theodore, 158
Gregory, Mary J., 157
Grotius, Hugo, 162, 174, 176, 177n6, 179nn36, 37
Gruen, Lori, 35
Gwynne, Peter, 66
Gyges, ring of, 113, 117, 165

Halaby, Najeeb, 139n9
Hall, David, 100
Hampshire, Stuart, 193, 196nn17, 19
Happiness, 2, 3, 18, 72, 90, 117, 122. *See also* Good
Hare, R. M., 34, 137, 139n13
Harman, Gilbert, 34, 51
Harris, Eric, 103
Hedonism, value (or hedonist theory of the good), 16, 68–82, 122
  dominant-end versus exclusive end, 73, 79
  negative, 74
  psychological, 69, 79
Hedonistic defense of psychological egoism, 105–106
Hedonist paradox, 72–74
Heil, John F., 99
Helm, Paul, 65
Hentz, Claire, 139n7
Herman, Barbara, 158
Hill, Thomas, Jr., 158